D1569376

My Name Is

and I'm a Recovering Legislator.

Memoirs of a Louisiana State Representative

by

Ron Gomez

For information contact:
Zemog Publishing
P.O. Box 81397
Lafayette, LA 70598
Phone: 337-406-5600

Second Edition

Library of Congress Card Number: 00-102416

ISBN: 0-9700156-0-7

Foreword

Over the years, a few political reporters have written highly readable books about the Louisiana Legislature and the sometimes noble, occasionally bizarre and often outrageous things done in the name of law making. Yet a journalist can only probe so far before he hits the invisible, inviolate wall that stands between legislators and the Fourth Estate, and hence the public. An inside "source" may provide interesting, even sensational information, but such leaks are almost always self serving. They usually reveal only what the source needs to publicize to reap personal benefits.

Except when reporting on open sessions, the view of even the most able of journalists is always that of an outsider.

Legislators have tried their hands at writing about things that happen on their side of the wall, but seldom have they had the skill to craft an interesting, readable narrative. None has produced a book that illuminates all the dark corners or lifts us high enough to see over the wall. Each legislator owns a share in the wall and has a vested interest in keeping it strong.

The journalist's view is restricted; the politician's view is selective.

This book then, plows rich new ground. Written by a skilled journalist who later served honorably and effectively in the Louisiana House of Representatives, it offers a unique double-barreled perspective. Almost like a second self, the Journalist Ron Gomez was obviously there watching with the calm, practiced eye of the reporter even when Lawmaker Ron Gomez was neck deep in the bloodiest of political frays.

Ron's multiple talents and wide-ranging background enhance this dual perspective. While he observed with a reporter's skill, what he saw could be assessed and analyzed from the viewpoint of a successful, conservative businessman.

Former owner of three radio stations and currently owner of a travel agency, partner in an advertising agency and a government issues-management consultant, he could weigh the responsibility and accountability of government against proven business practices. What the scales revealed makes for fascinating reading

The Legislature is a great stage and seldom has anyone reported so adeptly on the histrionics and humor of it. We see it through the perceptive eyes of Ron Gomez the Entertainer, a vocalist with the voice and style of a professional who sang in nightclubs and did stand-up comedy in his early years.

The pace of the book is reminiscent of Ron's days as a network-quality radio play-by-play announcer. Unencumbered by pretentious literary devices, it moves fast, hits hard, and puts you at the scene as expertly as a good radio sportscaster makes his listeners "see" the long, spiraling pass and the incredible interception.

As with all the other accomplishments of his life, Ron was a highly effective legislator. His powerful intellect, mastery of words and innate leadership qualities produced countless benefits for his local constituency and for the state as a whole.

In an arena where a little corruption can bring a lot of rewards, he performed with unyielding integrity.

I have seen him as the lonely warrior stumping the state, not for political office or personal gain, but for desperately needed governmental reform.

I have seen him bypass the retirement benefits and other perks of public office.

I have watched him give legislative scholarships to poor African American students when many of his colleagues were passing them out to children of affluent political supporters.

I have seen him drive home to his wife at night while many other legislators lived like bachelors in Baton Rouge throughout the session.

I am not surprised that Ron has written an excellent book. In more than four decades of friendship, I have never seen him settle for anything less.

Bob Hamm
author, humorist and
chief editorial writer,
Lafayette Advertiser

ix

For Nanette, Jimmie and Larry and especially for
Gregory who just needed more time.

"We live for those we love."

I

"Mama, I won!"

"Mama, I won, I won the election!"

Silence.

"Mama? Did ya hear me? I won the election."

"Ronnie?"

"Yeah, Mama, I wanted you to know that I had won......"

"Where are you calling from?"

"I'm at that ESSO station, you know, on Government Street, on the corner across from school. They wouldn't let me use the phone in the principal's office 'cause I wasn't sick, but, I had to call you."

"Ronnie, you'd better get right back across that street before you get in trouble. I'll talk to you when you get home."

So much for an early lesson in knowing your priorities and the relative importance of a political victory.

It was spring of 1951. I was 16 years old and finishing my junior year at Baton Rouge High School. I had just been elected president of the Student Government Association. I, little Ronnie Gomez, 118 pounds of confidence and ambition, had just defeated the star fullback of the Bulldog football team.

Now, please don't get me wrong. My mother was not uncaring, uninterested or cold-hearted. Far from it. She was a homemaker totally dedicated to loving and caring for her husband and five children.

It was just that, well, she was in her mid-fifties, (I was the last of the five, eight years behind the youngest.) While I was still in high school, all of the others were married, with children. All of my siblings were achievers in varying degrees and had brought home many honors and accomplishments over the years. When it came my turn, she had "been there -- heard that."

But her main reason for admonishing me to get back on the school campus was that my mother lived her entire life guided by a narrow band of beliefs that served her well and were instilled in all of those she loved. The first rule was: Obey all rules. Rule two was: see rule one.

In her world, the primary and most important rules were those laid down by the Catholic Church. Equally inviolate (if they were not in conflict with the church rules) were those mandated by governments, schools, institutions, employers and society. Therefore, the winning of some school election by her sixteen year old son absolutely did not justify breaking the rule of not leaving the campus before school was out.

My mother, Anastasie Marie Alleman Gomez, was born near a south Louisiana crossroads she referred to as Brusly-McCall. I could never find it on a map and other people just called it "back o' Donaldsonville." She and her six siblings were brought up speaking only French. In the demanding environs of a hard-scrabble farm life she got a bare-bones elementary school education.

She married Laurence Fletcher Gomez while in her early twenties. He had just returned from serving in the infantry in France in the closing days of World War I. My father was from a similar background: nine siblings (two others had died at birth,) French-speaking until school age, from a dirt-poor sugar cane farming family from "back o' White Castle" and even less educated than she was.

I never thought about it while growing up, but now I marvel that this under-educated farm couple moved to urban Baton Rouge early in their marriage and were able to lift themselves into a respectable, middle class environment while raising five children.   They gave each of us a solid home built on honesty and integrity.   While they were not able to provide college funding, each of us was given the opportunity to continue to live at home while attending college or working for the best education we could attain.

They had moved to Baton Rouge in the early 1920's so that my father could go to work for the newly built Standard Oil of New Jersey (later ESSO, even later EXXON) refinery. Early in his employment there he suffered a concussion from a falling pipe and, after recovering, decided there might be safer ways to make a living.   Fortunately for the family, he found employment with the United States Postal Service.   I say fortunately because just a few years later the "Great Depression" hit and an undereducated, untrained man such as he would have undoubtedly found very hard times.   Instead, being a government worker, he was steadily and securely employed through those bleak years.   Postal workers were woefully underpaid then, but there was job security.

He became a rural letter carrier working out of the downtown Baton Rouge Post Office which is now the posh Baton Rouge City Club.   In those days rural carriers purchased and maintained their own cars.   His route was almost 40 miles long and most of it was on gravel or dirt roads.   Of course there was no air-conditioning in cars back then.   He'd leave the house at 5:30 in the morning, sort and pack his mail for the day at the Post Office and hit the road.   He'd usually get back home about 2 or 2:30 in the afternoon, eat lunch and head back to the Post Office to unpack the outgoing mail he had picked up and presort whatever had arrived during the day for the next day's delivery. His day would finally end about 5 P. M.   He followed that routine for 38 years and when he retired, following a heart attack at age fifty-nine in 1956, his income was still less than $5000 per year.   His retirement income was a little over $200 per month.

The car he drove on the route was the only one we had. It was just as well because my mother had given up driving after she had an accident in her early years. She was a prodigious walker and bus rider. The other four children were born and raised during the years my parents lived in two different homes within a couple of blocks of each other, one on Washington Street, the other on Highland Road in Baton Rouge. The location was almost equidistant between the Louisiana State University campus and downtown Baton Rouge. My mother would often take some of the kids for a shopping trip by walking the mile and a half into downtown or, if she felt she could afford it, taking a city bus. I was born in the house in the 1800 block of Highland Road. I was the last baby her doctor delivered at home. From then on hospital birth was required.

My sister Dorothy (Mrs. Jack Frazee of Baton Rouge) tells me that when Huey Long was assassinated in September of 1935 and his body lay in state in the magnificent State Capitol building which had been completed just three years earlier, my mother put me (age 10 ½ months) in a stroller and took us down to the Capitol (about two and a half miles one way) to stand in line with thousands of people and shuffle by to view the body. It wasn't that she or my father were great admirers of the flamboyant governor, she just instinctively knew that this was an historic event and wanted to be a part of it. Naturally, I don't remember anything about it but I can see where I picked up my innate curiosity.

We lived on Highland Road until mid 1941. By then that area had suffered from what is now called "white flight." For several years, we were one of the few white families left in the neighborhood. That didn't seem to bother anybody in my family too much but it was time to "move on up." My earliest playmate was my next door neighbor Joseph. He and I never really realized that the difference in our skin colors could be important.

When we moved to the "suburbs" I was six. It was like moving to a different country. Actually, our new address, 2012 Ferndale Avenue in University Gardens subdivision, was only about three miles from Highland Road. University Gardens was a newly developed, middle-income subdivision with 1200 to 1500 square foot frame homes just across University Lake from LSU. The house and lot together cost $4900. To my ultra-conservative mother, we had just taken on the national debt.

World War II broke out in December of that year. I remember well the family sitting around our big console Philco radio on December 8th to hear President Franklin Delano Roosevelt intone the famous "...day that will live in infamy" speech.

Within a year, my two brothers, Griffin and Hewitt, had enlisted in the Navy and Army respectively, each intent on entering flight school. Griffin, twelve years older than me, went on to become a Navy pilot serving in various capacities including instructor and ferry pilot and flew four-engine R5-D transports from Guam to China for a period of time following the ending of the Pacific war. Hewitt, ten years my senior, became a navigator in the Army Air Corps (predecessor of the U. S. Air Force) and was a crew member of a clandestine group attached to the 8th Air Force in England. They were called "The Carpetbaggers" and flew black-painted B-24's on low-level night missions dropping supplies behind the German lines to resistance fighters. You probably never heard of them. The missions were so secret that the Army would never acknowledge them. However, after the war, they received the highest unit commendations awarded by France and England.

Meanwhile, back on the home front, my two sisters, Dorothy, eight years old when I was born, and Elaine (Mrs. Beno Cortelloni of Baton Rouge,) the eldest of the five at fourteen years older than me, lived at home with our parents. In 1943 my mother decided it was time to go to work to pay off this enormous house debt. Being an excellent seamstress, she was immediately hired in the fabrics and notions, or "piece goods," department of Rosenfield's, a prominent downtown department store.

Not being a driver, she walked a half mile every morning, six days a week, rain or shine to catch a city bus to work. In the afternoon, heat or cold, same long half mile back home. No one then had ever heard of a day care center or after school care service so I was pretty much on my own in the late afternoons, answerable of course, to my sisters. Elaine had been working for some time and it wasn't long before Dorothy took summer employment and then, on graduating from high school in 1945, began business college.

During the summer, with no one at home, mama took me to work with her. Sort of. My mother and I would walk to the bus stop, ride downtown and she would go to work. She'd give me 25 cents. In those days the movie theaters would start their first screenings at about 10:00 A. M. There were only two in downtown Baton Rouge at the time, the Paramount and the Louisiana. Another, the Hart, opened just before the end of World War II..

Every day, five days a week, I'd go to a morning movie. Admission was nine cents. Popcorn and a cold drink cost five cents each. I was then expected to return six cents to my mother. Saturdays, I would spend at the downtown YMCA on Fourth Street. Of course, movies only changed about every two weeks at the theaters so that meant that I had to see the same one at least five times. Hey, it was a good life. Kids nowadays buy the videotape and do the same thing. I could do reenactments of whole movies while imitating the voices of the actors.

After the movie, it would be around noon. I'd go back to Rosenfield's and my mother and I would go to the employee's lunchroom and eat the brown bag lunch she had prepared that morning. Many days I would relate for her, almost word for word, the story of the new movie of the week. In the afternoons I was allowed to go the five or six blocks to the State Capitol building to play on the grounds. I had to walk through the school grounds of Catholic High School which was then located on North Street. There was some playground equipment on the school grounds which occupied some of my time, but the real kick was exploring the Capitol and its surroundings.

I was absolutely fascinated by that place! I could make up great wartime or cowboy scenarios while running through or pretending to hide out in the eight acres of maze-like gardens in front of the Capitol.

The old arsenal building on the East side of the Capitol, now a museum, was then abandoned but I found ways to squeeze through crevices in the crumbling walls to get inside for more fun and games. And wandering the marble and brass-embellished halls inside the incredible Capitol building was like being in wonderland. I was even allowed to go to the observation tower on top of the Capitol and look out on the beautiful oak-laden landscape of Baton Rouge nestled against the muddy Mississippi River. I'd take a break from all this action occasionally and sit in the balcony of either the House or Senate chambers and watch the old men shout and argue. With some sort of predestination, I preferred watching the high energy activity in the House. The Senate was too somber and staid.

My father died in 1964 at age 67. In spite of their relatively low income during their working years and their meager retirement, their house and car were paid for and there were virtually no unsettled debts. My mother lived almost twenty years longer to age 87. Up until her last three years, she maintained her curiosity and involvement with current affairs. She read newspapers and magazines daily and never missed the evening TV news. Unfortunately, a series of strokes robbed her of most of her hearing and sight in her final days and her quality of life had ebbed greatly. Amazingly, her frugality enabled her to leave a small nest egg of cash to be distributed to the brothers and sisters.

*   *   *

June, 1979:

"Mama, this is Ron (my all-grown-up name) how ya doin'?"

"OK, just my knees and legs hurtin' all the time. What's goin' on with you?"

"Well, I wanted to tell you about a decision I've just about made before you hear it from anybody else. I'm seriously considering running for State Representative."

Silence. Oh, oh.

"Mama, you there?"

"Yeah I'm here, I think you'd be crazy to do that. If you're not careful, you'll end up just as crooked as all those other politicians."

Well, I did and I didn't. I ran. I won three elections for State Representative from Lafayette Parish, served on a governor's cabinet for two years and lost an election for Mayor of Lafayette by 166 votes. But I never forgot her warning. The honesty, integrity and humility of this saintly woman as well as my father's simple but solid principles were pounded into all five children with regularity.

The pursuit of lofty goals such as trying to provide good honest government can sometimes be daunting. The tide always seems to be running against you. I greatly appreciated the message John Maginnis, columnist and author, wrote in his book *"Cross to Bear"* when he autographed it for me in 1992: *"To Ron Gomez - a long-distance swimmer against a very strong tide. Keep stroking."*

Sometime the temptation to relax, roll over and go with the flow was awfully strong. But, there was always something stronger: the look in my mama's eyes when I had disappointed her, her throaty Cajun-accented voice when she admonished me for poor judgment, or worse, the feeling of knowing I had broken one of her rules and had to face the consequences. Even after she was gone, she was always there, whispering in my ear and tugging me away from temptation (well, most of it) by my coat-tails.

I've lived a life like most others with ups and downs and victories and failures. I did a lot of foolish, irresponsible things in my personal life, but, in the area of politics, I think I can truthfully say, "Mama, I made a lot of mistakes, but they were honest mistakes and I didn't end up 'as crooked as all those other politicians' and it was because of you."

I must admit I learned more in those twelve years in public office than I had in all the rest of my life. I met dedicated and interesting people who became life-long friends. I acquired more insight into human nature and the machinations of government than I ever thought possible. When people have asked if I was ever sorry for entering politics, I often replied, "I don't regret getting into politics one bit. I learned a lot. What I learned about government was priceless. What I learned about some people's principles and motivation was forgettable."

My earliest ambition was to be a radio announcer, specifically, a play-by-play sportscaster. I was fortunate enough to fulfill that ambition at an early age. In my thirty-five years in the broadcasting industry, I worked in almost every position, commercial announcer, disc jockey, copywriter, news and sports reporter, TV news and sports anchor, talk show host, play-by-play sports announcer, sales representative, manager and, finally, owner of three South Louisiana radio stations, KPEL and KTDY in Lafayette and KTQQ in Sulphur.

None of those positions was more satisfying than news reporting and play-by-play sportscasting. I guess because of that, during my twelve years in politics, I always felt more like an observer, a reporter, than a participant. I suppose it was also my reluctance to think of myself as a politician.

That is why I began to chronicle some of these observations and experiences. Most of my memories of the ten years I served in the state legislature and two years as a member of a governor's cabinet are filled with that wonderful human trait that makes life livable, humor. Somewhere, early in life, I decided that you can't trust a person who has no sense of humor.

Some of these experiences also reflect a bitter disappointment in learning of the cynicism, greed and self-serving motivation which invades many human endeavors but seems to be even more prevalent, more malignant or maybe just more magnified in politics.

I can not vouch for the *total* accuracy of all that is related. I will tell you that what I relate is factual to the very best of my memory, my files, newspaper clippings and my observations as a reporter. In some instances, rather than hurt someone's feelings or reputation, I'll change or just skip actual names.

But, why even bother to record what, to many, may be trivia or, at best, somewhat interesting and entertaining anecdotes? Perhaps to provide a little better understanding of the unreported and unrecorded experiences of a legislator. Perhaps a reader might get a glimpse behind the scenes and even have a more empathetic feeling for those who seek and hold public office. It could be that all your suspicions or concepts of the back rooms of politics may be validated. It could be they may be shattered.

Notable quotes from the legislative halls:

"If it weren't for the Rural Electric Association, we farmers would still be watching television by candlelight!"

Anonymous

II

"We have lived long but this is the noblest work of our lives"

I have always been absolutely fascinated by the Louisiana State Capitol building. Perhaps it is because we're almost the same age. It was completed in 1932. I was born in 1934. Remarkably, it only took six months longer to build the capitol than the nine months it took to deliver me. The title above was composed by one of the architects for the skyscraper building, Solis Seiforth. It is the opening line of an inscription carved on the left side of the front portal of the building.

My fascination may also be tied to the fact that I first saw this awesome structure from the bed of a baby stroller when I was less than a year old. Think about that. Though I don't remember it, the sight of this gray limestone building rising 450 feet into the sky, surrounded by and embedded with giant sculptured figures had to make some strong images and lasting impressions on a young mind. I'm not saying that this was some giant cosmic encounter, but I did end up spending an inordinate amount of time during my life in and around this monument to Huey Long.

As I've previously related, the Capitol and its gardens were an enchanting playground for me when I was 9 and 10 years old. On many occasions through the years I have acted as a tour guide for visiting friends and relatives, pointing out the intricate brass work, showing them the gouged marble caused by flying bullets the night Governor Long was assassinated. I was in that building daily during the mid to late 1950's, covering news as a radio reporter. And finally, I was one of the "old men" I had watched as a child, serving ten years in the House of Representatives and two years as a member of Governor Buddy Roemer's cabinet. Through all those years, this incredible edifice never ceased to amaze me. Even today, every time I'm in or around it, I see something I had not noticed before.

In the late 1950's, Bob Hope came to Baton Rouge with a road show for a one night stand. He held a press conference on the top floor of what was then the Heidelberg Hotel (later the Capitol House). As a rookie reporter, I was there with my trusty Wollensack audio tape recorder. Hope minced into the room with his patented strut and suddenly stopped as he looked out of the bank of windows on the north wall of the room. There, about a mile away, stood our state Capitol building, a tapered, slim tower standing thirty-four stories tall and outlined against the swirling smoke of the ESSO refinery behind it. Hope turned to the crowd of reporters with a naughty leer on his face and said, "This damn city's got a hard-on!" Of course, that was a part of the interview that was never heard. We wouldn't even dream of using "damn" on the air then, much less a sexual reference.

The Capitol building owes not only its existence but also its design to the "Kingfish", Huey Long. It is his monument and memorial. He is buried on its elaborate grounds. (Some say they were inspired by the French Sun King Louis XIV's gardens at his palace at Versailles.) The larger-than-life bronze statue of this amazingly complex man, Huey Pierce Long, stands in the center of the gardens gazing eternally at his tower.

The Capitol was built about the same time as several other "skyscrapers" around the nation. The Empire State Building in New York was completed in 1931 and its neighbor, the Chrysler Building opened in 1932. In addition, the Nebraska State Capitol, which strongly influenced Long and his architects, was completed about 1930.

None, that I know of, was completed as quickly as this one. Construction began October 16, 1930 and was completed *fifteen months later.* It was formally dedicated in conjunction with the inauguration of Huey's hand-picked successor, Governor O. K. Allen on May 16, 1932. Huey had already moved on to higher aspirations by being elected to the United States Senate. Not only was it opened then, but it was completely furnished and replete with dozens of immense statues and thousands of square feet of sculpted friezes and profiles depicting the history of the state.

To me, a visit to the Louisiana State Capitol building is always an adventure. From the forty-nine monumental Minnesota granite steps leading to the front entrance, to the two story high, 4200 square foot, elaborately marbled Memorial Hall, to the sculpted figures that stand four stories high on the exterior corners of the building between the 22nd and 25th floors, it is a marvel.

I would walk the halls as a kid just to look at the pelicans, frogs, sugar cane, swamp plants and other symbols of life in Louisiana engraved in bronze on every railing and door knob. Even the air vents are incredibly intricate bronze carvings. I must admit, I also took a closer look (when no one was watching) at the two huge murals on the East and West walls of Memorial Hall. The first time my mother walked me through this area, she admonished me not to look up. The murals, depicting the Goddess of Agriculture and the Goddess of Knowledge, feature very well-endowed nude women. It was the avant-garde style of 1932 and definitely not my mother's idea of art.

Later, as a reporter, I still marveled at the one mural which had been preserved in the old Supreme Court chamber on the fourth floor, now the governor's press room. This one depicts, as several others did, a passage from the Bible. Do you suppose that could be done in a government building in today's politically correct society? (Later, a second mural was uncovered during remodeling and restored to its original brilliance in a hallway on the other side of the fourth floor.) These murals were part of a set which included those covering the walls of the original governor's office and reception room on the first floor but were painted over or destroyed over the years.

As a state representative, I was drawn almost daily to some component of the building I had not noticed before. There is so much detailed art it is mind boggling. It has been said that it epitomized the end of the Beaux-Arts architecture tradition in America.

I would recommend to anyone interested in the art and architecture of Louisiana's Capitol a book by Vincent F. Kubly, published in 1977 by Pelican Publishing Company of Gretna, Louisiana entitled *"The Louisiana Capitol."*

For whatever reason, I have had a relationship with this building all of my life.

I have always been particularly impressed by the sentiment of one inscription carved into the cornerstone on the Southwest corner of the base of the building: *"We live for those we love."*

Notable quotes from the legislative halls:

"If Thomas Jefferson was alive today, do you know what he'd be known for? He'd be known for being the oldest living human being."
                              Representative Dennis Hebert

III

"How the hell did I get here?"

I had always been vitally interested in politics and government. I was a delegate to Pelican Boys' State in the summer between my junior and senior year in high school and had been elected to the House of Representatives and then as state treasurer in that nine-day long mock-government exercise. Much of my radio and television career had involved reporting on government and politics. I had participated in election campaigns for other people, but I had never truly considered running for public office until I was forty-four years old in the summer of 1979.

I owned an ill-conceived, under-funded and thus short-lived advertising agency in Baton Rouge when I was twenty-five years old. I handled all of the advertising for the mayoral campaigns of Bill Bernhard (first primary) and "Apple" Sanders (runoff) in 1960. In subsequent years I had done volunteer work for several candidates, most notably Senator and later gubernatorial candidate Edgar G. "Sonny" Mouton, after moving to Lafayette in 1961. And, of course, my radio and television news reporting included coverage of the legislature for WAIL and WJBO in Baton Rouge. I had traveled to Galveston to cover Governor Earl Long's involuntary commitment to a mental hospital, his controversial release and bizarre tour of the west. When I moved to Lafayette, I continued day to day reporting on radio (KVOL and KPEL), and later television (KATC). Back then, no one could afford specialists so I covered state government and Lafayette and southwest Louisiana politics in addition to sports. But, never did I consider myself a candidate for public office.

The domino effect in 1979 did it.

Edwin Edwards had served as governor since 1972 and, because of term limitations on Louisiana governors, could not run again. There were a host of candidates for the open position, one of which was Edgar G. "Sonny" Mouton. Mouton had served as senator for Lafayette Parish since 1966 and as representative prior to that.

Allen Bares, who had been elected to the House in 1972, decided to run for the Senate seat being vacated by Mouton. This left the District 44 House seat open.

By May of 1979 three candidates had announced for the District 44 race. They were elementary school principal Harold Hollier; Mary Regan, a registered nurse and wife of a prominent Lafayette psychiatrist; and a black businessman and community activist, Larry Rochon.

As a voter, I was not terribly enthusiastic about the choices we would have.

One night in mid-June, I attended a Mouton-for-Governor rally at the Lafayette Municipal Auditorium. During the course of the evening, an old acquaintance, Paul Taylor, asked if I would come out to the parking lot to talk with him and some of his friends. Paul was an administrator in the Lafayette Public School system and the friends he introduced me to were all educators and prominent leaders in the black community. They told me they were not impressed with the announced candidates for District 44. They asked if I would consider running.

I asked them why they would support me when Larry Rochon, a highly visible, outspoken and ambitious member of the black community, had already announced. They dismissed that and said, "We know he can't win and we want somebody who can win and who we know we can talk to." All of us realized that, considering the political dynamics within the black community, their support would have to be kept quiet until after the first primary, assuming of course that Rochon would not make the runoff.

My first thoughts were negative. I had just come off a very active year as president of the Greater Lafayette Chamber of Commerce. (That title was changed to "chairman" in the subsequent restructuring of the chamber.) Our radio stations were growing and prospering. I was 44 years old, the four children were all out of the nest. It was time to smell some roses.

On the other hand, maybe this was a way to finish a project I had started in early 1978 as chamber president: the building of a multi-purpose assembly center in Lafayette.

Each year, back then, the chamber president presided over a "goals" conference at which the program of action for the coming year was adopted. It was common practice for each president to pick one major project to be his primary goal.

Many in the community felt that Lafayette desperately needed a facility which could handle large convention exhibit space, community assemblies and major entertainment events. At the same time, the University of Southwestern Louisiana's (now the University of Louisiana at Lafayette) basketball program had long since outgrown Blackham Coliseum, a rodeo arena with a dirt floor, which seated just over 8500.

The mayor of the City of Lafayette at the time was Kenny Bowen. Bowen had served since 1972 and had proposed the building of an assembly center early in his administration. Unfortunately, his plan had many flaws. First, it was to be built downtown which would require extensive and expensive demolition of existing buildings. Second, no provision had been made for planning or funding the infrastructure and parking needed to serve such a facility in the downtown area with its cluttered, narrow streets. Third, the proposed center would seat only about 7 or 8 thousand which would not have been an improvement over the capacity of the existing coliseum. And fourth, the funding for the project would come from an increase in sales taxes which had to be approved by the voters. The whole package was doomed to failure from the very first announcement. Bowen was trying to sell a "watermelon" package by promising the use of portions of the tax proceeds to every possible constituency. A group of citizens organized to fight the proposal and used as their motto: "No penny for Kenny!"

The proposition was soundly defeated by the voters.

At our 1978 goals conference, the chamber membership agreed with me and made the building of an assembly center for Lafayette its top priority. My concept was to make the project a joint venture between the city and state. I knew it would be a great asset to the city. In addition, I had been broadcasting the radio play-by-play of USL athletics since 1961 and had seen other facilities all over the nation. I wanted USL basketball to have a first-class arena in the twelve to fourteen thousand seat range.

Herbert Heymann and I had been friends for a number of years. Herbert's father, Maurice, a Polish immigrant, had come to Lafayette as a peddler and had the vision and talent to build, among other things, a great department store, a nursery and, ultimately, the Heymann Oil Center. The Oil Center was his answer to the needs of a booming oil exploration industry in the mid '50's. He heard that some of the major companies were planning to move to a central location in south Louisiana and that Abbeville and Lake Charles were being considered. Maurice came up with a plan that fit right in with these adventurous oil men. First, he built a club. The Petroleum club. It was a club with membership restricted to men involved full time in the oil and gas industry. It had everything they wanted. Fine food, especially steaks, a men-only bar, and private areas for a little card playing and wagering.

He took the nursery that he owned just on the outskirts of the city and adjacent to the university campus and converted it into a grid of streets and started building office space. It was about a mile long and a half-mile wide. He would only rent the space, not sell it. That suited most of the clients just fine since they were so dependent on ready cash for their drilling deals. He would build to specific needs of the clients and soon had filled the area with hundreds of oil and gas related offices. Major companies and single-office independent geologists and landmen came to the Heymann Oil Center. Retail stores, restaurants, motels and other services followed. Our radio station moved from downtown Lafayette and was closely identified with the "second center" of Lafayette. Maurice Heymann capped off the project by donating land for the Lafayette General Hospital then surrounded it with lease space for medical offices.

The former peddler had become extremely successful with all of his endeavors but he continually gave back to the community and the University of Southwestern Louisiana. His philanthropy is legendary, and yet, the legend was only the tip of the iceberg. Much of his largesse was known only to the recipients as he was a very private man.

His son carried on in that tradition and grew to fill his father's giant shoes in the same quiet, unassuming way.

Herbert had called me shortly after I was elected president of the chamber. He congratulated me and said he wanted to help me in any way he could. He said, "You know I'm not much on attending meetings or working on committees but, find a job you want done and I'll get it done."

After the goals conference, I mulled the possibilities of accomplishing our number one priority, the assembly center. I decided the only way we had a chance was to form a coalition of the City of Lafayette, USL and state government.

At lunch one day at the Petroleum Club, I spotted Herbert and asked him to join me. I outlined the general idea of combining the needs of the city and the university in this one facility. I suggested that perhaps the city could provide some funding if we could convince the state legislature and administration to provide the majority of the money, say two-thirds or three-fourths, on the premise that it would be home to USL basketball, graduation ceremonies, assemblies and numerous university-related functions. One big selling point to the state would be that it could provide the majority of the funding for construction of this much-needed addition to its University, then turn over the facility to the city which would be responsible for its operation and maintenance. It would be a unique and mutually beneficial arrangement.

Herbert enthusiastically agreed to take on the project and we called it the Assembly Center Task Force. It was a task force composed of one person. That's the way he liked to do business.

The city voters had recently approved an $8 million proposal to renovate the nearly thirty year old Lafayette Municipal Auditorium and provide for underground and multi-story parking and a slight expansion of the exhibit hall. Many, including Herbert and me, thought it was another bad idea from Mayor Bowen and, like so many other projects during the acrimonious administrations of Bowen, it was going nowhere. First, the auditorium expansion did nothing to provide the large seating capacity needed to attract major entertainment shows or exhibits. And, like the earlier downtown auditorium proposal, this one provided no improvements for access to the present facility which was surrounded on three sides by two lane roads and residential and medical buildings.

After several weeks of off and on conversation, Herbert came up with what he called a "five-card flush": 1) The city could convert the $8 million auditorium renovation bonds to use as its matching fund for the new project. 2) We would get an appraisal on the market value of the current municipal auditorium.   3) Lafayette General Hospital, which needed expansion room and abutted the municipal auditorium complex, would be offered the opportunity to buy the property at the appraised value. 4) The university would support the concept with a letter pledging a parcel of land necessary to build the new facility. 5) We would approach the legislative delegation and the governor with the idea of the state providing up to three-fourths of the funding.

Herbert arranged for a confidential appraisal of the auditorium. It came in at $3.5 million. He approached the hospital administration with the appraisal and got a letter of intent, approved by the hospital board of directors, to purchase the property at that price. We got written assurance from bonding authorities that the $8 million could be converted to use on a new facility without an additional referendum. USL President Dr. Ray Authement drafted a letter pledging the land. We talked with Lafayette Senator "Sonny" Mouton, a leader in the state senate and confidant of the governor. He liked the idea. He talked with Governor Edwin Edwards who said he would support it if the legislature approved it.

Herbert and I knew very well that selling the auditorium to the hospital was a bizarre idea, but proposing such a move was a way to get the whole concept off dead center. When we approached the chairman of the auditorium commission Frem Boustany, we were met with open-mouthed incredulity. We were proposing to sell Lafayette's "gem?" Were we crazy?

We brought the "five-card flush" to the Lafayette City Council. In a somewhat rancorous meeting, members of the auditorium commission, notably Mrs. Gloria Knox (known as the "Little General") were aghast at the suggestion of selling the existing auditorium. Some members of the council sat in disbelief and Mayor Bowen was in his usual confrontational, self-serving and cynical mode and said none of this was feasible and would never be done. We were almost laughed out of the room.

After the meeting, an astute political observer and old friend of mine laughingly told me, "You'll never pull this off. You know why? Nobody can make any money off of it. First, the land comes from the university free and nobody can make a real estate sale or commission. Second, without a new bond election there won't be any attorney fees to be made. And last, no local contractor is big enough to handle a project of this size."

Herbert and I agreed the selling of the auditorium to the hospital was probably too far-fetched to pursue but we continued to sell the city-state partnership angle.

Senator Mouton and the House delegation, Allen Bares, Mike Thompson and Luke LeBlanc were ready to run with the legislation though LeBlanc was somewhat lukewarm (no pun intended). Luke, the oldest of the delegation and a product of the police jury system of parish government, was very possessive of projects within his district. It did not matter that this wasn't just a road or drainage proposal. USL and the proposed site were in his district and he didn't like the fact that we initiated something without giving him the lead.

It wasn't an easy sell in the legislature but Mouton and the delegation got a small appropriation placed in the planning and design phase of the next state capital outlay budget. The original rough estimate was for a $24 million facility. The city would be asked to pay only one-third of that to get virtual ownership of a major facility. Bowen and the city council were jammed. How could they turn down such an offer?

It was not just coincidence that the estimate of total cost *just happened* to be a perfect fit for a one-third to two-thirds split if the city *just happened* to have $8 million available. The absolute truth is that nobody knew what this project would cost. The $24 million was merely a convenient figure to start. It would later prove to be an embarrassment.

With the initial money in hand, an architect was chosen and the site selected. The architect chosen by the state was Neil Nehrbass of Lafayette, who, coincidentally, was Senator Mouton's first cousin and had made healthy contributions to

Edwin Edwards' campaigns. The site was adjacent to Cajun Field, the USL football stadium.

A design committee was jointly named by the university and the city and success appeared imminent.

But now two key players were leaving the scene. Mouton's candidacy for governor would remove him from his powerful position as a leader in the Senate and his chances of being elected to the state's top spot were extremely slim. Edwin Edwards, who had pledged his support, would no longer be governor.

"Maybe," I thought, "if I can be elected to the House of Representatives I can continue to push the project from inside."

I came home from the Mouton-for-Governor rally and opened a tentative discussion with my wife about the possibilities and problems of running for state representative. Naturally, there was some initial reluctance bordering on disbelief, but Carol, my best friend, most trusted advisor and sometimes harshest critic is always supportive, many times even when I'm dead wrong. She said, "Well, if we're going to do it, let's make sure we do it right."

I said, "I'm still not sure, let's think about it."

Carol and I were not in the habit of taking long vacations then. We were both actively engaged in management, sales and programming of our radio stations and I was still broadcasting USL sports as the "Voice of the Ragin' Cajuns." That, in itself, ruled out any time off, including weekends, from September through February. We usually just took two or three "long weekends" a year. We decided to go to Cancun, Mexico for three or four days and make the decision while on the trip.

I took a Chamber of Commerce membership roster along with me and, as we lay on the sun-drenched beach, scanned it to try to determine what kind of support I would have from the business community.

We decided to make the commitment.

When we got back, I wrote up an announcement and sent it to the Lafayette Daily Advertiser. It was printed July 1, 1979.

You understand, I had not contacted the usual suspects: currently-elected public officials, potential contributors or political action committees. I had only called my mother. It was about as dumb a way to start a campaign as you'll ever find.

When I arrived at the radio station Monday morning following the Sunday publication of my announcement, I was amazed to find a $500 campaign contribution on my desk. It had been dropped off by my friend and local business entrepreneur Leon Chastant. At that time, the campaign contribution reporting laws required that only contributions of over $500 be reported. I decided then it would keep things simple if I accepted no contribution over that amount. I found out quickly that it also made it a lot harder to raise significant campaign money with that limit. But I was fortunate. Business associates, colleagues in the Chamber of Commerce, relatives and friends were amazingly generous and we got the campaign underway.

It didn't take long to discover that my late entry and failure to notify some important people of my intentions had created some problems.

Unknown to me, several of my good friends, who were very involved political activists, had been seeking a candidate to support. They had talked with a number of people but their first choice was Don Higginbotham. At the time, Don didn't feel as though he could sacrifice the time from his family or his work. Ironically, he ran ten years later and succeeded me when I resigned to take the cabinet position of Secretary of Natural Resources.

My friends told me they never thought that I would be interested and, after Higginbotham and others were eliminated, had committed to support elementary school principal Harold Hollier from the small town of Broussard in the South of

Lafayette Parish. About a dozen or so were part of the agreement and were truly distraught about the bad timing, but could not break their pledge. I told them I fully understood and hoped they could be free to help in a second primary. Most of these people were old hands at politics and very well connected. They could have made things very difficult for an amateur like me. Harold is a fine person and a good educator and we remained casual friends after the election, but frankly, I believe some of his supporters, our mutual friends, gave him less than one hundred percent after I announced.

Our campaign strategy was simplistic. No consultants. No staff. Carol was the de facto campaign manager and I was the treasurer and candidate. We would walk the district and knock on as many doors as we could. We would hold neighborhood coffees throughout the district and use mass media only in the last month of the campaign.

I quickly discovered something very surprising about myself. I found it extremely difficult, almost impossible, to stand before people and talk about myself. At candidate forums, a moderator would invariable ask each candidate to address the audience and tell them about his or her accomplishments. I would literally choke while trying to do this. I could hear my mother admonishing me, "Don't go around bragging on yourself."

One night the four candidates for state representative from District 44 appeared before a neighborhood gathering in the Huntington Park area of south Lafayette. When my turn came I stood and started, "My name is Ron Gomez and I served last year as president of the Chamber of Commerce, I've recently been named as Louisiana Broadcaster of the Year." By then my voice had shrunk to a hoarse whisper. I could barely continue and had to cut my presentation off short.

I was furious with myself. Here I was a "professional communicator" who could describe football and basketball action for three hours at a sitting, host a radio talk show and deliver speeches for the chamber. I had been master of ceremonies for innumerable banquets, beauty pageants and other events all over the state. When the kids were small and the income even smaller, I had even worked as a stand-up comic, impersonator and singer in night clubs in West Baton Rouge parish and had fronted my own jazz and pop musical group as a singer for several years in Lafayette. I had interviewed governors and celebrities from Bobby Kennedy to Ronald Reagan. I could do all that, but I couldn't talk about myself. I guess I had been hiding behind a microphone too long.

When we got in the car heading for another such meeting in North Lafayette, I told Carol, "I can't do this. I'm just embarrassing myself every time I try it."

She said, "Then don't. Don't talk about yourself. People already know who you are. Talk about what needs to be done in the state. Talk about what you feel the role of a representative should be, what you want to do in government."

That was the magic formula. From that point on I ignored the biography and concentrated on the philosophy.

Another aspect of my personality which I had never acknowledged was that I really was shy about approaching strangers or introducing myself to new people, especially if they were involved with other activities or engaged in conversation with others at the time. Again, my mother had drilled into us that we should never, never, "push yourself on other people."

A wise old Cajun man admonished me about that attitude early in the 1979 campaign. Again, I was attending a Mouton-for-Governor rally. This time it was held at the country home of a local car dealer and there were close to 200 people in attendance. My wife and I joined the crowd milling around in the house and on the grounds. Naturally, we gravitated to a group of people we knew and talked with them for some minutes. I left the group to find refreshments. An older gentleman, probably in his mid-70's, approached me at the bar. In a wonderfully thick Cajun accent he said, "You're Ron Gomez aren't you?"

"Yes sir, I am," I said.

"And you're running for what, representative?"

"Yes sir, that's right."

"Well," he said, slowly shaking his head, "You ain't gonna win like this."

That seemed like a challenge of some kind and I asked what he meant.

"I been watchin' you. You come in with that pretty wife of yours. You go straight to some people dressed nice like you, probably friends and people who're already gonna vote for you. And, you stop right there. You ain't talked with nobody else in ten minutes. How you gonna get all those people that might *not* know you to vote for you?"

Defensively, I said, "Well, this *is* 'Sonny' Mouton's party and I don't want to intrude."

"Man, this is a *political* party and you are now a *politician*. That's what you are when you say you're running for something. You know what you gotta do?" He started rapidly moving around in a circle with his right hand extended and pumping up and down. "You gotta shake a hand, shake a hand, shake a hand. Then you go to the next bunch and shake a hand, shake a hand, shake a hand. And, you don't stop until you done shook every hand in here. And, when you leave, If you see more than two people standing on a street corner, you stop your car, get down, and shake a hand, shake a hand, shake a hand. You check the papers and if anybody in District 44 dies you go to the funeral whether you know'em or not. You make sure you're standing outside the church after every wedding in the district. And, my man, you don't stop doin' that until the night of the election. Now, put down that drink, shake my hand and get on with the rest of this crowd!"

I got better at the handshaking part but I never could do the funerals and weddings. I led the first primary with 42% of the vote. Mary Regan, the only Republican in the race, surprisingly nosed out Harold Hollier with just over 20%. Rochon ran a close fourth. My political friends who had committed to Hollier, were obviously relieved with the outcome. They were now free to help in a second primary.

Mary Regan had been a volunteer nurse in the medical station at the State Capitol for several years and used that service as an example of her experience in the legislature. She would say, "Many times legislators would come to me for aspirin or with some type of illness and, in the course of the conversation, would ask my advice on an upcoming bill. A lot of times I would hear my own words come back during the debate on the bill. So, I thought, why not run for representative?"

Mary had a very sweet demeanor and I really didn't look forward to having to debate her throughout a second primary.

I did the math on the first primary results and decided to call her. I said, "Mary, I'm prepared to make this run and win but I hope you understand what you will have to do to win. You'll have to get all of the black vote and half of Hollier's vote or vice versa and I don't think you can. I think you know you can't do that. You can save us all a lot of time and money if you pull out of the race." I guess that seemed a little audacious to her but it was the truth.

Her closest advisor was the owner of the advertising agency placing all of her media buys and she had convinced Mary that she could win. She told me not only would she not resign from the race but, in fact, she would win. That decision ended up costing her a lot of personal money.

My media advisor (and wife) Carol decided it was time to soften my image. I had been campaigning as a solid businessman with strong history of community service. Now we recorded a soft and fuzzy TV spot. My daughter Nanette and son-in-law David were the proud parents of a beautiful baby boy born October 13th. He was only two weeks old when we videotaped the new commercial. I was seated in an old wooden rocker on the front porch of our country home. Erik was sleeping, swaddled in my lap, as I intoned, "This is my grandson Erik, he's one of the reasons I'm running for state representative...." As luck would have it, just as the camera moved in for a close up of Erik's cherubic face, he experienced a gas pain and, as babies do in such a situation, broke into a beautiful smile. It was dynamite.

One of the most hilarious moments of the campaign came in a candidate's forum before a civic club. The Beaver Club of Lafayette was and is noted for its boisterous membership and its sometimes irreverent treatment of guests and/or speakers. It is not unheard of in a Beaver Club meeting for the guest speaker to be pelted with napkins tied in a tight ball-like knot. In spite of its rowdiness, its membership includes outstanding community leaders and it is extremely effective in community service and has done many wonderful projects over the years in the city of Lafayette. I was a long-time member of the club and had served on its board of directors for seven years.

Mary and I were invited to appear at a meeting. Little did I know what my colleagues had planned.

The Beavers always start the meeting with the singing of "My Country 'tis of Thee." That is usually done in at least three different known musical keys and several in between as well as in several tempos - all at one time. As the last words of the song fade someone invariably yells, "Play ball." After the luncheon meal, the president of the club stood to introduce us. "Beaver members, today we have the privilege of hearing from the two candidates in the run off election for state representative of District 44. In alphabetical order, they are, Ron Gomez," the members sat in utter silence, no expressions crossed their faces, "and Mary Regan." The room erupted in wild applause. The members jumped to their feet shouting. Napkins were thrown in the air. I looked over at Mary. She had this surprised but smugly naive look on her face as if to say, "OK, Ron Gomez, you won't even win in your own club." She had no idea how devious these guys could be.

I spoke first. When I finished there was again stony silence. Mary stood and started her presentation. She was interrupted by applause after every other sentence. You'd have thought it was the State of the Union address. There was another standing ovation when she finished.

We were then open for questions from the audience. I was asked a series of innocuous queries such as, "How old are you?" "Where do you live?" "Do you like country music?"

Mary got questions such as, "Don't you think your profession as a nurse makes you more caring and sensitive than someone who is just a disc jockey?" "Don't you believe it is time for more women to be elected to the Louisiana House?"

Finally, Jim Miller, an attorney who has the dead-pan comic delivery of Johnny Carson, solemnly asked, "Mrs. Regan, how would you describe your philosophy?"

Mary was really pumped by now. She had this bunch eating out of her hand, right? She paused for a long time, swept the audience with eye contact and proudly announced, "Eclectic!". That did it, even the Beavers couldn't carry on the charade. When the laughter was over the meeting was adjourned.

It is hard to describe the forces and emotions that drive a candidate for public office as the campaign reaches its closing days. "Have I seen everybody I should have seen?" "Did I knock on enough doors, shake enough hands?" "Should I have run that last series of ads?" "Should I have run more?" After several months of almost non-stop activity, it is all about to come to a screeching halt - the election.

My last scheduled campaign event was a chicken barbecue at a bar in the black section of the town of Broussard. It had been arranged by my dear friend Alton Malveaux whose wife Leona had worked for many years with Carol and me at our radio stations.

There was a good turnout at the barbecue. There was no way I could match the eloquence of a couple of dynamic black preachers Alton had recruited, but the reception was good and I was confident.

Driving home afterward, however, questions kept racing through my mind. What else could I do? What bases weren't covered?

As a Republican, Mary Regan was not likely to get much black support. On the other hand, Republican gubernatorial candidate Dave Treen was locked in a runoff with Democrat Louis Lambert. Would there be some effort to get black voters to go Republican?

If there is a last-minute power play, I figured, it can only happen through the vote haulers.

I turned around and headed back toward town.

In my previous years of reporting on, and involvement with, Louisiana politics, I was somewhat familiar with the practice of "hauling" votes. Though a questionable exercise, it was still legal and operated predominately in the black community. Candidates paid a group of drivers to provide transportation to the polls on election day. Theoretically, the drivers did not pay their passengers to vote. They only provided a service.

In Lafayette there were several "agents" who were paid a lump sum to dole out to each driver. The amount paid per driver, $25, $50, $100 or more, depended on the number of voters a driver was known to have delivered in previous elections.

Drivers had a list of voters to transport on election day. The agent gave each rider slips of paper with numbers printed on them. These were the approved ballots.

In Louisiana's election system, each candidate is assigned a number by which he or she is identified on the voting machine. Those candidates financing the hauling operation get their numbers printed on the ballots. Drivers give these ballots to their passengers as they are delivered to the polls. Those being hauled are expected to pull the levers on the voting machine next to those numbers.

The campaign organizers would also arrange for a service station or two in the area to provide gasoline for the fleet of cars throughout the day. They'd roll in and out like a stock car pit stop.

In many cases, voting commissioners were part of the operation, actually going into the voting booth to "assist" some of the hauled voters, or to "check the machine." Actually they were randomly checking to see that the right levers were being pulled.

The "agents" knew their drivers well and the drivers knew their riders would pull the right levers, most of the time. An "agent" could lose credibility with his political clientele quickly if he didn't deliver the votes.

I had not contributed to the hauling operation, but friends among the operators had told me that, since I was seen as a sure winner – and other candidates had underwritten all the costs – they would include my number on the ballots for free. And after all, I was a Democrat running against a Republican.

Through the urging of "Sonny" Mouton, who had run poorly in the first primary for governor and endorsed Dave Treen in this general election, the group in charge of the hauling operation, though almost unanimously Democrats, had agreed to work the system for Republican Dave Treen. I have no idea if Treen or his key people in the state-wide campaign had any knowledge of this. I believe it was initiated locally. There were some in the group who could benefit greatly from a Treen election.

In those final hours before the election, I headed for the hub of the hauling operations. I figured if a move was being made in the black community, it had to be coming down now. My concern was that, if a switch in numbers occurred, my number might not be on a revised ballot.

I drove to a rent house owned by an elderly black woman said to be among the best-known and most reliable agents. She called herself "Big Anna". She was a former teacher who had been on the front lines of the civil rights movement. "Big Anna" controlled a couple of dozen drivers. She was big and brash and when she smiled, she displayed her pride and joy. Her four upper front teeth were capped in gold and each one displayed the icon of a suit of a deck of playing cards: a heart, a spade, a diamond and a club. Seasoned campaign organizers figured, in her prime, she could deliver a solid block of 500 or more votes in any election. While covering previous elections for radio and TV, I had seen "Big Anna", wearing her trademark wide-brimmed, black, man's hat, hauling the votes. Regular as clock work, she would deliver a new, packed carload to the LeRosen School precinct about once every forty-five minutes.

It was after 11:00 P. M. when I arrived at Anna's "safe house." The ballots would be distributed here to the drivers. My mission was merely to make sure that my number was on those ballots and my opponent's was not.

I had been told that Anna liked Scotch whiskey and her particular favorite was Cuttysark, so I had picked up a fifth on the way.

The block was buzzing. Over a dozen cars, mostly older and in various stages of disrepair, were parked along the curbs. Groups of black men were talking among themselves on the sidewalks or in the street. Many had beer cans, plastic cups or bottles wrapped in brown paper bags their hands. As I started up the walk to the house, I spotted a candidate in the Senate race coming down the walk from the house. I said, "Hi, I see you're checking the ballots, too."

He didn't even slow down, said, "Yep." And headed on to his car.

The front door was open and I walked through to the kitchen where Anna was stirring a huge black iron pot.

I caught a glint of gold as she grinned at me and said, "Hey honey, want some white beans and rice? They good."

I said, "No, thank you Anna, but I brought you something." I gave her the brown bag containing the Cuttysark.

Anna's eyes lit up, "Well man, ain't you something. You sure know how to treat 'Big Anna' right."

While Anna was serving beans and rice to a couple of drivers who wandered into the kitchen, I walked into another room where a group was gathered around a large table. They were talking and laughing while they worked, steadily marking something on each ballot. I waved hello and they all gave me a big greeting. I was obviously one of their benefactors.

As they became more comfortable with my presence, I moved closer to the table for a better look at the numbers on the ballots. My number was there, the last one on a string of about six. But just as interesting was the fact that, although the strips had been professionally printed, the group was busy changing one of the numbers with Marks-A-Lot pens. They were blacking out the number seven and writing in number five.

Dave Treen's number was "7". Louis Lambert, the Democrat, was "5".

I hung around long enough to see several hundred ballots changed and to assure myself that my number was still on the ballot.

A couple of days after the election, I learned from a credible source in the black community the "rest of the story."

At about 9:00 P. M. on that election eve, two of the local Treen supporters had delivered the printed ballots with Treen's number "7" at the top of the list. They also delivered a very large sum of cash. They didn't get what they paid for.

Did one of Lambert's Democratic supporters outfox the foxes? Did "Big Anna" decide on her own to stay with the Democratic party?

Treen still carried Lafayette Parish, though not as big as expected and without a substantial black vote. Nonetheless, certain individuals involved in the Treen support group in Lafayette did get prominent positions in his administration.

Statewide, Treen eked out a 50.6 % to 49.3% victory over Lambert.

In the local House districts, Luke Leblanc had been unopposed, Mike Thompson fended off a strong challenge from Mike Leblanc to win a third term by just over 800 votes. Just to the north of us, Raymond "La La" Lalonde shocked veteran legislator Walter Champagne with a razor thin 81 vote victory. Allen Bares defeated Pat Juneau 54% to 46% to take the Senate seat vacated by "Sonny" Mouton and,

I won the election over Mrs. Regan by 4342 votes with better than 76% of the vote. Even though the results of the election proved I had not needed "Big Anna's" help, I am still grateful for the lesson in hard core politics I learned that night – all for the price of a bottle of Scotch.

In March of 1980, I stood on the floor of the Louisiana House of Representatives in that magnificent State Capitol that had fascinated me since I was a child playing in its halls, corridors and gardens. I raised my right hand, took the oath of office and wondered, "How the hell did I get here?"

Notable quotes from the legislative halls:

"I can't believe that we're going to let a majority of the people decide what is best for this state. That's not right!"

Representative John Travis

IV

"How does it feel being on the 'other' side?"

Since I've "been there, done that," I've often said, "Everyone should run for public office at least once." Even more enlightening, if not practical, everyone should *serve* in public office at least once.

Believe it or not, this is not said cynically, sarcastically or totally in jest. I truly believe we would have a stronger democracy; undoubtedly a much more aware, informed and sensitive electorate and, ultimately, a more responsive, more efficient system of government. I've even advocated (jokingly) that one of the prerequisites of having the right to vote would be to spend at least one week watching, in person, a governmental body, such as the Louisiana Legislature, in action.

In spite of the trite saying, "Two things you don't want to watch being made are sausage and laws," it is an experience, an exercise that should be a part of every citizen's life adventure.

When you put your name, reputation, family, and beliefs on the line as a candidate, you get to meet many wonderful people. You find a lot of love and friendship, sometimes when you least expect it. But, you also expose yourself to media, cranks, and eccentrics and, you virtually forfeit personal privacy. If you are of a competitive nature, as most candidates must be (and I certainly was,) the campaign progressively becomes all-engrossing. By the last week of a campaign you have decided, "I must win." Or, unfortunately for many, "I'll do anything to win."

If you are uncomfortable in crowds, as I have always been, it can be excruciating. And, yet, you're meeting many interesting people you would never otherwise know and you're discussing subjects and problems which you had never explored.

You're finding out what true loyalty and friendship can be — as well as betrayal.

In the past several decades, "walking door-to-door" has become an expected, no, *demanded* ritual for candidates in localized elections. My opinion, before becoming a candidate was, "Wasn't mass media invented to substitute for this?" A district such as state representative will have 15 to 25 thousand residences, homes or apartments. In spite of my misgivings, I was determined, and expected, to visit every one, personally.

I had to kick-start myself to hit the pavement in early August (for the mid October primary.) I chose to start in a low-income, urban area of the district and knocked on my first door at about 5 o'clock on a swelteringly hot afternoon. I didn't keep score, but I would guess that by eight that night I had visited maybe 90 homes. Nobody was home at almost half of them. I left a brochure with a hand written note. When people did answer the door, probably 10% understood what the hell I was talking about when I handed them a campaign brochure and said, "Hello, I'm Ron Gomez, I'm running for state representative and I'd appreciate your consideration and your vote in October." Maybe one of that 10% asked me a question or two. Some of those asked who else was running. Occasionally someone asked about party affiliation. A lot asked if I was a lawyer. The rest took the handout without a word and shut the door.

About a third of the way through the evening, I noticed that a young black woman had been tracking me for the last block. I would knock on a door, leave a campaign flyer or make my pitch, walk out of the yard to the sidewalk and proceed to the next house. If I had talked with someone at the preceding house, I would look back and see the young woman knocking on the same door. After a dozen or more houses, I waited for her on the sidewalk. She very shyly approached me and I said, "Why are you following me to these houses?"

She said, "Well, I'm selling some chocolates for my school, and I just figured, if I followed you, you'd find out who's home and who's not."

Smart kid.

You never know what you'll awaken when you knock on a strange door. As I walked up on the porch of one home I noticed that, while the screen door was closed, the wooden door was open. I naturally assumed there was someone home and knocked on the door sill. I suddenly heard rapidly approaching scratching and clicking sounds and a low rumble. As I looked through the screen I saw a huge black dog scrambling toward me, his nails slipping and sliding on the hard wood floor. He was hurtling toward the door. I started to run, then realized that the screen door might be unlatched and the dog would come crashing through it. I braced the bottom of the door with one foot and the side with both hands just as the dog hit the door. It bounced off the door frame then pushed its foaming muzzle against the screen and started a menacing growl. Now what do I do? I couldn't tell if the screen was hooked and obviously no one was coming to the door from within.

I waited. So did *Cujo*. After several sweaty minutes, I eased the pressure off the door and pulled it slightly to ascertain that it was hooked. Praying that it was a well imbedded, strong hook, I backed slowly away from the door, off the porch and out the gate. The growling never ceased. Needless to say, my friend with the chocolates didn't visit that house.

After a couple of more days of "walking," I realized that, even if I did this four hours a day, every day for the remainder of the campaign, it would be impossible to cover more than half of the voters door-to-door. And there were also meetings, coffees, teas, forums, phone calls, fundraising and other campaign activities to fit in.

Carol and I got out a map. We charted what I called "pebbles and ripples" areas. We figured that if we hit one neighborhood in one area each day those visits would ripple out for several blocks. Neighbors would mention to neighbors that we had been there and, hopefully, the word would spread. We would then hit another neighborhood on the other end of the district the next day and let the ripple effect take place again. By alternating areas we could cover most of the district and word of mouth might fill in the gaps.

To make it more efficient, Carol would walk one side of the street and I the other. If a voter insisted on talking to the candidate or if Carol ran into an old acquaintance of ours or a problem or question she felt I should handle, I would simply cross the street. One of the added benefits of walking door-to-door is that I lost 12 pounds by election day.

There were three significant things I learned when I became a "politician":

1) Most people don't understand the differences in political offices and believe that being elected makes you a full-time (meaning 24 hours, 7 days,) grossly overpaid public servant;

2) I truly didn't realize how much distrust and stereotyping there was of people running for or serving in public office (and this was back in the late '70's); and

3) Your friends and associates in the media suddenly consider you an adversary.

First. People would talk to me about the pot holes on city streets, garbage collection problems, Social Security matters, foreign affairs. All politicians were the same. There was no differentiation in duties and areas of influence. A police juror, a congressman, a city councilman, a state representative were all politicians and thus public servants available to solve any and all public (and some not so public) problems.

In addition, most people thought that, being a politician, I was also an attorney. I was asked by almost every person I met for the first time if I was a lawyer. I hate to tell my attorney friends, but when I told the voter I was not a lawyer, they almost gave a sigh of relief and the conversation became a lot more friendly. There were many who assumed without asking that I was a lawyer. Many of these then proceeded to ask for legal advice on divorce and child custody laws, real estate questions and even asked if I could notarize a document for them while I was handy.

If you are fortunate enough to be elected, you get phone calls at any and all hours with the same type questions and pleas. One elderly gentleman knocked on my door at 5 A. M. one cold, sleety January morning. When I groggily answered the door, he started begging me to please get his grandson out of jail. The teenager had been picked up for possession of marijuana overnight by local law enforcement officers. I sympathized with him. I had personal experience in my own family with that problem, but I tried to explain that, as a state representative, I had no authority in a matter such as this. He held out a large paper sack and said, "Take this, and I know you'll find some way to help me." He left my door wiping tears from his eyes. When I opened the bag, very carefully by the way, I found about three pounds of cleaned and dressed rabbit meat.

Naturally, when you're serving in an elected position, you want to help even in situations beyond your area of influence. I followed up most of such calls and pleas with phone calls to others who were in charge of such situations. I'd simply state the problem, give them the person's name and number and ask that they talk with them. If the problem could be handled legally and ethically, fine, if not, at least someone had responded. I guess at least 70 percent of my constituent-response time was spent on subjects totally alien to the work of a state representative.

Second. Once you've announced your intention to run for public office, your phone, your business, your restaurant table, and your home all become public domain. Even stranger, after you have taken the oath of office, it is as if you had no prior life and no previous achievements. You are now and always will be a "politician." This was brought home to Carol and me in a startling manner.

A couple of months into the first legislative session, Carol was having lunch in a Lafayette restaurant. I, of course, was attending the session in Baton Rouge. A prominent local banker passed Carol's table and stopped to chat. He asked, "What are you doing with yourself now that Ron's running around with all the chicks in Baton Rouge?" Now, I believe Carol and I have always had an exceptionally good marriage. We both were successful and respected in our business dealings. Being in a high-profile career such as broadcasting, we were both very aware of public opinion and public perception. We have always been very attuned to the fact that it is easier to spread rumors about well-known people than about total strangers. Still, this question to Carol came as a shock. I was elected, a politician, therefore I was now a suspected womanizer and not to be trusted.

This stereotypical grouping was also one of the reasons I drove round-trip to Baton Rouge almost every day of the session. I didn't need the speculation, suspicion, much less the temptation, generated by attending one of the numerous nightly parties held for legislators by lobbyists during the session. And, admittedly, I liked visiting and conversing with my wife in the evenings and sleeping in my own bed at night.

I even had guys with whom I had played tennis for years commenting on my line calls on the court. "Did you call that shot out?" "Yea," his partner would say, "you know you're playin' with a politician now." I know most of it was just kidding around but I also know that most kidding and humor has a basis in truth. Besides, there were others on the tennis courts who didn't know me. They started giving me some suspicious looks when they found out there was a "politician" lurking among them.

Third. I had been in broadcasting since I was 18 years old. I was 45 when elected to the House. As I've previously related, I'd served in every possible aspect of the broadcast profession except engineering. I'd covered state government at the Capitol with many of the same veteran reporters who were still on hand when I took office.

On inauguration day, while walking through Memorial Hall between the House and Senate chambers, I ran into Bob Courtney. Bob, blessed with a massive, yet pleasing, bass voice which he used equally as well speaking or singing, was a reporter for a Baton Rouge TV station. We shook hands momentarily and Bob boomed, "Well, Ron, how does it feel to be on the other side?"

I said, "Bob, I haven't changed. I'm still running the radio stations and still believe in the same things."

He looked at me as if I'd just crawled in under the door sill and said, "Yeh, we'll see."

A couple of years into my first term, about 1982, my 22 year old son Jimmie was named as a defendant in a million dollar lawsuit stemming from an automobile accident. The accident was very minor with very little physical damage to the cars and no discernible personal injuries at the scene. Tort law in Louisiana being as it was, the other party, a physician, sued, claiming incapacitating injuries had surfaced later. As it developed, the suit was really filed to take advantage of the plaintiff's own "under-insured motorist" policy. My son, 22 years old and owning very few worldly possessions, was carrying only minimum insurance coverage. My advice to him was to let the insurance company handle the defense. Don't even hire an attorney.

The day the trial opened, I had just gotten home from the legislative session in Baton Rouge and was watching the ten o'clock news on a Lafayette TV station. My mouth dropped open when the reporter read a story that said, "The son of Lafayette State Representative Ron Gomez of Lafayette has been hit with a million dollar lawsuit as the result of...." I was stunned and outraged. As an experienced news reporter and radio station owner, I knew that civil suits involving minor automobile accidents were <u>never</u> covered by the local TV stations. In addition, my adult son driving his own car with his own insurance, had absolutely nothing to do with me.

I called the news director at the station. I had known this person for twenty years. I said, "I am absolutely shocked. First, why are you covering an automobile accident civil suit on your news, and second, why did you feel obligated to identify me in the story. This is an adult who had an accident with another adult. I'm not involved."

I was told, "Ron, you're a politician now. As the old saying goes, 'if you can't stand the heat, get out of the kitchen.'"

In spite of incidents like that, in the 12 years I spent in public office, I had very few complaints about media reporting of my activities. With the exception of the daily newspaper in Lafayette, who's management opposed me for personal as well as political reasons, the bulk of the reporting was fair. I did find many reporters were somewhat guarded about seeming to be too friendly with me. I suppose some of their peers may have accused them of consorting with the enemy.

I was disappointed many times with the lack of professionalism exhibited by some of the journalists covering the legislature.

Too many times, while looking for a hook to hang a story, a reporter would focus on the negative. Time after time I would marvel at legislative reports which quoted almost every *opponent*

of a bill which had been successfully passed but gave only a line
or two to the *proponents'* arguments.

Once I was handling a relatively non-controversial bill. I
don't even recall the subject. It had easily passed the House and
I watched as the Senate passed it by a vote of 38 to 1. Why that
one Senator was so adamantly opposed to the bill, I don't know.
It might have been pay back for a prior incident with the Senator
handling the bill. Who knows? He went to the mike and made a
blistering speech against it. That night, the local TV reporter
appeared on video tape from the capitol. She said, "In spite of
staunch opposition, the Louisiana Senate today passed Lafayette
Representative Ron Gomez' House Bill XXX. Senator Nabob of
Natterville led the opposition." The camera then focused on the
lone opposition Senator for twenty seconds of coverage. He told
of the horrors which would be foisted on the people of the state
because of this vile piece of legislation. Not one sentence was
uttered explaining the good features of the bill and why it had
passed both houses so overwhelmingly.

Another of my pet peeves involved reporters from outside of
Baton Rouge who were sent to the capitol, told to get a story on
such-and-such a bill and to get back with video tape by mid-
afternoon. In many instances they would shoot a few seconds of
tape setting the scene in the chamber or committee room, then
have a shot of the reporter standing in front of the capitol briefly
outlining the subject and, maybe, insert a 10 second comment
from one of the legislators. They would then proudly close with,
"Reporting live from the capitol in Baton Rouge, I'm Scoop
O'Day."

Meanwhile, back in the Capitol, all hell would break loose.
A major debate might ensue. The bill which Scoop had reported
on may be amended beyond recognition and proponents and
opponents would end up actually switching sides on the final
vote. The legislator who was lucky enough to get the 10
seconds "face time" may have voted totally opposite to the

position he stated on tape several hours earlier. But the folks back home got only the 45 second "we were there" coverage. Try to explain something like that at the next Rotary Club "Meet your legislator" luncheon.

One last whiny complaint. The news reporting occupation is not much different from other professions. The Peter Principle applies. Many times good reporters are rewarded by promotion to better-paying, shorter-hour jobs as editors, commentators or broadcast anchor positions and novices are put in their places on the beat. The Peter Principle, first outlined in a book by Dr. L. J. Peter, theorized that eventually, everyone is promoted until they reach their level of *incompetence*. Many times this produces the same affect referred to in the computer world as GIGO: garbage in, garbage out. If the data going in is wrong, it will not come out right. Thus, an ill-prepared news reporter with little background knowledge of legislative procedure might bring back flawed information which finds its way through the process to print or air time and is incorrect or, at best, misleading. Similarly, in the fast-moving and volatile setting of a legislative session, an inexperienced reporter may not recognize the changing dynamics and bring in erroneous reports.

Many TV news directors recognize this problem and have tried a different approach. They will send one of these neophyte reporters and a cameraman out armed with two or three questions prepared by the news director. The reporter's job is to corner a legislator from their coverage area and get on-camera comments on the news director's written questions. The problem with this approach arises when fast-breaking events at the capitol make the prepared questions virtually obsolete. Meanwhile, the cub reporter has been programmed like a cruise missile and is determined to fulfill the stated mission.

For instance: In 1986, I was handling an explosive package of bills aimed at reforming the tort (negligence) laws. This was the opening stage of what has come to be called "lawsuit abuse reform." The House Civil Justice Committee was stacked against the package. Almost all of the committee members were plaintiff trial attorneys in their real lives back home. A series of hearings was set and we proceeded with over twenty grueling hours of committee meetings in a three day period. The famous, self-styled consumer advocate Ralph Nader was hired by the Louisiana Trial Lawyers Association and flown to Baton Rouge to testify against the bills. There was standing-room-only in the committee room at all times. The mood was highly adversarial, abrasive and tense.

On the morning of the third day, the committee was to vote on what remained of the package of bills. The tort reform legislation had been thoroughly gutted. A young reporter from one of the Lafayette TV stations, on her first assignment in Baton Rouge, approached me as I stood on the side of the committee room watching the members making their final statements before voting. I was pretty wrung out by the ordeal. The reporter said she was on a tight schedule and could I step out into the hall for a quick interview? There were already several other TV stations from around the state set up in the hallway outside the committee room waiting for the final vote on the tort package. Numerous print journalists were in the room. I explained to her that we'd get a final vote in the next few minutes and I would meet with all the reporters at the same time to comment on the results.

The members' speeches droned on. She came back. "I'm really pushing my deadline, could you please come out for just a minute?"

I told her I knew we'd finish very shortly, I couldn't leave the room, and until the vote was taken, there really was nothing to say, she would be going home with half a story. (In my heart I knew none of the remaining bills stood a snowball's chance of coming out of this committee.)

Finally, inevitably, the bills were killed and the committee adjourned. I went out to meet the reporters in the hall. There were about five TV units and a dozen or so other radio and print reporters waiting as I got started. I gave them my comments on the committee's actions, my speculation on what the proponents of the lawsuit abuse reform package may do to try to salvage it and said I'd answer questions. I asked them to please allow me to let my home town TV reporter ask the first question since she was on a tight schedule and had been waiting patiently for almost two hours.

She made sure her camera was operating, then glanced down to a rumpled piece of paper she held in her slightly trembling hand. She then read the question she had been programmed to ask, "I'm sure you've heard that an Iranian Airbus has been shot down by the United States missile ship the *USS Vincennes*. Since you are handling this package of bills dealing with liability laws, do you think the United States should accept liability for this loss?"

I didn't know whether to laugh or cry. I hated to see her embarrassed in front of this group of reporters. They could sometime be heartless, even to their own. I reached up and covered the lens of her camera with my hand and said, "Let's start over." I took my hand down. Without waiting for her to speak, I looked into the camera and said, "That's a very good question. Yes, I do believe there is strong support by the people of this state who want to see the civil justice laws applied more fairly. I believe the package of bills we introduced were not given a fair hearing considering the make-up of that committee and blah-blah-blah-blah-blah."

She was not to be denied. "One more question," she said. She proceeded to read from her note sheet, "how will these bills you've introduced affect television stations in libel and slander suits?" Of course we were arguing bills on liability, not libel. I took the same approach and gave her an answer more fitting to the real issue.

I hope she told her boss that she took the initiative to ask those "good questions" instead of the ones given her.

Notable quotes from the legislative halls:

"This is the Senate.   We play the rules by the game."

Senator Larry Bankston

V

"My damn dog ate it!"

Carl Gunter was a big man. Some might even use the description "raw-boned" though his obviously hard musculature had become, at age 41 in 1980 slightly layered with softer tissue. Still, he had the build of a hard-working farmer and outdoorsman. When you saw the large, rough hands, the square set of his jaw and heard him talk, you knew he wasn't somebody you'd want to mess with.

Carl was a farmer from Central Louisiana, an area known for its tough, fundamentalist, rural inhabitants. He was a member of a pioneering Rapides Parish family. Though farming was his primary occupation, he had obviously been successful in real estate development and lived in a large, beautiful home that he had practically built by himself. He had been elected to the Louisiana House of Representatives in 1972 and, in spite of the best efforts and campaign finances of the Louisiana Association of Business and Industry and other conservative interests, he was reelected four times serving 20 years.

His ultimate defeat was as much a result of a few typically blunt, intemperate remarks he had made over the years on the floor of the House as it was the efforts of his political detractors and his opponents.

For instance: during a debate involving the laws dealing with abortion, the House was deciding whether or not to agree to Senate amendments which would allow an exception to the law to protect the life of the mother but not allow one for rape and incest. Carl decided to tell the House that, as a farmer, he didn't think incest was all that big a deal. He said all this talk about inter-family relationships didn't distress him too much, "Cause ah got to thinking the way we get thoroughbred horses and dogs and cattle is through in-breeding. Maybe we would get super-sharp kids." Except for a collective gasp, the House was silent. Television cameras were rolling and reporters were scribbling.

During that same legislative session Gunter got up to take some shots at a bill that my Lafayette colleague Don Bacque was sponsoring. The bill would give a wife the right to reject a husband's sexual advances. Gunter talked about his wedding and remembered his wife promising to "love, honor AND OBEY!" He bellowed that when a wife marries a man, "She knows what he is when she takes the oath, and if she doesn't like being roughed up, she can leave." Another time he took the wrath of the feminist movement when he opposed the Equal Rights Amendment in biting, homespun remarks on the floor of the house: "There ain't no way to make people equal, one's born a man and one's born a woman."

In his first term he unsuccessfully argued against a school program: "This is just another deal to create some deadhead jobs. Maybe there's some way you can teach somebody to manage a child who can't be managed at home, but I don't know what it is."

When I first started serving in the House in 1980, our daily schedule began at 9:00 in the morning at which time routine and housekeeping affairs were handled, committee referrals, second readings, introduction of bills and other innocuous procedures. We would break for committee hearings at about 10 A. M. and reconvene, usually at 2 P. M., for floor debate on bills reported by committee.

I decided to use that morning hour in my first few weeks to get acquainted with other members and be sure they got acquainted with me. I'd roam up and down the aisles, shaking hands, getting names right and repeating mine, exchanging news, pleasantries, gossip and rumors.

One Monday morning I noticed a small crowd gathered around Carl Gunter's desk. Eight or ten representatives were listening intently as Carl related a weekend incident. As I moved into the circle, I noticed a blood-caked bandage on Carl's index finger, or what was left of it. It was obvious that he was missing the first joint of the finger. Carl was telling the group that he had been doing some work on his farm that weekend with an ax and had accidentally chopped off the end of his finger. "Just cut it clean off," he said.

The listeners were amazed, alternately suppressing smiles or laughs and expressing sympathy. One of the bunch finally said, "Well Carl, why didn't you pick up that piece of finger and get yourself to a hospital? You know they can sometimes sew them things back on and they take."

Without a blink Carl said, "I tried to, but before I could get to it, my damn dog ate it! I chased him for twenty minutes 'fore I caught him, shook him upside down by his hind legs, but he wouldn't spit it out!"

Once, while I was handling a bill during floor debate, Carl rose from his desk to question me. He said, "You know what Mr. Gomez? I don' know if I can trust a man what speaks smooth like you. You know, when a man never even says 'uh' ever so often when he's talkin' there's somethin' that bothers me." Of course he knew my broadcasting background but, he needed to rattle my cage a little.

I said, "Well, uh Mr. Gunter, uh if it'll make, uh you vote, uh for this, uh bill, uh I can talk like this, uh another hour."

Let me explain something else about Carl Gunter. He had what urban people call "street smarts," that innate ability, also common to many rural folk, to smell a phony an acre away, to be suspicious of everyone who didn't dress or talk like him and to cut to the heart of a matter with cold precision. His politics were populist in nature. He was regularly graded high by organized labor and low by business and professional associations.

One of the capitol's most astute journalists and most colorful columnists, John Maginnis, annually compiled a "best and worst of the legislature" list. It wasn't terribly scientific and was somewhat opinionated, but he did talk with legislators, other journalists, lobbyists and legislative staffers in arriving at his much-awaited column at the end of each session.

After the 1985 session, under the heading *"Best bill killer"*, Maginnis wrote, *"Rep. Carl Gunter of Deville knows more ways to kill a bill than the lobbyists know how to introduce them. The rhetorical heir to Earl Long, Gunter has the plain talk and pea-patchisms to puncture opponents' slick and sloppy arguments. He may not know all of Roberts' Rules, but he has a flair for the dramatic, as when he preserved a quorum on an important vote by calling for the state police to round up ducking legislators. A labor representative, Gunter is totally unintimidated by any form of arm-twisting, from gubernatorial on down. When not disposing of (legislative) garbage, he takes care of mundane local bills for his police jury and school board – unglamorous chores that he takes very seriously."*

The reference by Maginnis to the move by Gunter to preserve a quorum occurred on one of the most bizarre nights I ever spent at the legislature.

On a Friday night late in the 1985 session the House was trying to work its way through the last few bills left on its calendar. Most were instruments which had originated and been passed by the Senate.

One of the problems which precipitated the weird sequence of events was the absence of Speaker of the House John Alario. The speaker was a master of adding just the right degree of levity to defuse almost any potentially explosive situation. The situation was about to become explosive. John's father had died the day before and the funeral was scheduled for Saturday in Westwego, LA.

In those days, it was not unusual for the House to work late each day in the closing days of a session. We would also usually convene on weekends in order to take action on bills still working their way through the legislative process. Fridays, however, were the exception and we usually adjourned in the early afternoon. This day we planned to work until about 5:00 P. M. Most of the House members were planning to go to the senior Alario's funeral so a Saturday session would be impossible and we were scheduled to return for a Sunday session.

Speaker Pro-tem Joe Delpit of Baton Rouge was acting speaker in Alario's absence when a heated debate broke out just before 5 P. M. An Edwards' administration-backed measure, which had been extremely controversial for several years, would make the State Superintendent of Education an appointed rather than elected position. Under the provisions of the administration's bill, the Board of Elementary and Secondary Education (BESE) would appoint the superintendent. It must be noted that the BESE board had members appointed by the governor as well as elected members but was generally considered to be easily manipulated by the governor. The Senate was sitting on the bill waiting to be assured that the House would grant it confirmation authority on the appointed Superintendent.

Lafayette Senator Allen Bares had introduced a companion bill which would give the senate the authority to confirm or reject a BESE appointment. Some of us in the House had felt the Senate had gone too far in previous mandates to give them sweeping confirmation authority. We were determined to hold the line on further meddling by the Senate.

In addition, Republicans, moderates and conservatives in the House were still hopping mad over Edwards' veto of the repeal of Louisiana's onerous "Prevailing Wage" law. Business and industry had been trying to repeal the law for years and had finally forged a coalition which accomplished that in both the

House and Senate. The law mandated that an area's "prevailing wage" be used to determine labor costs on all state construction contracts. In practice, the prevailing wage used was invariably the labor union scale for the area. This effectively took competitive labor costs out of the bidding equation and drove state contracts up costing the state an estimated 30 to 50 million dollars in additional construction costs annually. Edwards had again sided with organized labor and the AFL-CIO boss Victor Bussie when he vetoed the repeal.

Given the lateness of the hour, the fact that it was a Friday and the impending Alario funeral the next day, many House members had already left for the day. Sensing that there would not be the necessary 53 votes needed to pass the measure, the house floor manager for the Bares bill, Raymond Laborde, moved that the matter be placed back on the calendar to be debated on the next legislative day. Those of us who wanted to kill it objected. We wanted to force it to come up for a vote with a short house and little chance of getting the needed 53 votes.

Of the 105 members, only about 60 were still in attendance. To conduct any kind of business requires a quorum, 53 members present and voting. Laborde knew the bill was in serious trouble. He took the mike in the well of the House and pleaded with the remaining members to let him put this important item back on the calendar for future proper consideration. Meanwhile, mini-conferences broke out all over the floor of the House, members' under-the-desk phones were ringing and pages were racing around delivering messages. Suddenly a dozen or so administration-friendly members scurried out of the chamber. Speaker Pro-tem Delpit hastily declared that there was not a quorum present and the House would adjourn until Sunday. The bill would be automatically carried over.

"Hold on," someone shouted, "You can't have a vote to adjourn if there ain't no quorum." It was Carl Gunter.

Pandemonium. Members were shouting, Delpit was hammering the gavel and parliamentarians were tearing through copies of the House rules and the Constitution of the state. Representative Ed Scogin, the crotchety old republican from Slidell roared, "I'm tired of being run over by the administration."

After several minutes, Gunter got the attention of the speaker pro tem and was recognized to speak. The House quieted to a low rumble. Carl was holding a copy of the Rules of the House and quoted a seldom-noticed section that *required* the speaker to order any missing members to return to the House in order to form a quorum. (There is still some controversy over when the rule had last been used. One report said it was during the administration of Governor Jimmie Davis in the early 1960's but Jack Wardlaw and Ed Anderson of the New Orleans *Times Picayune* reported it had last come into play during Earl Long's last term in the late 1950's.)

Gunter demanded that Speaker Pro-tem Delpit immediately order the sergeants-at-arms *AND* the state police to begin the roundup. After a lengthy conference with the official House parliamentarian, House Clerk Alfred "Butch" Speer, Delpit agreed. He was still treating this as a big joke. "Okay," he said, "Where should they look?" Members yelled suggestions: their apartments, their hotel and motel rooms, popular eating and watering holes such as Del Lago, The City Club, The Camelot Club, Giamanco's, The Pastime, The Place, Zee Zee Gardens.

"Just send the state troopers to go get'em," Gunter roared, "We ain't gonna adjourn."

Some members still in the Capitol building heard the melee and wandered back in. Another quorum call was ordered, 48 members present. Those present were ordered to stay. Some sidled out, others returned. Another quorum call: 50 present.

Over the next two hours no less than six quorum calls were taken without success.

In an effort to hold the members who were still in the chamber, the state troopers on security duty were ordered to close and guard the doors, to turn off the elevator which ran down from the coffee lounge to the first floor and the basement exits and not to allow anyone to leave. Lobbyists and spectators were ordered out of the chamber. Some retreated to the balcony overlooking the House and watched in awe and disbelief. One group of tourists, visiting from out-of-state stayed throughout the wild evening. What a vacation story they took home from lovely Louisiana. We were prisoners in our own house.

Someone complained that some of the representatives were using their phones to call missing members and warn them of the dragnet taking place throughout the city. The presiding officer ordered the phones to be shut off.

Usually, as each daily session was winding down, I would call my wife to let her know we were about to adjourn and give her some estimate of when I would be getting home in Lafayette. When the debate on this particular bill had started, I assumed we would deal with it quickly and be on our way. I had called Carol about 4:45 and told her I'd soon be crossing the swamp and should be home by 6:30 or so. I called again about 6:00, during the heat of the proceedings, and erroneously speculated we'd get this over with by 6:30 and I'd be home by 8:00. It was now after 7 o'clock and I couldn't use my desk phone or any other phone in the chamber nor could I leave the chamber.

I even tried a little subterfuge and a test of the state troopers' resolve. There were two rest rooms in the coffee shop lounge just off the chamber. I walked into the lounge for a moment, than walked back to the rear of the chamber. I told the trooper on guard I desperately needed to use a rest room and both in the lounge were occupied. He sadly shook his head and said, "Sorry, Representative, orders are orders."

"What are you going to do, shoot me?" I asked jokingly.

He paused for a second, did a slow Jack Benny-like take and said, "I don't know."

The situation became more insane. A quorum call was taken and indicated 54 members present and voting. Finally. The question on the floor to vote on the confirmation bill was ordered and a vote taken. Only 52 machines were voted. People were beginning to talk in terms of binding, gagging, handcuffing or even lynching some members. Groans, moans and worse broke out again.

Representative Sam Theriot of Abbeville yelled, "Call Rambo to get us out of here!"

Representative Raymond Jetson of Baton Rouge came walking into the chamber announcing, "I want to make it perfectly clear that I was not arrested. I turned myself in."

Representative Alphonse Jackson of Shreveport, an Edwards floor-leader appealed to the House to stop game-playing. "Let's adjourn and come back when tempers are at a lower level. We might do something we will regret."

"The game was played on us," said Rep. Quentin Dastugue of Metairie, referring to the prevailing wage veto by Edwards.

Finally, at about 8:15 P. M. it appeared the required number of representatives were back on the floor. Some, who had been rounded up at various clubs and bars, were, almost literally, *on the floor*.

The vote was taken and the bill was rejected 28 – 26. We were free and the object of all this rancor, the Bares bill was killed.

But even after such an uncanny night, Edwards and the Senate prevailed. Alphonse Jackson resurrected a bill he had introduced granting the Senate confirmation power just as the Bares bill had. It passed the House on Sunday 62-37. With that assurance, the Senate passed the governor's bill to make the Education Superintendent appointed by a vote of 34-3.

I can't say that Carl Gunter and I ever became friends though I believe we shared a mutual respect. That was all I ever really expected from my colleagues in the House. It occurred to me early on that, though we each represented 105 different areas of the state and varied greatly in education, intelligence, age, philosophy, religious beliefs and any other demographic category a census bureau could conjure, we were each elected from a district with roughly 45,000 citizens. Whether I shared Carl's beliefs or he disliked the way I talked, we realized that we both got to the House the same way and for the same reason: we were there to represent the people of our respective districts. I hoped that all the other members of the House practiced that philosophy.

Carl Gunter died of cancer in the summer of 1999 at age 60.

Notable quotes from the legislative halls:

Two days after a "shoot a carjacker" bill was passed, a bill placing longer sentencing on carjackers was being debated :

Representative Kip Holden: "Are we going to enact these penalties before or after we shoot the carjackers?"

Representative Peppi Bruneau: "Mr. Holden, this bill will only apply to the ones we miss."

VI

"....an embarrassment of riches!"

1980 was a heady time to be entering the state legislature in Louisiana.

A Republican governor had been elected for the first time in 100 years. (The last time was under "carpetbagger" rule during reconstruction after the Civil War.) Edwin Edwards was leaving office after eight prosperous years and oil prices were floating in the $30 per barrel range leading long-time House Appropriations Chairman Kevin Reilly of Baton Rouge to bemoan, in his best John Kennedy Boston Brahmin accent, that the state was "suffering an embarrassment of riches."

Dave Treen did not win the 1979 gubernatorial election easily and some felt that, had it not been for the bitter contest over the runner-up spot in the first primary, he would not have achieved that historical victory.

Former Lieutenant Governor Jimmy Fitzmorris and Public Service Commissioner Louis Lambert (who later would return to a seat he had vacated in the Senate) were virtually tied for second place when the final count was ended in the first primary. Voting irregularity charges started flying and legal action was filed by both sides to decide the issue. The wrangling continued for two weeks before it was officially decided that Lambert would be Treen's runoff opponent. The bitterness had spread to other Democratic candidates Paul Hardy, former House Speaker E. L. "Bubba" Henry and Lafayette Senator Edgar "Sonny" Mouton. In the meantime, Dave Treen and his Republican supporters were serenely and steadily campaigning for the governorship. By the time it was decided that Lambert had placed second, there were only a couple of weeks left in the campaign. One by one the bombs started to fall on Lambert as Fitzmorris, Hardy, Henry and Mouton, all Democrats, did the unthinkable and endorsed Republican Dave Treen for governor. Even with their support, Treen's victory was not overwhelming and the legislature remained solidly Democrat. Starting the 1980 term, not one Senator of the 39 was a Republican. Only 10 of the 105 House members were GOP. The elected Lieutenant Governor Robert "Bobby" Freeman and all the other state-wide elected officials were also Democrat. In contrast, when Murphy J. "Mike" Foster III took office in 1996 as the third elected Louisiana Republican governor, one-third, thirteen members of the Senate and 27 members of the House were Republican. (Foster switched to the Republican party during the 1995 campaign. Former Governor "Buddy" Roemer was a Republican when he left office but had been elected as a Democrat in 1987.)

Treen quickly installed two of his key supporters, John Cade of Alexandria and William "Billy" Nungesser of New Orleans, as his top aides. Cade, quiet, acerbic and impersonal was untitled but obviously Treen's closest political advisor. Nungesser, red haired, florid-faced and a typically gregarious New Orleanian was Executive Secretary and Chief Executive Assistant.

The "turncoat" Democrats who had endorsed Treen were also quickly rewarded with appointments. James Fitzmorris, Jr. became Executive Assistant for Economic Development, a newly created position. Edgar Mouton, former Lafayette Senator, was named executive counsel to the governor. Former House Speaker Bubba Henry took over as Commissioner of Administration. Paul Hardy moved into the powerful position of Secretary of the Department of Transportation and Development. One appointment that surprised everyone and angered many of the staunch Republicans was the naming of George Fischer as

Secretary of the Department of Health and Human Resources, one of the largest departments in state government and one which controlled an enormous budget in state and federal funds. Fischer was a prominent member of the Edwin Edwards administration and a long time confidant of the former governor.

As I began my first term as a state representative, I thought I knew a lot about the legislative process having observed and reported on it for many years. But my first meeting at which only legislators were present was an eye opener. It was a meeting of the Acadiana area legislators prior to the inauguration to decide various things such as preferred committee assignments and who we would be backing for speaker of the House.

Jesse Guidry of Cecilia was generally considered the dean of the Acadiana area delegation. The proliferation of "caucuses" had not yet spread through the legislature. The Jefferson Parish delegation was the first to unite, hire staff and acquire office space. Today, the legislature is splintered into a variety of "caucuses": rural, black, women's, big and small municipalities and Acadiana. Juba Diez, Manny Fernandez and I jokingly called ourselves the "Hispanic Caucus." Jesse had served for eight years as a St. Martin Parish police juror before being elected to the House in 1973. Elias "Bo" Ackal, Jr. of New Iberia was another of the area legislators who had been closely allied with Edwin Edwards since being elected to the House in 1972 and was considered one of the leaders in the House.

During the meeting we were told that "Bo" would prefile House Bill 1 of the 1980 regular session. This would be a bill to raise the pay of legislators effectively immediately. At the time Senators and Representatives received $16,250 per year base pay and $50 per diem while in session or attending committee meetings. The per diem averaged about $4 to $5 thousand per year. I balked. "I didn't even know how much this job paid when I started running and I'm certainly not going to vote for an immediate pay raise with my first vote as a state representative!" I said.

"C'mon Ron," Jesse Guidry said, "this is how the deal works. You get this done early and people will forget all about it in four years when you run again."

Some of the older members, notably Luke Leblanc of Lafayette, said us new guys had to vote for it to help the older ones build up their retirement benefits. I later found out that Luke had no intention of voting for the pay raise, and didn't. He just wanted to make sure the rest of us did so he could get the benefits of it.

Long story, short: the pay raise passed with three or four votes to spare. I didn't vote for it. Neither did Luke. The bill was severely amended in the process so that the increase was not very significant. The base was raised to $16,800 and per diem to $75. There was a convenient ruling that members could not refuse to take the raise. I had my net-after-taxes increase calculated and contributed that amount annually for the ten years I served in the House to the Southern Consumers' scholarship fund in Lafayette, a black organization which financed college scholarships for meritorious and needy black high school graduates.

Another topic of that first organizational meeting of the Acadiana delegates was the "railroad bills." It seems that former Lafayette Representative Richard Bertrand was on a session-to-session retainer from some of the railroad companies to lobby for their interests. However, he was only retained if bills were introduced which threatened the companies in some way, costing them excessive money or sanctioned new, onerous regulations. To help out their old colleague, a member of the delegation each year would introduce such bills. There really was no intent to pass any of them.

One of the ways the railroads would counter any adverse legislation was to move a string of club cars onto a siding by the

Baton Rouge Memorial Stadium about a mile from the Capitol. They would invite legislators to the plush club cars for lunch or dinner, usually serving steaks and adult beverages and, as a unique offering, always had a large supply of Macadamia nuts laid out as snacks. Don't ask me why Macadamia nuts. Cigars for the legislators were also a big item with the railroads.

John N. John, a veteran representative from Crowley, was the designated railroad bill author. (The senior John, killed in an automobile accident in the early '80's was the father of former state representative and current 7th district Congressman Chris John.) He would introduce the bills. The railroads would respond to the threat and Bertrand would get a lobbying contract for the session. We were told that if we were on a committee which heard the bills we should vote for them. That would insure that they would be brought to the floor of the House for debate and further guarantee that the railroaders would take the bills seriously and move the club cars into Baton Rouge.

Rep. John would take over from there. He was a master at delaying a vote on the bills. They would work their way up the calendar and be scheduled for debate and John would take the floor, "Now, you know I want these bills to get a fair hearing, but how can I compete with those big, rich railroad companies with their Macadamia nuts, their big "ceegars" and their big thick juicy steaks. I'm just gonna ask you to put these bills back on the calendar so we can wait to see if they'll run out of all those steaks and things and we can concentrate on doing the right thing." John could delay the final vote for weeks. After every one had been well dined and wined he would claim that he just could not round up enough votes for the bills and would table them. "But, I'll be back next year," he would say. Some of the legislators even applauded his performance.

I only recently learned that there are now laws in some states against just such activities. The practice is called "bellringing." According to a recent newspaper report, several legislators in another state have been indicted for the practice of introducing or threatening to introduce legislation merely for the benefit of a lobbyist's shakedown of a client. How they hope to prove such a charge is beyond me. After all, as Jesse Guidry told me it was "just done in the spirit of fun."

I had ambitiously stated that I'd like to serve on the Appropriations Committee (the money spending panel.) Of course two-thirds of the members of the House had the same request. That assignment, obviously was out of the question. However, with the help of "Sonny" Mouton, Governor Treen's newly designated Executive Counsel and Republican Mike Thompson of Lafayette, my seat mate in the House, I was assigned to the House Committee on Commerce and the House Committee on Ways and Means. Both were important and extremely busy committees. Ways and Means met on Monday and Tuesday mornings and Commerce on Wednesday and Thursday. As a freshman, I was expected to also help fill out one of the committees that met on Fridays. Only a couple of low profile committees met on Friday and nobody wanted those assignments. I was put on the Retirement Committee. That was a little ironic since I had chosen not to participate in the legislative retirement program. I considered the job of state representative to be part-time and not deserving of a retirement benefit. Besides, I figured we all had or should have regular full-time employment to provide for retirement benefits.

The chairman of the Retirement Committee was the legendary Shady R. Wall from West Monroe. He swore Shady was his real first name. He also claimed he was the only member of the legislature who could prove he was legally sane since he had spent some time in a mental institute and had a certificate of release to prove his soundness of mind. Shady had run for governor at one time. He had dabbled in real estate, advertising and "investments" and he had married well and become the President of a bank in West Monroe. He loved guns and firearms and kept a cache of them in his apartment at the

Pentagon Barracks adjacent to the Capitol. He reportedly had a bowl of hand grenades displayed on a dining room table like a still life display of fruit. He had also reportedly fired a pistol at a representative who made the mistake of incurring his ire. Seems this colleague and several others were playing a childish prank on Shady one night and got caught. They were fleeing the scene when Shady opened fire. Luckily, he missed. No one is quite sure whether that was intentional.

When I met Shady in 1980 he was 58 years old and his thick wavy hair was totally gray. A tall, well proportioned man, Wall dressed with a flair. He wore white linen suits, brightly colored ties and ankle high boots. It was not uncommon for him to have a small revolver in an ankle holster tucked inside a boot. I had seen earlier pictures of him as a younger man. He was quite dashing with a dazzling smile. But his most arresting features were his eyebrows. Even after he had turned prematurely gray, his eyebrows were thick and black. They also were shaped like an upside down V and, combined with eyes that seemed to dance crazily when he grinned, gave him a devilish look.

One day in the House, Shady was at his desk, leaning back in his chair and talking on the phone. Carl Gunter, big, rawboned farmer from Deville, walked by his desk and playfully reached under and jiggled the cradle that held the hand set. That inadvertently disconnected the call. Little did Gunter know that Shady was conducting a meeting by conference call with his bank board in Monroe. Shady's volcanic temper erupted. He leaped out of his chair and immediately reached for the small, derringer-sized pistol in his boot holster. Gunter, unaware of the problem, was already several strides up the aisle and John Ensminger was just behind Shady. The sergeant-at-arms on that side of the floor was nearby. Ensminger, the sergeant-at-arms and several others grabbed Shady and prevented him from doing whatever he intended to do with that pistol. Gunter was escorted to the speaker's office and Shady was asked to leave the chamber.

About a half-hour later, my curiosity took over. I went to the speaker's office to see what was happening. Gunter was sitting in a chair. He was rigid. His face was prodded by a tic in the left cheek. His jaws were clenched. Tears were in his eyes. I thought, "What a wrenching experience," and patted Carl on the shoulder and said, "He didn't mean it Carl. It's going to be all right."

He brusquely shoved my hand away and said, "It ain't all right. No body pulls a gun on me and gets away with it."

We didn't see much of Shady on the floor of the House the rest of that session. In the meantime, the sergeants-at-arms and state police were always hovering near Carl Gunter. Time, of course, healed the problem but it could have been a nasty incident.

Shady ruled the Retirement Committee with an iron hand. It was his committee. In spite of the criticism he took for his dictatorial methods, it was grudgingly admitted that Shady had saved the state millions of dollars by killing hundreds of special interest retirement bills. At that time, every group in state government had its own separate retirement system. The teachers had one, the state police another, judges had their own, district attorneys, clerks of court, assessors, all with their own retirement systems. Each had different rules, different investment plans. Each employed a staff, each had paid actuaries. It was a mess. It hasn't changed much.

According to the Rules of the House, the author of a bill has sole control of that bill. House Committee chairmen are obligated to schedule all bills assigned to their committees in a timely fashion. The author of a bill requests a hearing and only he/she can bring the bill up before the House for debate once cleared by a committee.

The rule of the Shady Wall Retirement Committee was that only Shady Wall could be the author of a bill dealing with retirement. Thus, he was in total control of every bill that came before his committee, no exceptions. If you wanted to introduce legislation dealing with an area of retirement you went to confession with Father Wall. He was one of the few House members who had a private office in the Capitol at that time. In fact he had a suite of offices on the ground floor. Long before the Capitol was wired to bring the audio proceedings of the House and Senate to almost every office, Shady had speakers in his office bringing him the audio proceedings of the House. He was rarely in the chamber unless he had bills to present. If you needed to see Chairman Wall you made an appointment and went to his office. If he blessed your idea for new legislation *he would introduce the bill, drafted the way he wanted it and under his name.* He would then decide whether the bill would be heard by his committee, advise the committee how he wanted them to vote on "his" bill and then decide whether he wanted to have it passed by the House. He did it all rather good-naturedly if somewhat sardonically.

In July, following the 1982 regular session, the now defunct weekly newspaper, the *Baton Rouge Enterprise* ran a feature called "The '82 Legislative Awards." One of the dubious awards was for the "worst committee in the Legislature." Though first place went to the Senate Labor and Industrial Relations Committee, the House Retirement Committee ran a close second. Explaining their choice, the *Enterprise* said, *"Shady Wall's Retirement Committee isn't so bad, except that it's not a committee, it's Shady's classroom. 'Now you listen up, gentlemen while I explain this to you' is Shady's means of dealing with his bored and unruly children."*

"Mr. Gomez," he said in one of my first meetings, "Now you're just a freshman here and don't fully understand what most of this stuff is about. Most of those people sitting out there consider themselves experts on retirement. They're not. They're just hired guns trying to milk the system. Some of them are called actuaries, that's a hi-falutin' title that says they can predict the future. They can't. They lie. Now, I'm gonna show you how this works. I'm gonna call Mr. Graves up here to tell us about this next bill. Mr. Graves, come up here."

An elderly man rose and came to the witness table. He looked as though someone had been beating him with a whip or was about to. His rheumy eyes were downcast, his complexion gray, his hands trembling slightly.

"Mr. Graves here is one of those actuaries, now tell us what this bill does Mr. Graves," ordered the chairman.

"Well, Mr. Chairman," he started in a wavering voice, "as you know, this bill doesn't really do much, it just straightens out a little problem we have in St. Helena Parish..."

"Now you see Mr. Gomez," Wall interrupted, "he's lying already. This damn bill would open up the retirement rolls for two dozen new people to come in and cost the state thousands of dollars. Counsel, put this man under oath, swear him in!"

It would go on like that hour after hour every Friday morning. Brow beating and insulting, Shady would weed through the bills to be heard. Every so often we were allowed to vote on one. In truth, he killed a lot of bad legislation. One could only wonder if his methods were totally necessary.

But, Shady wasn't blindly committed to "good government."

Early in that 1980 session, several state elected officials had prevailed upon Chairman Wall to introduce a bill dealing with their retirement system.

The venerable Treasurer of the State of Louisiana, Mrs. Mary Evelyn Parker took the lead to present their case. She was speaking for the other state-wide elected officials such as Lieutenant Governor "Bobby" Freeman, Secretary of State Jim Brown, Superintendent of Education J. Kelly Nix, Agriculture Commissioner Bob Odom, Insurance Commissioner Sherman Bernard and Commissioner of Elections Jerry Fowler.

Mrs. Parker's health was not good at the time and she addressed the retirement committee in a strained, shaky voice, "Gentlemen, all we want is fairness and parity. You all know that since the mid '70's the retirement system for state officers like us has not been fair."

As she continued her presentation, I leaned over to Loy Weaver, seated next to me, and asked him to what she was referring. Loy, from Homer, a really nice guy, one of Governor Treen's staunch supporters and floor leaders, former special agent with the FBI, was beginning his second term. He explained to me that a major change had been made in the retirement system for some elected officials in the mid '70's. Loy suggested that it was a quid pro quo to give the legislators a good reason to vote for the huge change in oil severance taxes which Edwin Edwards had pushed through. Naturally, the oil industry had put tremendous pressure on the legislators in opposition to the change.

Most of the retirement systems were based on a "2 ½ times" formula. The number of years of service was multiplied by 2 ½ times. That would become the percentage of base pay which would be paid as retirement benefits. The base pay would be the average of the highest paid three years. Thus, a teacher who's highest three year average pay was, say, $20,000 and had served thirty years would multiply thirty times 2 ½ to arrive at 75%. Her annual retirement would then be 75% of $20,000 or $15,000.

The law was changed for the governor, state judges and legislators only. Their formula would be 3 ½ times. They would also be vested after only 12 years service and could start receiving the retirement at age 55. By the way, not only salary was counted, legislators could also add in per diem income. Therefore, a governor, judge or state legislator with 20 years service would multiply 20 times 3 ½ and receive 70% of their highest three year average pay and could start receiving it at age 55.

Naturally, the rest of the elected state officials felt slighted by this sweetheart deal and wanted "fairness and parity."

By this time in my legislative training I had learned to draft amendments. As Loy grinningly finished his explanation, I grabbed an amendment form and proposed to change the bill at hand. My amendment would grant fairness and parity. It would reduce everybody, governor, judges, legislators back to the 2 ½ formula. I passed it up to the Chairman's desk. Shady looked at it then looked at me over his granny glasses, smiled pityingly, arched those great peaked eyebrows and shook his head, "No."

I had one advantage. Because of the appearance at the committee of so many elected officials, we had a good contingent of media covering the meeting. Normally, the media avoided the proceedings of the Retirement Committee like a lecture on ant farming. I raised my hand and asked to be recognized by the chair. Shady ignored me. Some members of the media started getting interested.

"Mr. Chairman," I said, "as a member of this committee, I believe I have the right to submit an amendment. You have that amendment at your desk and I insist that it be heard."

Shady made a big show of searching his desk to no avail and held up his hands as if to say, "I find no amendment." Mrs. Parker and the other state officials were anxiously conferring at the witness table trying to figure out what in tarnation was happening in Chairman Wall's sacred chambers.

I grabbed another piece of paper and quickly wrote out the same amendment to the bill and brought it to Mr. Wall's desk.

Under his breath, Shady said, "You don't really want to do this Mr. Gomez."

"Yes, I do!" I said.

Shady banged the gavel and announced, through clenched teeth, "This meeting is adjourned."

Naturally, the media reporters wanted to know what I had done and I told them.

When the House started convening for the afternoon session, I walked into a thunderstorm. All of the older members of the House, led by my Lafayette colleague Luke Leblanc, were waiting for me. Buster Sheridan, Earl Schmitt, Ty Cobb Lanier all wanted to know what the hell I was trying to do to their retirement benefits. I tried to explain my motives and that, even if my amendment had been adopted, they would be "grandfathered" in under the old formula. They were in a state of high anxiety to say the least.

Needless to say, the "fairness and parity" bill never came up again before the Retirement Committee and the good old boy system rolled along until 1996 when a new flock of reform legislators finally did away with legislative retirement. Of course, with the passage of term limits by this same group, the retirement question was almost moot.

Though I knew that "Awards" articles such as the one quoted above from the *Baton Rouge Enterprise* were written somewhat tongue-in-cheek, I was pleasantly surprised, and honored when they named me "Rookie of the year" with the following explanation: " *'As close to perfect as any freshman to come down the pike in years,' says one veteran lobbyist of Ron Gomez. He surprised many observers with the easy passage of a host of reform bills opposed by architects. He goes out of his way to help everyone. If anything, he needs to be more selective for maximum effectiveness."*

Interestingly, at least five "veteran lobbyists" told me "very confidentially" that they were the source of the above quote.

Notable quotes from the legislative halls:

"I know you're worried about being a hypocrite for voting for this, but that's our job!"

Representative Francis Thompson

VII

"You mean a person can get away with telling a lie on the House floor?"

I devoted my first session in the legislature to learning. As much as I thought I already knew about the process, I had already found out, in the pre-session meetings, how much I didn't know. I only introduced one bill that first session. It was a relatively non-controversial law dealing with taxation on aviation fuels. A professional pilot friend of mine had explained the problem and I decided it was a worthwhile effort. It passed with ease. Wow, I had written a law.

I had gotten two choice committee assignments - Commerce and Ways and Means, and, of course the not-so-choice Retirement Committee.

In those days each year's session was open to all types of bills. Since then the legislature has adopted, by a citizen-approved Constitutional amendment, a schedule which allows only "fiscal" matters (budgeting, taxation measures) to be introduced during shorter sessions (45 days) in even-numbered years. All other types of bills may be filed in only odd-numbered years, but these sessions would last the traditional 60 working days in an 85 day period. Dan Juneau and my friends with LABI, most conservative legislators, most lobbyists and Governor Mike Foster are all big supporters of this relatively new process.

I was not in the legislature when it passed but I didn't like it from the beginning and spoke against it at several civic club appearances in Lafayette. It was not the only time I've ever been in the distinct minority. Proponents argued that this schedule would have the legislature meeting for much fewer days over the course of several years and thus save money in legislative and legislative-support budgets. They also argued that limiting tax and budget proposals to every other year would focus attention on these important subjects without the temptation of vote trading on other matters.

My fears were twofold. First, I didn't like what it did to new legislators every four years. A candidate campaigns for office in an odd-numbered year, probably commits to supporting or introducing legislation to fulfill his/her promises and the wishes of the constituency, then finds that, under the new schedule, those promises can not be kept for over a year and a half since the first session of the term falls in an even-numbered year and is for "fiscal only" matters. Second, under the "even-odd" system, a governor can call a special session at any time, any year to consider matters which he wants. Under the law, a special session can consider only the legislation included in the "governor's call." Therefore, a governor can control the entire agenda of a special session. Theoretically, the legislature can also call itself into special session and set its own agenda. It has never happened in the history of the state.

The result of the "even-odd" system is that there have been special sessions called in practically every "fiscal-only" year and the legislature has been in session more days than before. In addition, during the even-year sessions there are only two or three committees involved in fiscal legislation in either the Senate or House and the rest of the members have virtually nothing to do during the first half of the session which is devoted to committee hearings on the budget and other fiscal matters. I've heard that the average handicap of the golfing members of the legislature has been considerably reduced since the new schedule was adopted. There have been several unsuccessful attempts to amend the session schedule. Some would reverse the years allowing fiscal only items in odd-numbered years and vice versa. Other bills have been introduced to revert to the old schedule while still others have several variations of both systems. Governor Mike Foster is a big proponent of the present system and so far has helped thwart any attempts to change it.

*   *   *

My seat mate, Republican Mike Thompson of Lafayette was my chief mentor during my first session in the legislature in 1980. He had coached me on some of the more subtle rules of the House. One of the prime rules was that only members could address the House from the podium in the well (the lower section in the front of the House between the members' desks and the speaker's and clerk's platform) unless an exception was made by a vote of the House to suspend the rules. This was usually done only for the governor's state of the state address or for visiting dignitaries. Through the ten years I served we had everybody from presidential candidates, movie and TV celebrities to Mother Teresa address the legislature.

One mid-afternoon, after we had been in session about six weeks, I looked up when I heard a strange voice coming over the speaker system. There, standing at the podium, was a nattily dressed man of about fifty. He was very well-spoken and seemed quite comfortable addressing the House. A nice looking guy, if you liked the big-hair style of the mid '50's, he was explaining a bill to the House. I had never seen him before in my life. I looked at Mike Thompson who was serenely reading over a piece of legislation. I said, "Mike, who is this guy? Isn't this against the rules?"

Mike started laughing, "Naw, that's Eddie Bopp. He's a representative from the New Orleans area but he hardly ever comes to the session."

I was amazed, "How does he get away with that?"

I made it a point to meet Bopp that day and saw him only a few more times during that first term. He was a very pleasant, very erudite man from an unusually diverse district in greater

New Orleans known as Arabi. He had been elected in a special election in 1978 and to a full term in 1979. He had a law and a pharmaceutical degree and co-owned a drug company, had an apartment business and was a bank director. The legislature was most definitely a sideline. His laissez-faire attitude toward attendance soon caught up with him. He was defeated in 1983 by a bar owner named "Bud" Ripoll who was in turn taken out in 1987 by Ken Odinet, a construction engineer/contractor who was also executive director of the St. Bernard Parish Water and Sewer Commission. Reapportionment in 1990 somewhat smoothed out the demographic anomalies in the district and Odinet was reelected in '91, '95 and '99. I believe that is a new longevity record for District 103.

I got a major surprise early in my first session in the spring of 1980 when I learned that, while all committee hearings were recorded and transcribed, there was absolutely no record of anything said during debate on the floor of the House. The exception, of course, would be the unofficial notes or recordings of reporters or TV cameras.

I found this out as I was listening to debate on a bill early in that first session. One of the opponents took the mike and used some "facts" which I knew to be untrue. I went to the clerk of the House and asked how I could get a transcript of the remarks. I wanted to see if I was right about his facts. David Poynter, the clerk at the time, told me there was no record. None.

I said, "You mean a person can get away with telling a lie on the House floor?"

Yep!

During my third term, while I was serving on the House Executive Committee, I tried to get funding appropriated to purchase an audio recording system for the House. It could easily be done for a relatively modest amount of money. I believe it would have served the legislators and the public well and eliminated much of the truth-bending during House debates.

The whole question got side tracked when another member of the Executive Committee insisted that a television recording system be installed instead of the voice-only I was advocating. While very desirable, gavel to gavel television recording of the House proceedings would have been infinitely more expensive than audio-only. By the time we had priced various systems and argued the merits and disadvantages of either, I was leaving the House and the matter was dropped.

My dear friend Hunt Downer from Houma, who served as speaker pro tem of the House during the Roemer administration from 1988 to 1992 was elected speaker in 1996 when Mike Foster became governor. He obviously stepped on some toes of those who like status quo but he instituted some first-rate changes which made the House more efficient, more accessible to the public and included a complete restoration of the magnificent House chamber. He also brought the House up to date with computers and a new communications system on every desk. And, along the way, Downer instituted a videotaping system of all House proceedings. Now, they're on record.

Shortly after the fall '99 elections, Governor Foster yielded to pressure from Downer's critics and withdrew his support for the speaker. Deeply disappointed, Downer magnanimously withdrew his campaign for reelection as speaker. The governor's choice to succeed Downer was Representative Charles Dewitt from Lecompte who started serving in the House at the same time as I did, 1980.

*   *   *

As I stated earlier, I was beginning to find more and more things that I didn't know about government.

Let me give you a good example of why I and others in public office tend to become cynical.

Shortly after I was elected, a friend came to me and asked for my assistance in a state-related matter. He said he wanted me to help an acquaintance of his get the state light bulb procurement contract. I had no idea what he was talking about. He told me that, during the previous eight years under Edwin Edwards, an individual, operating on a personal contract, handled all light bulb purchasing for the state. This person hired two men who divided the state equally. Each would travel a circuit of his part of the state on a regular year-round basis and inventory the neon tube and light bulb supplies of all state buildings: hospitals, office buildings, motor vehicle offices, highway department division headquarters, vocational-technical schools - every state building. They would file regular reports with, let's call him the LBPC (light bulb procurement chief), who would then order the needed supplies from a major manufacturer, such as General Electric to drop-ship the light bulbs to each facility. He did not have to have a warehouse or ever even handle the product. For this service, my friend told me, the LBPC received approximately $200,000 a year in commission from the manufacturers. He paid each of his inspectors $50,000 a year and kept the other $100,000 or so for himself.

It seems the LBPC had died just before Edwards left office and his wife had taken over the operations. But, my friend said, she had no political ties to the Republicans or Dave Treen, thus the position should be wide open.

I went to Billy Nungesser, one of Treen's closest advisors and said, "Billy, I can show you a way to save the state $200,000 a year." I told him of the arrangement and suggested that, surely, the state could do its own inventory, make a deal with the light bulb manufacturers and convert the commission procedure to a discount for the state. They did it. I believe that lasted until Edwin Edwards came back into office in 1984. I'm sure we then had another LBPC named though I was certainly not privy to that agreement. To put the enormity of the light bulb use in the state in perspective, I recently read that Lafayette General Hospital had 14,000 light bulbs in its facilities. The state owned New Orleans Charity Hospital is about three times the size of the Lafayette hospital.

Then there was the state public school text book procurer. This person had a lock on this sweet deal for years. Each year, all of the public schools in the state would place their orders for the text books needed for the school year. Only this one person could handle the orders. The publishers shipped the books to him for warehousing and distribution and paid him a handsome commission. I never met the man but he must have had a lot of stroke. Representative Kathleen Blanco of Lafayette and I sponsored a bill to allow either the individual school boards or the State Department of Education to buy directly from the publishers and take the commission in the form of a discount. It was big money. Believe it or not, we could not get the bill passed by the House during Edwards administration.

Now, project those two small slices of a state budget into the hundreds of potentially similar areas: paper supplies, office equipment and furniture, computer systems and their maintenance contracts, automobile and truck purchases and maintenance, specialized uniforms and on and on and on.

Suppose you have exclusive access to supplying the state with "frog eyes" – those reflective squares used to mark the shoulders and center lines on highways. Can you imagine what kind of commission you could make if the state replaces all of its "frog eyes" just every four or five years? They have.

One year, all the state police "bubble gum machines" (the flashing and whirling light arrays on the top of police cars) were replaced. Were they all broken? Were they all obsolete?

Once you've finished imagining all the areas in which you could make big money out of Louisiana state government, project that to a huge state like Florida, or Texas, or California. Then, to really make yourself crazy, project that to the rake-offs that can occur on a budget the size of the United States Government.

Now, try to figure out how to stop that kind of abuse!

*   *   *

During my first session, two items became the focus of my involvement: funding for the Assembly Center in Lafayette (eventually named "The Cajundome,") which I had envisioned as a joint effort between the city, university and state; and, a bill that started off very quietly and innocently and erupted into a war among the horse racing tracks in the state.

Robert Adley was, like me, starting his first term in the legislature. Robert was only 32 years old at the time but carried a lot of personal and governmental experience. An ex-Marine with a ramrod straight posture on his slim 5' 8" frame, Robert had served on the Bossier City Recreation Board as well as on the Civil Service Board. He was a past state president of the Jaycees and had served three years on the Bossier City Council when elected to the House. His boisterous laugh could be heard throughout the chamber but he could also be an intense, persuasive speaker.

Robert had introduced a bill on behalf of Louisiana Downs, the plush horse racing facility located in Bossier Parish owned by the DiBartolo family. The DiBartolo's were extremely wealthy entrepreneurs who had made their early fortune in shopping center developments and had moved on to varied ventures including ownership of the National Football League San Francisco 49'ers.

The purpose of Adley's bill was to grant Louisiana Downs more racing dates each season. The legislature had always held regulation of horse racing very possessively in spite of the fact that Louisiana had a very active Racing Commission.   In addition to the ultra-modern Louisiana Downs in Bossier, there were two tracks in the New Orleans area; (one being the venerable and world famous Fair Grounds,) one in Vinton, just outside of Lake Charles; and Evangeline Downs in Carencro in

Lafayette Parish. Racing was a big industry in the state. Since then, the horse racing industry, breeders, riders, trainers, grooms, suppliers and track workers, have been seriously impacted by the legalization and expansion in the state of numerous other forms of gambling. ("Gaming" as the legislature has defined it - gambling, you see, is in violation of the State Constitution.) Race tracks have now become a haven for video machine gambling and have spawned satellite locations for off-track betting and video gambling. Recent legislation has authorized large scale slot machine establishments at tracks in Bossier and St. Landry Parishes which has prompted the relocation of the entire Evangeline Downs facility from Lafayette Parish.

Visitors to the Capitol and legislators who were not familiar with the legislative facilities prior to 1984 would be shocked to revisit a committee hearing in those days. The more important committee rooms were on the ground floor but were little better than drab, stark meeting rooms with no amenities. Most had no sound systems and visitors were sometimes hard pressed to follow the proceedings. The lesser committees met in the basement. These rooms featured concrete floors, exposed water pipes and electric conduits criss-crossing the ceilings, caged light bulbs and folding chairs for the attendees. Natural light came from a small transom-like window set at ground level just below the ceiling on the outside wall. Inmates from nearby Hunt Correctional facility were used for janitorial duties in the Capitol and its complex of buildings. The committee rooms could easily have served as holding cells for the prisoners at night.

Speaker John Hainkel started the renovation process which produced beautiful first floor committee rooms each featuring native Louisiana woods such as Cypress, Oak, Pine and Pecan. Speaker John Alario topped Hainkel's efforts with a complete new complex in what was the basement and sub-basement. The new addition, named "Alario Hall" (after his father since it is not lawful to name public facilities for living people) is state of the art in comfort as well as audio-visual facilities.

Adley's bill came before the Commerce Committee in the stark committee room setting of 1980. He called the owner of the track, Edward DiBartolo, Sr. to the witness table. A dapper little man in a dark, expensive suit, it was obvious DiBartolo, a close friend of Edwin Edwards, was accustomed to much more luxurious surroundings. With a self-confidence that seems to rise exponentially with the number of millions of dollars a person possesses, he took control of the discussion and expounded on the wonderful things Louisiana Downs had done for the state and, in particular, for Northwest Louisiana – the employment, taxes, entertainment. It was all true. But, somewhere during the discussion, I realized that the dates to which Louisiana Downs wished to expand would overlap a large portion of the dates now reserved for Evangeline Downs in Lafayette.

Evangeline Downs was truly not in the same class as Louisiana Downs in facilities or the size of its purses and thus in the quality of the horses it attracted. It was always struggling to turn a profit for the owners. Still, it had been in existence since 1965 and, I thought, certainly deserved to have its racing dates protected. Louisiana Downs, with its more up-to-date facilities, had successfully created large attendance drawn from northwest Louisiana, Arkansas and Texas, particularly Dallas. That gave it the advantage of offering much larger purses to the horse owners and trainers. If it started racing on the same dates, as this bill would permit, it would severely diminish Evangeline Downs ability to attract the better horses and, consequently, the betting crowds.

Most of the committee was surprised, maybe even annoyed, at the opposition I raised to the bill and it was passed "favorably".

Seeing how easily the bill had passed the committee, I decided to find out if anybody else cared about the conflict with Evangeline Downs and whether it was worth a fight. I personally had little interest in horse racing and had only attended the Lafayette facility a few times. I called Charles Ashy, an old friend and manager of Evangeline Downs. He seemed to be surprised that the measure had gone through the committee so easily and that it appeared to have strong support in the House. I asked him if I should continue to oppose it and try to get the Acadiana delegation solidly in opposition. He said yes and said he would contact some of his counterparts at the New Orleans tracks for support. (Delta Downs in Vinton only ran quarter-horse races and was therefore not negatively affected by Louisiana Downs' move since they were primarily a thoroughbred track.)

Looking back on this whole episode, I still can't truly tell you how the players were lined up. As it turned out there was a lot of subterfuge and, I think, a little suppressed amusement at watching this naive freshman take on some powerful, unseen forces.

Nonetheless, the Acadiana delegation *seemed* to share my concern and indicated they would be in opposition to the Louisiana Downs proposal. The large delegation from Jefferson Parish was solidly in opposition due to the lobbying of the management of Jefferson Downs. The vote was getting tight.

Adley presented the bill on the floor of the House. He did an excellent job of pointing out Louisiana Downs' superior facilities and geographic distance from the other tracks. Several Jefferson Parish legislators, some from Acadiana, notably Harry "Soup" Kember of White Castle and I, took the mike in opposition.

After a loud and lengthy debate, the final vote was taken.

Here's where it gets a little dicey.

The machine is opened. Members push the green or red buttons on their desks to indicate a yes or no vote which shows up with a corresponding light on the large board mounted above the speaker's podium. The machine stays open 10 or 15 seconds until the speaker intones, "Are you through voting? The clerk will close the machines." As I scanned the lighted voting board, I suddenly realized that Representative Jesse Guidry's light was green, indicating a vote in favor of Adley and Louisiana Downs. That couldn't be right. Guidry was the leader of the Acadiana delegation. I looked down to his first row seat and saw Jesse tilted way back in his swivel chair with the phone pressed to his ear. The green light on his desk was lit. The seat next to his, Sam Theriot's, was empty. His light was green. The two seats behind him were also empty. Both lights were green. l yelled at Jesse to no avail as the machine was closed to further voting. I looked back to the vote board, the bill had passed by two votes. Suddenly, Theriot emerged from the lounge with a cup of coffee and strolled over to talk with Speaker Hainkel.

I was totally confused and, as it turned out, totally naive. Later, it was all spelled out to me. Joe (her preferred spelling) Wood, a long-time and very effective lobbyist was a tall, buxom, platinum blond. Her office was two blocks from the Capitol in the picturesque Spanish Town section of Baton Rouge in an old frame residence called "The Green House." It wasn't that she raised plants there, it was just that the house was painted green.

Joe had a list of very substantial clients who, along with a couple of other lobbyists, financed the operations at the Green House. It was open for lunch every day during the legislative session and featured the wonderful "down-home" cooking of a creole chef. Pork roast, baked chicken, smothered okra, crowder peas, red beans, ham hocks and smothered pork chops were regular menu items. Every day thirty or forty legislators, lobbyists, their guests or hangers-on would stroll over to the Green House and enjoy a great meal and a respite from the pressures of the Capitol. There was no charge for the meal to legislators. No lobbying was allowed during the lunch hours. Of course their was a sign in the dining area reminding everyone of the businesses or industries who made it all possible. Refreshments were available as well as free cigarettes and cigars.

The house was also available to legislators and lobbyists for fund raising events during other hours of the day or night as well as to groups wishing to entertain legislators. Lobbyists sometime used it for strategy sessions away from the Capitol. It was an ideal setting for Joe and her associates to cement lasting friendships. Joe's lucrative lobbying career came crashing down in 1995 when it was revealed that the federal government had included her in their gambling investigation. Her office and home were raided and her records and computers were seized. Though she was never indicted, the feds had caused irreparable harm to her reputation and her business.

Joe was a quietly effective lobbyist. Naive as I was, I didn't realize that she had been working on behalf of Adley's bill for her client the Hotel-Motel Association. More important, Joe and Jesse Guidry were obviously *very* close friends. In fact, following Jesse's divorce a couple of years later, they were married. When the vote on the bill was called, Jesse had simply voted all four of the machines for Wood, her clients and Lousiana Downs. Theriot and the other two, of course, loudly proclaimed they didn't know the vote was being taken and certainly would not have voted for it. They denied that they had "taken a walk." I was livid.

People called Jesse Guidry a lot of colorful Cajun names. Sometimes he was the "old Gator," other times the "old Possum." Well, the old Possum asked for a moment of "personal privilege" at the mike. This is a request for time to address the House on special matters other than regular business.

Jesse, in his quiet, soft, Cajun-accented drawl explained that he had taken this important phone call just before the vote and wasn't paying much attention to the proceedings. He really thought the vote was being taken to "call the previous question" (bring the matter to a final vote.) He noticed his seat mates weren't around but figured they would surely want to end the debate and call for the final vote to defeat this bad bill, so he just reached over and voted them "yes" like himself. They had all pledged to vote against the bill. With a slight smile (or was it a smirk?) on his face, he apologized to the House, looked around, shrugged his shoulders as if to say, "Whatcha gonna do?" and sat down. There was a smattering of light applause for his performance and not a few suppressed snickers.

I was still boiling. I now realized the extent of the betrayal. I looked over at Robert Adley who appeared as confused and outraged as I was. He talked to a couple of lobbyists over the rail, slammed his fist into his hand and marched down to the mike.

There was total silence in the chamber as Robert started speaking in a small, hurt voice. Most of the members knew or had now been told how the four votes from the "solid" Acadiana delegation had been ripped off.

After a couple of minutes of proclaiming his pride in serving in the legislature and his respect for all of his colleagues in the House, Robert said, "But, I don't want to win like this." He then asked the House to reverse the action and put the bill back on the calendar for another, later hearing. It took some unusual parliamentary maneuvers to fulfill his request, but it was done.

That was the mark of a big man. Robert Adley had my respect for life. He subsequently became a floor leader with me during the Roemer Administration, suffered through the personal tragedy of losing a brilliant teen-age son, left his seat in the House to run unsuccessfully for governor in 1996 and has still managed to maintain a highly successful career in the oil and gas industry. He also still has the "fire in the belly" which may get him back into the political arena in the future.

Robert tried to revive the bill a few days later but, with every one painfully aware of the previous fiasco, it failed. Robert later told me that Joe Wood was furious with him and told him, "Once you win a vote you never go back, no matter how you won it!" In 1981, he sponsored much the same bill. By that time the tracks had discussed the matter, some compromises were made and Adley's Bill 952 was finally passed and became Act 726 of the 1981 regular session.

The main priority for me in that first term, funding for the Assembly Center in Lafayette would take considerably more time and create a lot more anxiety.

Notable quotes from the legislative halls:

"I don't know anyone here that's been killed with a handgun!"

Representative / Reverend Avery Alexander

VIII

"It is possible this project may exceed the funds allocated!"

The Assembly Center concept had been the target of heated discussion and opposition since it had been introduced as the top priority of the Greater Lafayette Chamber of Commerce during my term as president of that organization.

Some of the opposition was predictable and politically or economically motivated, some was unexpected, some was legitimate.

Then-Mayor Kenny Bowen didn't like the plan because it replaced his idea of a similar (but much smaller) facility in downtown Lafayette which had failed to gain approval of the voters. The Lafayette Auditorium Commission feared that it would replace the 2300 seat theater and adjacent ballroom of the Municipal Auditorium. And, of course, my friend had nailed it when he told me it would never be built because the plan did not include real estate commissions, bond attorney fees and locked in contracts for local architects, engineers and contractors.

However, once the initial hurdles were cleared and actual planning of the project got underway, all of the members of the Lafayette Auditorium Commission served diligently and admirably on the "Multi-Purpose USL Civic Assembly Center Planning and Design Committee." (Thank God the name was finally changed to "The Cajundome.") The chairman was Glynn Abel, former USL Dean of Men and formerly manager of the city municipal auditorium. Other Design Committee members were members of the Municipal Auditorium Commission Louis Mann, Mrs. Gloria Knox, Richard D. Chappuis, Sr., Willis

Ducrest, Frem Boustany, Sr., and the manager of the auditorium Frank Bradshaw. Glenn Menard, Raymond Moore, Jr., and Dr. James Caillier, Jr. represented USL and Michael Hopkins, was assigned by the Chamber of Commerce.

Shortly after it was announced that Lafayette architect Neil Nehrbass had been selected as the designer of the building the first shots were fired. Although the state Architectural Selection Board, in open meeting, awarded the contract to Nehrbass and Lee Architects, several of his peers openly questioned Nehrbass' ability to handle such an immense project. They had a good basis for their anxiety since Neil had never taken on such a colossal building. He was known, rather, for his non-traditional and sometimes avant-garde designs.

Nehrbass and I had been acquainted many years and he recognized my passion for this project. We talked at great length about the building and the uses for it. Neil was the consummate artiste. He dressed flamboyantly, chain smoked gold tipped, pastel-colored cigarettes which he imported from England and was definitely not a sports fan. He had never attended a USL basketball game. But he was enthusiastic about his new project. When I told him about the new domed facility, the Mississippi Coast Coliseum and Convention Center, which had recently opened in Biloxi, he immediately drove to Mississippi, visited the building and made contact with the architect.

I related to him my admiration for Madison Square Garden in New York City and its excellent sight lines from every seat in the house. He hopped a plane for New York and spent a week haunting Madison Square Garden and everyone connected with it.

When the 1980 USL basketball season opened in "the rodeo barn," Blackham Coliseum, Neil was there. He, naturally for Neil, was dressed immaculately. His bright tie, pastel blazer, tie tack, cuff links and reptile skin shoes made a real fashion statement among the T-shirt and jeans crowd. After the game, he stopped at the broadcast table where I still hung out even after I no longer broadcast the games. He was really excited to have seen the game (his first ever) and gotten a feel for the crowd.

Neil called and visited with me on a regular basis throughout the summer, fall and winter of 1980 and 1981. He assured me he was making great progress and that the plans would be finished by February, 1981 and the bids would be "in the money."

The question was, how much money. We had started out with that somewhat nebulous figure of $24 million, $16 million in state funds and $8 million from the City of Lafayette. Nobody really believed that would be the figure. Truthfully, nobody really yet knew how much it would cost.

The Treen administration had inherited a huge number of building projects to which Edwin Edwards had promised state funding. The Assembly Center in Lafayette was one. To his credit, and discomfort, Governor Treen tried to honor all of the commitments throughout the state. As always, Edwin had been very generous with promises. As fate would have it, many of the projects which were in the planning stages when Edwards left office were fully funded and begun during the Treen years. Then, they were completed just in time for a triumphantly re-elected Edwards to show up and cut the ribbons.

We in the Lafayette delegation were selling this project as a unique joint effort between a state, its university and a city. Not only would the City of Lafayette contribute to the cost of the building, it would also assume the responsibility of operating and maintaining the facility. No other such facility or building had ever been built on a Louisiana university campus with this unique arrangement. We thought we were in good shape and anxiously awaited the release of the governor's Capital Outlay Bill. This is one of the two budget bills configured by the governor's office each year in the state. The General

Appropriations bill is the operating budget and the Capital Outlay bill is the infrastructure and building budget.

The Treen administration staff seemed to find the pace of state government faster than they anticipated. Part of the problem was that the entire staff of the "fourth floor" (governor's main floor at the Capitol) were new to their jobs. Another problem was Dave Treen's maddening habit of meticulously picking over every item that crossed his desk and insisting that everything cross his desk. Moving from the pace of a congressional office in Washington, D. C. to the Louisiana Governor's office during the midst of a legislative session proved to be daunting. Legislation that could take up to a year to pass congress would routinely whisk through the state legislature in a month or less.

Many of the administration's package of bills were hastily drafted. Some were mere skeletons for legislation that the governor's people hoped to flesh out as they moved through the system.

While all this was unraveling, the House and Senate leadership got into a major rift and decided to split the Legislative Council. This was the staff of the legislature. The Legislative Council drafted all the bills, amendments, did the technical checking, staffed the committees and generally were the working experts and paper pushers who kept a legislative session together. The Council worked for both the House and Senate but many observers felt the Senate and its President dominated the staff.

Speaker John Hainkel and Senate President Michael O'Keefe could not have been more different. John was an outspoken, conservative Democrat (who would soon switch to Republican), and was destined to become the first man to serve as both speaker of the House (1980-1984) and president of the Senate (2000-) and the first Republican Senate president in history. In 1980 he felt the Speaker of the House should have more to say about the running of the Council. O'Keefe, the epitome of the slick Democratic ward-boss, was not about to give up control. (O'Keefe would later be twice convicted of federal crimes and serve prison time.) The end result was the splitting of the Council. There was now a Senate Council and a House Council. The Senate paid more money and worked fewer hours and thus had their pick of the current staff. The net result was a bitterly split staff that did not coordinate legislation and almost doubled in size and budget. Senate staff routinely refused information to me and other House members when we called requesting details on bills filed in the Senate.

One of the many casualties of this first session bedlam was the Capital Outlay bill, the spending plan for the concrete, bricks, mortar and tar in the state. This is where the funding for the Multi-Purpose Assembly Center would be placed.

The much-delayed and long-awaited bill was finally released late in the session on a Thursday afternoon. My seat mate, Mike Thompson and I hastily thumbed through the bulky document looking for the line item which would set the project in motion.

The Capital Outlay bill is generally composed of six sections: cash and priorities one through five. The cash section appropriates money for immediate needs such as projects under construction or ready for instant start up or emergencies. Usually bonds are sold to finance priorities one through four which supposedly fund projects to be started in each of the next yearly quarters. I say, supposedly, because such an ambitious schedule has rarely, if ever, been achieved. Priority five merely puts the state on record as approving future funding of a project.

The Lafayette project was not in the bill. Mike, being the experienced legislator having served since 1972, immediately got on the phone and started tracking down administration officials. He wanted to know what happened to the money for the Assembly Center. No one seemed to have an answer. Frustrated, he phoned the governor's appointments secretary and demanded an immediate meeting with the governor. He was told Governor Treen was tied up with appointments all afternoon. Mike looked at me, told me what she said, raised his eyebrows in query and said, "We'll be up there soon and we'll wait, if it takes all night."

Shortly after he hung up, Senator Allen Bares of Lafayette came ambling up to our desks. It was Thursday and, as usual, the Senate had adjourned for the weekend. Bares was heading home. Mike told him of the snafu in the Capital Outlay bill and our proposed stake-out of the governor's office. He said he'd pass and wished us luck.

Mike and I waited in the governor's outer office over two hours. Treen finally told his secretary to let us in but said we'd only have a few minutes.

We pleaded our case with every available argument. "This is the number one project in southwest Louisiana." "The City of Lafayette shares the cost, the University of Southwestern Louisiana gains a long-needed facility and the state walks away from the building on completion with no future operations, maintenance, repair or management costs. What a great deal for the state!" "If this concept is not initiated, the University will soon be prioritizing a similar facility with total state funding and with all the future revenue demands remaining as a state responsibility."

We almost cut our wrists and signed in blood that the total cost would never rise above $40 million. (That was a new figure which we thought much more realistic than the previous $24 million. The sharing formula would be three to one, $30 million from the state and $10 million from the city.)

The governor was very empathetic. He was under an enormous amount of pressure in this, his first session. The Capital Outlay bill was, in truth, bloated, mainly because of the unfunded promises the previous governor had made and which Treen was trying to honor. He said he would take it under consideration, confer with his Commissioner of Administration E. L. "Bubba" Henry and let us know.

Our problem, of course, was not the only one. Other legislators on both sides of the Capitol were raising hell about the bill: what it contained, what it didn't contain and the lateness of its introduction. Finally, the unthinkable happened. For the only time in my memory, the legislature ran out of time and adjourned *sine die* without passing a Capital Outlay budget.

The governor immediately announced that he would call a special session as soon as possible to handle the crisis. The session was called for September 2nd through September 10th, 1980. The further delay worked in our favor as we were able to enlist more support and assure the governor of the importance of the project.

When the new bill was produced, we all gave a sigh of relief. There it was, finally, in black and white. In the priority four section of the bill, *"For land acquisition, construction and equipping a multi-purpose civic, academic and community center at University of Southwestern Louisiana at Lafayette....$9,800,000."* And in priority five, with the same preamble: *"$20,200,000."* The state was committed.

To make peace with various delegations which were still complaining about being left out of the spending bill, an unusual section was added. Entitled, "Projects to be funded in the 1981-1982 Capital Outlay bill," this was sort of an IOU from the governor to assure those left out that they would be remembered next year. In that section the Lafayette delegation had the administration add, under the heading "University of Southwestern Louisiana", 1) Dairy Science Facility in St. Martin Parish and 2) Relocation of the Health and Physical Education Facility. We hoped that would quell some critics who were saying that the University's more important needs were being usurped by the Assembly Center project. It didn't.

With the funding now secure in the Capital Outlay bill, I would never have believed how tenuous the project still was and how close we would come to losing it over the next year.

In spite of architect Nehrbass' assurances, his self-imposed deadline for delivery of the final plans by February 1981 arrived and passed with no delivery.

On April 21, Nehrbass submitted a "budget summary" for the project which added up to $36,386,000. However he then added a second set of figures he called "alternates" which totaled another $4,100,000. These alternates were such "minor" things like seating, kitchen, specialized equipment, scoreboard and parking lot. We were now over the $40 million figure we had solemnly vowed not to exceed.

On April 28, the Planning and Design Committee chairman, Glynn Abel wrote to Richard Futch, the head of the state's division of Facility Planning and Control. In part he said, *"In view of the fact that the governor and the local legislative delegates have been emphatic that the budget of $30 million from the state and $10 million from the city (not be exceeded), we were expected to complete the project without requesting additional funds. It is already anticipated that there is a possibility of this project exceeding the funds allocated."*

Abel then advised Mr. Futch, for the first time, that the bid might best be held with several alternates added to the base bid.

By May 7th, Nehrbass had still not submitted the final plans. I wrote a letter to him co-signed by Mike Thompson. The letter said, *"Preceding the regular legislative session of 1980, the Center was tentatively funded at $24 million, $16 million in state funds with a matching $8 million from the City of Lafayette. Your (later) estimate was that the project, with 12,000 seats for basketball, would cost some $36.6 million. This, we were told, included a built-in inflation factor assuming bidding and construction would begin in the first half of 1981. That figure* *assumed a gross cost including all engineering and architect fees.*

"With the above, we approached Governor Treen. We added $3.4 million to the estimate, as a hedge against potential over runs. Thus, the governor and the delegation agreed the project would be funded with a maximum of $30 million in state funds and $10 million in matching city funds.

"We are now some three months overdue on your promise of having completed plans to Facilities Planning."

I proceeded to outline a meeting held with officials at Facilities Planning which could expedite the proceedings once the plans were delivered. The letter continued, *"One point that came as a surprise to us and has caused some consternation is that the gross figure for the project is now $40 million and includes only a two percent contingency figure. It appears that our request for total funding of $40 million has now been taken (by you) as an operating budget.*

"Neil, this project must not run over. It must be complete, turn key, all fees included in the $37 million range and with the capacities and functions as currently planned.

"This project is now going into its third year. We have put our full faith and trust, indeed bartered our integrity, on your abilities and your assurances. The bottom line is, we are looking to you to fulfill your obligations."

The Assembly Center project continued to take on more mystery and intrigue than a palace plot.

Finally, while the legislature was still in session in the summer of 1981, Neil delivered an entire set of plans to me, nearly 30 pounds of rolled up blueprint paper. He gleefully announced that he wanted me to have my very own copy on the same day he had delivered the original to Facilities Planning.

I waited about a week and called Facilities Planning to check on the progress of the review process. I was advised that they had not received the final plans. I was furious. I called Neil and was about to threaten him with a death worthy of St. Sebastian. He seemed to be almost in tears as he insisted, swore on his family that he had, in truth, made delivery of the documents the same day he had brought them to me in Baton Rouge.

A young man that I knew and trusted, I'll call him Ralph, was on the staff at Facilities Planning. We were in legislative session at the time and I called Ralph and asked if I could visit him during the noon hour. The office, in the Capitol Annex building just across the street from the Capitol, was practically deserted because of the lunch break when Ralph and I met. He said he wasn't sure about the delivery of the Nehrbass documents because it was the responsibility of another staff member. He suggested we take a look around that person's desk. We looked through numerous sets of plans, rolled and stacked waist high. Ralph then glanced under the man's desk. Rolled up and pushed against the wall, almost out of sight, was the set of plans for the Assembly Center. Had that been done on purpose? Was someone trying to sabotage the project by causing more delay? I'll never truly know and calling attention to it or pointing fingers would probably have caused even more harm.

I went back to the Capitol, waited an hour and called Richard Futch to inform him the plans were indeed in his shop and told him where to look. I also called Commissioner of Administration "Bubba" Henry (Facility Planning was under his supervision) and told him of the finding.

The usual procedures followed: detailed appraisal of the plans by Facilities Planning staff, recommendations for changes, changes resubmitted by the architect, etc. Finally, it was announced that bid specifications would be advertised beginning August 10th and would be received and opened on the project at 2:00 P. M., September 17, 1981.

By now everyone was getting antsy about the possibility of the bids coming in way over budget. The Planning and Design Committee had met in mid-July and was told by Nehrbass that there was a "possibility the project would exceed allocated funds." The committee recommended that the bid be separated into a base bid and five or six alternates.

The night before the bid opening I called Neil at his home. We had a long discussion during which he repeatedly tried to soothe my anxieties by saying, "This is a building you'll really be proud of."

I'd respond, "Not if it's so expensive it can't be built."

Neil, ever the flower child with the pastel cigarettes, would admonish me to think positive, think of the wonderful events and gatherings which would occur in this magnificent structure.

I finally said, "Neil, please tell me the truth so I can get some sleep. Is it going to come in at or below $40 million?"

Neil calmly and confidently said, "I guarantee it!"

The day of the bid opening arrived. There were only two bidders: Blount Brothers of Montgomery, Alabama and Algernon-Blair and Tudor Construction in a joint bid. Algernon was also based in Montgomery, Alabama and had constructed the University Medical Center (Charity Hospital) across from the Assembly Center site in Lafayette. Tudor was from Alexandria and its owner "Buddy" Tudor was a prominent Republican and major financial supporter of Governor Treen.

The lowest bid on the base and five alternates was $54,620,000!!!!

The maneuvering began. Blount Brothers had the low base bid at $41,950,000 and was low through the first three alternates: 1A) permanent seating; 1B) telescoping seating; 2) Kitchen. Their base bid plus those three alternates totaled $44,775,000.

The Algernon-Blair/Tudor combo was low on base plus alternates 1A, 1B and 2 as well as alternates 3) specialized equipment; 4) scoreboard; and 5) parking lot. Theirs was the $54 million plus I quoted above. I must say, I had a hard time envisioning the parking lot for a 13,000 plus seat facility described as an "alternate."

Governor Treen and his closest advisors were in a quandary. The options were: throw out all the bids, send the plans back to the architect for redesign and bid again at a later date; or, let a contract for the whole thing; or, accept the base bid and one or more alternates with the intention of funding the remaining alternates sometime during the three years of construction.

I could hardly look Dave Treen in the eye when we met with a group shortly after the bid opening. He muttered something to me that included the word "embarrassing."

Other voices chimed in. Lafayette architects Paul Emmer, President and Charles Beazley, President-elect of the South Louisiana Chapter, American Institute of Architects wrote a letter-to-the-editor and distributed a news release which said in part, *"State law makes it difficult to accept bids on the project and eliminate frills without eliminating other necessary items. Even if area legislators are able to raise another $8 million for a "bare bones" Civic Center, a very real possibility remains that future expenditures would be required to add necessities being left off now."* They made some very good points.

The Louisiana Architects Association, in what is believed to be an unprecedented action, passed a resolution against funding the project as bid. They also offered to put together a team of architects from their association to review the project. Some of the LAA's own members considered such action "a dangerous, if not totally unethical precedent."

As the storm raged into November, no decision had yet been reached by the Treen administration. Meanwhile, Neil Nehrbass received a letter from Jesse Cannon, Jr., the membership chairman of the American Institute of Architects offering him membership in the association for the balance of the year *at no cost.* (Yes, it seems our non-conformist architect had long ago shunned and therefore alienated the members of the association by refusing to join.) Mr. Cannon closed his membership offer to Neil with these possibly cryptic sentences, "Please weigh this offer carefully and give yourself the opportunity to affiliate with persons in your profession. I believe you will find the experience quite beneficial."

"Buddy" Tudor made a technically sound and impassioned plea to his friend Dave Treen and copied "Bubba" Henry and John Cade with handwritten notes pleading with them to intercede. His reasoning was that an award of the base bid without going up through alternate #3 would be "disastrous." As has been noted, Blount Brothers was the low bidder on the base and alternates 1A, 1B and 2. Tudor's bid would be low if the award included alternate 3. Still, Tudor was being very honest when he said, in his letter to Treen, *"The building, as drawn, reflects the needs of the Lafayette area, and it would certainly be a shame to build something less than that needed which might be outdated before completion. I realize that my arguments may be taken as being strictly self-serving, but I honestly must say that whether we are the successful contractor or not would in no way alter these facts. I know that this is a difficult decision for you."*

Nehrbass was busy on his own behalf enlisting letters from anybody and everybody willing including Bevely Latimer, Director of the Lafayette Natural History Museum and Planetarium (whose ultra-modern building Nehrbass had designed,) the entire Planning and Design committee, USL Professor and artist Elemore Morgan, Jr., and even the Bishop of Lake Charles, Jude Speyrer. They all wrote letters to the governor urging full funding of the project.

By law, a decision would have to made soon or the bids would expire.

With very mixed feelings, I wrote a personal letter to Governor Treen:

"I believe your choice of the word 'embarrassing' when referring to the bid prices on this project was very appropriate. Since I initiated the 'shared-cost' concept of this project while president of the Greater Lafayette Chamber of Commerce in 1978 and have been working since for its completion, I deeply feel that embarrassment as well as a sense of frustration." I reiterated the benefits to the state of the arrangement, *"..the state walks away from the building on completion with no future operations, maintenance, repair or management costs. This last fact alone seems to me to be worth the initial construction cost.*

"As we all know, facilities such as this rarely produce enough direct revenue to cover operations and maintenance. It is conservatively estimated that the Assembly Center will operate at $500,000 per year deficit for some years." (At least I was correct on one thing concerning this project. As it developed, the city's deficit averaged almost exactly a half-million per year for over ten years before the facility finally began paying its own way.)

I continued, *"I cannot stress too strongly the importance of full funding of this project at this time. While there is no excuse for the terrible miscalculation on the bid price, our failure to complete the concept will be equally inexcusable.*

"My recommendation is that we place the funds to cover the alternate bids in priority five of the Capital Outlay Budget during the Special Session so that the contracts can be let before the November 24th deadline. These funds would not be needed for at least two years and could be moved up in priority at that time.

"Believe me, I share your embarrassment and reluctance to bend some principles on this question. Your willingness to listen to the problems and alternatives has not gone without notice and appreciation in the Acadiana area."

The governor responded with a very cordial letter and assured me that a decision was imminent.

Throughout this period, a part of me despised the over-run and the fact that it appeared we had been deliberately misled. However, another part was saying, "If we do not get this project started now, it will never be done." I was not being clairvoyant but, within two years, with the crash of oil prices and the virtual collapse of state revenues, capital outlay came to a stand still and projects of this magnitude were not even considered for another 8 or 9 years.

The Lafayette legislative delegation met with Treen in his office shortly after that exchange of letters. The governor actually had a full set of plans for the building laid out on his desk and had obviously been meticulously studying them. He asked very specific questions as to why certain features and configurations were included. We urged the governor to make a positive decision and to let us set up a press conference in Lafayette for him to announce that decision.

The day was at hand. The decision was due. I got a call in my office in Lafayette from the governor. He said, "Ron, I have just a couple of more questions I want answered by the Lafayette delegation. Can you get Allen, Mike and Luke together and call me back within the hour?" I assured him I would and got on the phone to call the others.

Allen and Mike said they'd be in my office in 20 minutes, Luke said, "You've got my proxy. Whatever ya'll want to do."

We called the governor on my speaker phone. After a few preliminaries he started going over some of the same ground we'd covered for several months. Finally he said, "I want you to let me know exactly how you want to proceed on this contract, what alternates and so on and I want to be assured you're unanimous and I'll have your full support. Talk it over and call me back when you've decided." He hung up.

We looked at each other and didn't know whether to laugh or cry. He knew what our decision would be. He knew he had our full backing and that it would be unanimous. I said, "Well, shall we call him back?"

Mike Thompson, who knew Dave Treen better than any of us, said, "No, let's wait about an hour. If we call him back now he'll feel that we weren't deliberative enough. Let's make it look as though we had a long discussion." Mike suggested I write down some buzz words to use when we called him back. We decided to say that "after much deliberation" we had arrived at a conclusion which we felt was truly in the best interests of the state and our constituents and that it would be a project that we would all be proud of. We would mention leaving a legacy and so on.

About an hour later, I called the governor's office at the Capitol only to be told that he had already left and was at the mansion. I called the private quarters of the mansion and spoke to the first lady, Dodie Treen. She said that Dave was in the bathroom but she'd have him pick up on the phone in there. I didn't even want to imagine what he was doing. When he answered I slowly and painstakingly explained our "deliberations" which had come to the ultimate conclusion that the project should be fully funded immediately. We were on a speaker phone and the governor polled the three present: "Allen, you agree?'

"Absolutely governor."

"Mike, you're one hundred percent?"

"One hundred percent, governor."

"OK, let's do it," he said.

We told him we'd get with his appointments secretary to arrange the press conference as soon as possible.

On Tuesday, December 15, 1981 we had representatives from every media in southwest Louisiana gathered in USL President Ray Authement's conference room on the 2nd floor of

Martin Hall on the campus. Several dozen VIP's and wannabe VIP's were also on hand.

The governor's helicopter landed right in front of Martin Hall. Dr. Authement, Lafayette Mayor Dud Lastrapes and I met the governor as he ducked under the rotor wash. After a few moments of hand shaking and greetings, the governor looked at me and said, "Ron, I still have a couple of questions I need answered."

My heart stopped. Questions? What other questions could he possibly have? Was he studying the plans while riding the helicopter from Baton Rouge? I said, "Maybe I can answer them governor, but we should do it out here because we've got a ton of media people right up those steps."

Treen said, "Alternate 1A is for permanent seating and alternate 1B is for telescoping seating. Why do you have to have both? Couldn't we do away with the telescoping seating?"

I said, "The telescoping seating is the folding bleachers on the floor of the arena. They're folded out for use in the basketball configuration and folded back up when you need to use the entire floor of the arena for other functions. That's why it's called a multi-purpose facility."

That seemed to satisfy him and we started walking toward the building and up the winding stairway to the second floor. A crowd had gathered along the steps to greet the governor. I was thinking, "He said, 'a couple of questions.' When is he going to remember the other one?"

Among the greeters on the steps was Dean of Student Affairs Raymond Blanco, another was Neil Nehrbass. When the governor recognized Nehrbass he suddenly stopped and said, "Oh yes, there was one other question I need cleared up."

Before he continued, I looked at Blanco and said, "We need to go to your office immediately." His office was on the same floor but on the opposite side of the building from the conference room in which the announcement would be held.

I grabbed Nehrbass and a small group of us crammed into Dean Blanco's office. Nehrbass was so nervous his face had turned crimson and his fingers kept fidgeting with the pocket containing his British cigarettes. The governor looked at Neil and said, "In alternate 3 there is a provision for a conduit running under the floor the whole length of the arena. Now, if we don't award alternate 3 how are you going to handle the electrical wiring that goes in that conduit?" Who was this guy?

Neil almost collapsed with relief as he answered, "Oh governor, that's a small item, about $8,000. We can handle that with a change order."

The governor shook his head and said, "I don't like change orders. They can get out of hand."

Neil quickly said, "I guarantee you governor, I can take care of it without a change order." Great, another guarantee from Nehrbass.

With that, the governor seemed satisfied and we headed down the hall to the gang of reporters and others gathered in the conference room. I was walking next to the governor and, just before we entered the room, I whispered to him, "Be positive governor, this is a great thing you're doing."

The governor did a good job with the media. He knew the project particulars better than anyone in the room, probably even the architect. At one point Nehrbass was asked about construction time. He estimated three and a half years. The governor jokingly said, "Anything you can do to move that up will be greatly appreciated." He caught some surprised looks from the reporters and quickly said, "I do expect to be there opening night -- as governor." He added that, in any case, it should not take more than six years. That, of course was in reference to the number of years he would be governor IF he was reelected. Unfortunately, Edwin Edwards was the governor on hand at the opening ceremonies of the Cajundome.

The next day, a legislative budget committee unanimously approved Governor Treen's proposal to accept the low bid for the project plus alternates 1A, 1B and 2. The total contract of $44.8 million went to Blount Brothers Corporation of Montgomery, Alabama.

To this day I do not know how or why the decision was made to go with the base plus the first three alternates. It seems as though it would have been just as easy to go through alternate 3, raise the total to $53.35 million and award the contract to the Louisiana contractor "Buddy" Tudor and his joint venture. Who knows? It could well be that Dave Treen's overwhelming sense of integrity and propriety would not let him make that kind of decision in favor of a strong financial supporter.

The official groundbreaking ceremony took place on the site on January 27, 1982. The construction was finally underway. Throughout the three plus years, Neil would send me or bring me postcard sized, sometimes larger, charcoal or water color sketches of the project in progress. I still have over a dozen of them. In spite of the ghastly error in cost projection, he did truly design a magnificent building.

The building was dedicated on Sunday, November 10, 1985. The governor on stage taking credit for its construction was Edwin Edwards who, of course, had defeated David Treen in the 1983 election.

In spite of it all, I still marvel that this project went from conception in early 1978 to completion in 1985, just over seven years. I believe that must be some sort of record for the state of Louisiana.

When the final tally was taken in 1986 the Cajundome (as it was named by a select committee) cost $58,844,895. The City of Lafayette paid twenty-five percent of that and provided an additional $1.1 million for equipment. That's a giant leap from the $24 million first bandied about and is still hard for me to swallow, and yet... I must look at the finished product, a truly multi-purpose facility which has lived up to the description the Daily Advertiser used in touting the project as "the single most important component in the master plan for the future of this community."

In its first 28 days, the Cajundome drew 110,000 people to 21 events. Kenny Rogers and the Oak Ridge Boys were the opening attraction. They were greeted by an audience of over 13,400 fans. The Muppets entertained over 16,000 in 7 performances and USL Basketball played to more than 26,000 fans in their first four games.

In its nearly fifteen years of existence, the Cajundome has proven to be a truly multi-purpose venue: Graduation exercises for the university and area high schools; a visit by saintly Mother Teresa; Mardi Gras balls; the state's high school basketball tournament; banquets seating up to 1800 people; tractor pulls; ice shows; professional ice hockey; professional soccer; wrestling; boxing; civic club meetings and conventions; trade shows; rock, country and every other kind of musical concert and even a public hearing for a committee of the United States Senate. Entertainment names like The Eagles, N-Sync, Dionne Warwick, Kiss, Rod Stewart, Garth Brooks, and dozens of others have played to huge, appreciative audiences.

Now, mainly through the efforts of Lafayette Representative Jerry Leblanc, the addition of an exhibit hall will expand even further the multi-faceted uses of the Cajundome.

In his letter to Governor Treen supporting the funding of the building, professor, artist Elemore Morgan Jr. said, *"I would like to point out that our culture and the culture of other civilizations around the world would be immeasurably poorer if buildings had been constructed with utility and economics as the only consideration. ... I believe that officials of the State of Louisiana, the University of Southwestern Louisiana and the City of Lafayette have an opportunity to provide people in*

Louisiana with a building that will have special value for many years to come, beyond its practical uses."

Notable quotes from the legislative halls:

"What we're doing here is trying to change the 1974 Constitution... whenever that was passed, I don't know."

Representative Donald Ray Kennard

IX

"Still f------ the poor people, Gomez?"

Edwin Edwards could have done more than any one person in the history of Louisiana to change the course of the state, improve the educational system, reform government. He, more than any governor before or since could have taken this state, with its unmatched natural resources and excellent geographic location to its maximum potential. In his first term he truly sought to make significant and progressive changes. He had the charisma, the intelligence and, most of all, the communication skills to lead the people of this state as no one ever could or has, not even Huey Long.

He served four full terms as governor. No one has been elected governor as many times. He is still spoken of with reverence by many.

And yet, in my opinion, he squandered all of that and devoted his efforts to rewarding himself and his political friends. He posed as a savior of the poor and needy. Four terms and almost thirty years later, Louisiana still trails the nation in providing for and lifting its under privileged. He initiated historic changes in some areas of state government. Still, he left the state ranked near the bottom in the nation in everything good and near the top in everything bad.

After serving all but about eight years of his adult life in public office, he had somehow amassed millions of dollars in personal wealth for himself and many of his closest political cronies. And, he enjoyed bragging about it.

I suppose the political philosophy expressed to me by a long time Lafayette Parish police juror worked for Edwards, "If you can't help yourself and your friends, what's the use of being in politics?"

Indeed, when Edwards was first elected in 1971, he was considered a reformer. Young, energetic and charismatic, he immediately set out to accomplish something no other Louisiana leader had been able to do for decades: rewrite the state's archaic, voluminous Constitution.

The Constitutional Convention of 1973 reduced a bloated, excessively-amended, antique document to a streamlined instrument about the size of an issue of Readers' Digest. It greatly reduced the number of departments in Louisiana's state government. That was good. The problem was that it still contained arcane elements that were preserved by special interests (primarily those in government) and shackled future legislators' attempts at moving the state forward.

A Constitution, according to most knowledgeable observers, should be an outline, a guide, a framework.

The 1973 document still contained specific provisions such as the amount of homestead exemption allowed individual homeowners and the individual income tax *rates*. Any future tax reform could never be done by acts of duly elected legislators. It would require amending the Constitution with a two-thirds vote of the legislature and concurrence by the voters in a state-wide election. Louisiana's unique structure for the administration and governance of higher education was left virtually unchanged. Three separate boards would still exist thus maintaining the eternal turf battles between the universities and colleges to the overall detriment of the education system.

Still, the new Constitution was an improvement.

Edwards also restructured the taxation of oil produced in the state. The new law put the tax on the market value of oil rather than on the volume. As luck would have it, he did it just before the OPEC countries put the squeeze on oil imports into the

United States thus tripling and quadrupling the price of oil and related products.

Edwards appeared to be a prophet. The state was suddenly practically awash with oil money, from leases, royalties and product taxes. Unfortunately, this also made the state extremely dependent on the price of a commodity traded in a worldwide market. No one would face the fact that the tax structure left over from the days of Huey Long was unstable and non-progressive. Huey Long's populist practice was to tax businesses and "the rich" and thus be the hero of the "little man." Edwards' philosophy was not much different.

As one observer commented, the state was experiencing an "embarrassment of riches." With oil driven increases in state revenues it was easy for a governor to be a hero. "You want a new hospital in your district? You got it!" "Let's build a vocational-technical school in everybody's district!" "How about a special, lucrative retirement system just for legislators, judges and the governor? Done!"

It took less than ten years for reality to set in. When oil prices crashed in 1983 over 40% of the state's budget was dependent on oil and gas. Dave Treen was governor and struggled to avoid the inevitable cuts in state services.

When Edwards came back in office in 1984, he immediately pushed for tax increases of over one billion dollars. That was roughly the amount lost annually because of the downturn in the oil and gas industry. Still, the taxes he proposed were to be paid primarily by businesses.

Never would he consider reforming the unworkable tax system that included high sales taxes, no state property taxes, individual income tax rates unrealistically frozen in the Constitution, exorbitant and bizarre corporate taxes and the highest homestead exemption rate in the nation.

The legislature balked at swallowing the whole Edwards tax package. We "merely" raised about $650 million in new taxes.

Edwards said that wasn't enough and resisted all efforts to reduce spending.

About this time, he was indicted by a federal grand jury for trafficking in hospital permits and brought to trial. His first trial ended in a hung jury. He was retried and acquitted. But the trials were time-consuming and embarrassing to the state. Between the trials and the lack of money to continue his populist programs, Edwards seemed to lose interest in being governor.

Some people close to him urged him not to run in 1987. However a larger group, those who needed Edwards as governor to maintain their place at the trough, prevailed. He ran second to Buddy Roemer in the 1987 first primary and shocked his friends and the state by conceding the election and avoiding a runoff.

As I write this, he and his son and other close allies are on trial again. This time the charges are the result of numerous federal indictments following a massive federal investigation dealing with the granting of riverboat gambling licenses. Another trial, dealing with insurance regulation practices, is scheduled to follow this one. By his own count, Edwards, now in his seventies, has faced two trials and over 20 similar federal investigations in his political career. He has survived them all and no one is betting heavily against him this time. Convictions will require *unanimous* verdicts.

Somehow, his brashness and arrogance over the years, traits that would have destroyed the average politician, have only seemed to endear him to his core constituency: minorities, organized labor, Cajuns and lower-income voters. It is exactly those groups who suffered the most over the quarter of a century he was in and out of the governor's office. Except for some black leaders who attached themselves to his entourage and gained political clout and monetary rewards through favors and appointments, the minority population as a whole has made very little progress culturally, educationally or socially because of his leadership.

Organized labor, once a powerful force in the state, has fallen to its lowest membership count in history. And, overall, when he finally left office in 1996, the state was near the bottom in teacher pay and college and university funding (among other things.) It was also near the top in high school dropouts, teen pregnancies, welfare recipients, prison population and virtually every other negative category.

I first met Edwin in the early 1960's when he was a newly elected member of congress and I was a news reporter and morning anchor on the "A. M." program on KATC-TV in Lafayette. He was a good interview, charming, intelligent and blessed with that quick, clever Cajun wit that has served him so well over the years.

The last time I saw him in person was during the 1994 legislative session. I was standing outside a committee room in the Capitol with Dan Juneau, president of the Louisiana Association of Business and Industry. I was vice-president of marketing for LABI at the time and Dan was preparing to testify before the committee on a business-backed workers' compensation bill. Just days earlier, Edwards had announced that he would not be seeking re-election in 1995. He too was scheduled to testify, naturally, in opposition to Juneau's position on the bill.

Dressed casually in jeans and a plaid shirt, he came swaggering down the hall with his entourage. Seeing him approach, I decided to magnanimously say something nice about his decision to retire and wish him luck. I didn't get the chance. Ignoring my proffered handshake, he said, "Still f------- the poor people, Gomez?" I was shocked. Here was this pompous, arrogant, multi-millionaire still being the ultimate demagogue to the end. All I could say was, "You should be ashamed of yourself, governor."

"No," he shot back, "you should be ashamed of yourself."

Other than occasional meetings in social, political or news coverage situations, our paths didn't cross much after the earlier TV interview until I was serving in the State Legislature in the '80's. Edwin had served as governor from 1972 to 1980 and, under Louisiana law, could serve only two concurrent terms. When Republican Dave Treen succeeded him, Edwin let everyone know he was just in a brief, mandated hiatus and would be back.

He hosted a dinner at the mansion for the newly elected legislators and their spouses in early 1980, before the inauguration. In his brief remarks he confidently suggested that we "take good care of my state for the next four years and then I'll be back."

It was at that dinner that I discovered one of the roles I could play in the House. Interpreter. Edwin asked each of us to introduce our spouse and to make any remarks we thought necessary. My wife, Carol, and I were seated at a table with Billy and Dianne Atkins from Jonesville. Billy had a strong north Louisiana twang and said something like, "This is my wife Dianne and I'm really lookin' forward to workin' with ya'll."

The introductions went around the tables and Raymond "La La" Lalonde from Opelousas got up and said, in a rapid-fire, heavily-accented Cajun-english, "This is my wife Evelyn. Now, ya'll don't fool with my cock-fightin' and I won't fool with your business."

Billy leaned over to me and said, "I didn' unnerstan' a thang he said." That was my cue. I'd be an interpreter.

During Treen's administration, Edwin was never out of sight or out of mind. He still had access to high-placed appointees in various departments and the loyalty of a great number, if not the majority, of the legislature. During many floor debates on administration backed bills you could hear John Alario, "Bo" Ackal, Clyde Kimball, Raymond LaBorde and others discussing phone calls, lunches and meetings with "the governor" and you could see Edwin's hand in the tactics used to thwart many of Treen's initiatives.

Governor Treen tried to resurrect an old oil and gas taxing idea once known as "first use." Somewhat revised, it was now called the Coastal Wetlands Environmental Levy (CWEL.) Edwin took the opportunity to align himself even more closely with one of his natural constituencies, the oil and gas industry.

Long and bitter hearings ensued in the Ways and Means Committee chaired by John Alario and on which I served. Some of the hearings lasted well into the night. The battle had become so elevated that the committee hearing was moved to the House chamber to accommodate the hundreds of witnesses and attendees. Edwin Edwards was the star witness for the opposition.

As a member of the committee, and representing a district in Lafayette, the oil center of south Louisiana, I was opposed to the tax and had let the Treen people know it. The committee was deadlocked. As the hearing in the House chamber dragged on, I noticed that, one by one, the members who were opposing the bill were being called into the coffee lounge just off the floor of the House. Finally, my time came. I was summoned to the lounge and walked in to find Governor Treen and John Cade, his chief aide.

The governor spoke to me for a few moments on the merits of his bill. He assured me it would pass constitutional muster. He said the tax would be paid by out-of-state and foreign entities and not hurt our local oil and gas people. I told him again of the staunch opposition in my district, my personal misgivings and said I just could not vote for it.

Cade, a cold, acerbic man who had never given me the time of day in the halls, the elevators or the governor's office, suddenly said, "All right, Gomez, what do you want?"

I was a little stunned with the question, especially coming from a self-professed arch-conservative, good-government type such as John Cade. I simply said, "Mr. Cade, you can't build a bridge high enough or a highway long enough to make me vote for this bill."

Some votes were changed in the coffee lounge. The bill got out of committee and went to debate on the House floor. However, the administration knew enough about nose counting to know it could not pass as presented. The floor manager for the bill, Loy Weaver of Homer, had the unenviable task of introducing a surprise amendment that he hoped would keep the bill alive.

Throughout the committee hearings, the administration had strongly proclaimed that the $400 million or so which the tax was expected to produce was absolutely necessary to save, among other things, the state's education system. Nothing less would suffice. They also argued that, although the ill-fated "first use" tax of the 1970's had been declared unconstitutional after several years of litigation, there was no question as to this bill's constitutionality. Now, Weaver's amendment would reduce the tax to a mere $14 million or so in order to get it on the books to "test its constitutionality."

Many of us were outraged. What happened to the argument that all of the proceeds of the tax were absolutely necessary? What happened to the complete confidence that the levy would be constitutional?

I went to the floor of the House and argued against the amendment and the bill. I told the House, "I'm new here but I've watched this body for many years as an observer and newsman. I've seen a lot of bills which were called "watermelon" bills (swollen to include something for everyone) but this is the first watermelon bill I've seen that has shrunk to a kumquat. This is hypocrisy!"

The bill failed. A couple of days later I received a two page letter from Governor Treen and found out a little more about him. You could accuse Dave Treen of many things, but do not question his integrity. He had taken serious offense to my suggesting that his administration was guilty of hypocrisy and he let me have it with all his righteous indignation: *"When you use the word hypocrisy, Ron, you are making a statement about sincerity and integrity. For such a statement to come from one of a small group of people with whom I have been working and counseling on this legislation for a long time is difficult to understand. I accepted the fact that you could not vote for the bill, although I was not happy about it."* Then the typical political quid pro quo was raised. Treen wrote, *"Strangely enough, I had one legislator tell me he thought it was hypocritical for the Lafayette delegation to be solidly against CWEL when it had just recently come to the State for substantial sums for the Assembly Center and wanted a new, major, costly highway project. I counseled against characterizing anyone's motives in that way."*

Edwards took a lot of the credit for the defeat of the CWEL tax and, naturally, reminded the oil industry leaders of his efforts when he ran against and defeated Treen in 1983.

* * *

As the fall elections approached in 1983 I couldn't believe my good fortune, I had not heard a word, not a whisper of anyone preparing to run against me. I had already held a couple of very successful fund-raisers and felt I was well prepared and positioned for a campaign, but not having to hit the streets in the heat of summer was awfully enticing.

At that time qualifying for elections took place during the last week in July, approximately three months before the first primary in October. The legislature changed this in the mid '90's and put off qualifying until early in September, only about six weeks before the election. Many thought that would tend to shorten and thus make less costly election campaigns. The net result is that serious candidates still raise money and start spending it three or four months or more prior to an election. Other, less sincere or even decoy candidates can keep everyone guessing until virtually the last minute and seriously affect the dynamics of a race.

When qualifying week opened in July, 1983, I was at the court house early to pay my money and file. Then I waited. By Friday noon, the last day of qualifying, I was beginning to feel cautiously optimistic. No one had so much as mentioned anyone running against me. "Sonny" Mouton and Dickie Breaux picked me up at my radio station to go to lunch. "Sonny" of course was still connected with the Treen administration and Dickie was an ex-legislator who had served in a district which included Iberia and St. Mary parishes. He had gone through some personal difficulties, recovered and was now living in the Lafayette area. We had a long lunch and they dropped me off in mid-afternoon.

I had quietly placed a bottle of champagne in my office refrigerator for a celebration at 5:00 P. M. when qualifying closed.

At 4:45 the receptionist paged me to take a phone call from clerk of court Dan Guillot.

Dan came on in grave, dead-serious tones, "Ron, I hate to tell you this but you got somebody running against you." While he was talking I could hear "Sonny" Mouton joking and laughing in the background.

"Dan, I know you're kidding, 'Sonny' put you up to this. I can hear him laughing."

"No, no, I'm not kidding," he insisted.

"Well who is it?"

Dan said, "His name is Cleophile 'Bobby' Babineaux."

I laughed. "Now I know you're kidding. You couldn't get that name on a bumper sticker! Let me talk to 'Sonny'."

Mouton came on and I said, "What the hell are you guys up to?"

"Sonny" could hardly contain himself, "No, Dan's serious. Babineaux is head of the electrician's union in the Lafayette Trade Council and he's running against you. And, you know what else? John Breaux is running against Allen Bares for Senate, and so am I!" With that he exploded into laughter.

As it turned out, they were serious about Babineaux. Unfortunately for "Sonny" he got himself out on a limb with what started out to be a joke and well-meaning friends and old political allies convinced him he could retake his old Senate seat. Bares had won that position when Mouton vacated it to run for governor in 1979. This time Bares beat him badly to end what once was a brilliant political career.

The John Breaux everyone would immediately think of was the then-Congressman from Crowley, a former Edwards aide and now U. S. Senator. The John Breaux who actually qualified was John Richard "Dickie" Breaux. That part was all a big joke and Dickie Breaux withdrew his name a few days later. Dickie and his artist wife Cynthia now run a wonderfully nostalgic restaurant in downtown Breaux Bridge called "Cafe des Amis."

I, of course, was very disappointed with the fact that I was now facing a three month campaign, but we were ready to go. We drank the champagne anyway.

Monday morning a call came in from Harry DeLahoussaye, the head of the Lafayette Trades Council. This was the coalition of construction worker unions affiliated with the AFL-CIO. Harry was staunchly union but, in truth, a very gentle man. I had appointed him to the board of the Greater Lafayette Chamber of Commerce when I was president. We were respectful and courteous to each other though he abhorred many of my labor-management votes in the legislature and I disapproved of his blind allegiance to the president of the state AFL-CIO Vic Bussie.

Harry came to my office, closed the door and carefully sat down. He was a big man who had once done his fair share of manual labor but who had suffered from severe back ailments for several years. As we exchanged pleasantries, I noticed he was very studiously looking around at the various stacks of papers, trinkets and paraphernalia strewn over my desk. On later reflection, I realized he was probably looking for some sort of recording device.

In his slow, deliberate, Cajun accent Harry got to the point, "Ron, I believe we can help you out. If you'll just give me one thing, I can get Bobby out of the race."

"Oh, really?" I said, with some surprise, "and what would that one thing be?"

"Well, we know how you are about Right-to-Work and Prevailing Wage but if you'll just give us your promise of one vote on 'Agency Shop' I can call Vic and he'll talk to Bobby."

Right-to-Work had become the law in Louisiana in the mid '70's after a long and, some would say, bloody battle. It basically mandated that union membership could not be required as a criteria for employment. I was vice-president of Governmental Affairs for the local chamber the year it was made law. We were the first chamber in the state to make the passage of Right-to-Work our number one legislative priority.

"Agency Shop" was the union leaders' attempt to circumvent the Right-to-Work law. Under an "Agency Shop" law, if the majority of workers in a unit voted to join a union, all workers, even those who did not choose to join the union, would have to pay union dues.

"I'm not going to do that, Harry, you know that.".

Harry couldn't help himself, he had to play the hard nose union enforcer. He had seen "On the Waterfront" too many times, "I hate to see you say that, Ron, you're just going to make it hard on yourself and your family. It's just one vote." I told him no again, but he was persistent and wouldn't leave. I finally ran out of patience. "Look Harry," I said, "I'm not promising you or Vic anything. If you want to leave Cleophile 'Bobby' Babineaux stranded out there on a limb in a representative district which has less than 15% union voters, fine. I'm going to beat him so bad you and your union pals will never have any credibility in District 44. The next time you enter a candidate or endorse somebody you'll be laughed at. Now get out of here and let me get to work."

Harry did his best for his candidate. Bobby attended the first half dozen candidate forums then almost disappeared. The Daily Advertiser editorial writers did their best to make it look like a race. Could that be because I chose to use no newspaper advertising in my campaign? Several weeks before the election, Savez Vous, an unsigned front page commentary column, said,

" 'Bobby' Babineaux seems to be closing on Ron Gomez and it could be a close race." Wishful thinking. I won with 82 % of the vote. As "Cat" Doucet, long time Sheriff of St. Landry parish used to say, "We won in a mudslide!"

Notable quotes from the legislative halls:

"Where I come from, we use the newspaper classified ads for two things: to train puppies and line bird cages."

Representative Troy Hebert

X

"I know better than to talk to a good-government son-of-a-bitch like you."

While he was out of office during Treen's and Roemer's terms, Edwards was a frequent visitor in the halls of the Capitol. On one occasion, as I was leaving the House chamber, he was standing in a section in the back reserved for lobbyists and others to confer with legislators while the House was in session. I had seen him standing back there for some time talking with various members of the House. Dressed in his casual uniform of jeans and a plaid shirt, he nodded to me as I approached. I stopped, shook hands with him and asked, "What brings you to the Capitol today governor?"

"Just trying to help my friend Foster Campbell with his bill," he said.

Senator Foster Campbell of Elm Grove, just outside of Shreveport, always had some populist, usually anti-business legislation moving through the process. Persistent is his middle name. (His latest is a "processing tax", the grandson of "first use" and "CWEL".)

"Well, you haven't talked to me yet," I laughed.

As usual, Edwin was quick with the retort. "Ha, I know better than to talk to a good-government son-of-a-bitch like you," he said.

It was one of the better compliments I had while serving in the House.

While in office, Edwards rarely came to the House chamber. In fact, he rarely conducted business in the governor's office located on the fourth floor of the Capitol. He preferred the relative privacy of the office in the governor's mansion located within a half mile of the Capitol.

When you saw him in the back of the chamber you knew there was something brewing that: A) would financially benefit one or more of his friends (and thus himself;) B) would financially damage one or more of his enemies; C) would raise more state revenue for him to spend or D) all of the above.

I was chairman of the House Committee on Commerce from 1984 to 1988 (Edwin's third term.) Our committee handled bills affecting everything from banking laws to licensing of undertakers. Included in our domain was licensing of horse racing facilities and the like.

A small group of businessmen, one of whom was Senator Ned Randolph of Alexandria (later mayor of that city,) were promoting the establishment of Jai Alai Frontons in Louisiana. With little hope of success, Randolph introduced the bill in the Senate and, lo and behold, it passed with flying colors late in the session. It should be noted that, in the Louisiana Senate, a bill introduced by a Senator almost always passes with flying colors. Even if the majority of the Senators thought it was a bad bill, they would vote for their colleague and then let the House members from their district know that it needed to be killed. It is an interesting fraternity.

The Jai Alai bill was assigned to the House Commerce Committee. As I said, it was very late in the session, maybe a week and a half before sine die adjournment. I was racing to get all of the bills referred to our committee properly heard. My committee secretary notified me that she had not been able to find which House member would handle the bill on our side of the Capitol. I got in touch with Senator Randolph and he immediately sent one of his partners in the venture, Peter Tattersall, to see me.

He told me they had no House sponsor. They really thought the strong opposition by the horse racing industry, an ally of the governor, would kill or defer the bill in the Senate. Neither the horsemen nor the governor thought it had a chance and it had been practically ignored. Peter begged me to act as the bill's handler and just get it heard by the committee. Again, he really didn't think it would get out of committee but would at least like to make a presentation and perhaps lay the groundwork for another try in the future.

Gambling bills were not my forte. It should be noted that this was several years before the legislature decided that gambling was "gaming" and the mad rush for Louisiana to legalize practically every betting game known to mankind. But, I had seen Jai Alai in Mexico City and found it to be a tremendously exciting spectator sport featuring some of the world's great athletes. Picture an indoor, three-sided handball court almost 200 feet long and 50 feet high with spectators protected by a wire mesh curtain on the open side. The game is played with a rock hard ball a bit smaller than a baseball made of a rubber core covered with goat skin. The ball, called the pelota, is caught by the players in the cesta, an elongated, curved wicker basket about two feet long which is strapped to their arm. Then, in a powerful sweeping, windmill-like motion, it is propelled against the far wall at speeds exceeding 180 miles per hour. It is a real spectacle and, by the way, there is lively betting going on in the stands and at the wagering windows throughout the contests. Practically a national pastime in Mexico, Spain and some other Latin countries, Jai Alai is legal in Connecticut and Florida in the United States.

The promoter of the legislation was proposing a limit of only two facilities in the entire state and very stringent, controlled oversight. A percentage of the income from betting and attendance would be dedicated exclusively to the Louisiana state police budget. The state police, naturally, were in favor of passage.

I still wasn't crazy about the idea but thought, "What the heck, it's an orphan bill, it passed the Senate, it's late in the session, it deserves a hearing."

Of course the Commerce Committee members had a lot of fun hearing the testimony on the adopted bastard child and then gleefully put the monkey on the Spanish-surnamed chairman's back by passing the bill, almost unanimously.

With the accelerated action of the final days of the session, the bill quickly moved up the calendar and was scheduled for floor debate. I told any of the House members who asked that I had absolutely no personal interest in the bill, I was handling it as a courtesy and certainly didn't care how they voted.

Now the horse racing industry came to the post. They were actively lobbying the house members against the Jai Alai bill. The chance of passage was virtually nil. But, stranger things have happened.

The day the bill was scheduled for floor debate Edwin showed up in the chamber and took a seat in the back. As usual the sergeant-at-arms saw to it that there were two empty seats on either side of him. I was soon summoned to visit the governor.

I took the seat on his left, facing the chamber. He didn't even turn his head toward me, just stared straight ahead.

"Why are you handling this stupid Jai Alai bill," he asked?

I said, "Governor, it's an orphan bill that passed the Senate with a huge majority and the sponsors had nobody to handle it in the House. I just thought it deserved a hearing. The Commerce Committee members thought it was a great joke to get me to wrestle with it on the floor of the house. I'm not even asking anyone to vote for it."

"Did Randolph and his boys cut you in for a piece of the action?"

"Absolutely not!"

Now he looked at me with eyebrows raised, "Then you're stupider than I thought you were. Even in my craziest days I would never handle a bill like this without getting some kind of action. Pull the damn thing down," he said.

I said, "I can't do that. But, I know and you know it doesn't have a chance."

It didn't.

Another occasion that brought Governor Edwards to the floor of the House was the debate to ratify a new Superdome contract which he had negotiated with the National Football League's New Orleans Saints' owner Tom Benson. Benson had been making the usual threats, more and more common to NFL owners, of saying he was considering moving his team to another city. He was demanding a number of conditions involving the Saints' lease of the Louisiana Superdome as incentive for keeping the team in New Orleans.

In addition to the sweetheart deal he already had on the lease, Benson wanted substantial revenues from parking, luxury suites, concessions and advertising in the dome, not just for football season but year-round. Benson and his entourage were seated in the rear of the House chamber as the debate began.

Those of us who thought the state was giving away too much questioned what would happen should the Saints become successful on the football field. *(it could happen!)* With success would come increased revenues from all these peripheral sources. We asked why the state could not, at least, retain some of the increased revenue. The proponents said all of the revenues included in the contract were absolutely necessary and specifically quoted a figure on concession sales that they said was the minimum needed.

Representative Charles "Chuck" Cusimano, a diminutive fireball from Metairie, (now a district court judge in Jefferson Parish) heard the numbers and quickly drafted an amendment to the resolution. Cusimano's amendment would allow the Saints' owner to receive concession revenues only up to the figure his proponents had just quoted as the *minimum* needed. Anything over that would then be split 50-50 with the state. Sounds reasonable, right? The amendment passed by a slim margin and Benson and his entourage jumped out of their seats, shouted a few obscenities and something that sounded like "deal buster" and stormed out.

There was chaos on the floor. Speaker John Alario was banging the gavel and reaching for the phone under his desk. After several minutes, Alario hung up the phone, managed to get the chamber reasonably quiet and announced that the House would stand in recess. We were quite certain he had been on the phone with Edwards.

For the next half hour, Alario, the governor's floor leaders and sergeants-at-arms escorted a dozen or so representatives one by one out of the chamber. There was no sound of gunfire so it couldn't be a firing squad. Those of us not called got curious and wandered down the corridor and into the suite of offices occupied by the speaker of the House and his staff. (When the Capitol was first built, this was the governor's suite.) We found a short line of House members waiting outside the speaker's office. The governor was inside. They all looked like schoolboys summoned to the principal's office. All of the representatives waiting had voted for the offending amendment.

Within a half hour we were called back into the chamber where Speaker Alario announced that we would remain in recess to hear a short address by the governor.

Now this was utterly unprecedented. First, the governor was only invited to the floor of the House for a speech on the day of his inauguration and once a year for a "state of the state" address to start a regular session or opening speeches to special sessions. Second, the escapades of governors such as Huey and Earl Long in the past had persuaded the House to adopt very strict rules concerning the privilege of coming on to the floor of the House.

Only legislators and staff were allowed, no families, no lobbyists, no reporters, no governors. It must be noted that the Senate does not have a similar provision. Governors often wander the floor of the Senate, the lounge or the sofa-furnished sitting area at the rear of the Senate chamber.

Alario didn't wait for a protest to develop. He immediately called the governor to the floor of the House and banged the gavel for quiet.

I had never heard Edwards give such a disoriented speech. He looked shaken and was almost pleading as he tried to explain to us that the proposal he had presented could not be amended. Any changes in the document, such as the amendment we had adopted on concessions' revenues, he said, would amount to a deal breaker. The Saints would leave New Orleans. The nation would turn its back on us. The skies would darken forever. Little children would be crying in the streets. The city would dry up and turn into a ghost town. We would be the laughing stock of the NFL. (Had he seen any of the Saints' games?) He went on for ten minutes or more explaining step by step the process by which he had crafted this sacrosanct agreement.

As was customary for me, I was taking notes on the speech for future reference. When Edwards got near his closing I stopped and thought, "I couldn't have heard what I thought I just heard." I showed my notes to a representative seated near me and said, "Did I get this right?"

He said, "Yup."

Read this carefully. Edwards said, *"When I got around to changing this apples and oranges thing, that was the straw that helped the camel cross the river."*

Many referred to Edwards as a silver-tongued orator. Some just called him the silver zipper. But in this instance the silver plating sounded more like an alloy.

The governor left the podium. The speaker gaveled the House back into session. Representative Raymond Laborde of

Marksville stepped to the mike and moved that the previous amendment by Rep. Cusimano be deleted. The previous question was immediately called and thus precluded any debate or discussion. The vote was taken and the governor had changed enough votes to get the amendment stricken. It couldn't have taken more than a minute. Benson and the Saints, and some presume Edwards, were back in business.

*   *   *

Edwin Edwards was, and is good with the words, quick with the quip, one of the best. One could probably fill a chapter with the bon mots of Edwin Edwards. During the 1983 campaign against incumbent Governor Dave Treen, Edwards suggested Treen was so deliberative it took him "an hour and a half to watch '60 Minutes'." He was so certain of victory in one election that he told a reporter he could only lose if he was caught in bed with a dead girl or a live boy.

But one thing about Edwards constantly amazed me. He seemed to draw confidence and glibness from the size of the audience. I watched him captivate a crowd of over 10,000 people at USL's Cajun Field in Lafayette in the closing days of the 1983 campaign. Speaking from the back of a flat-bed truck, he had them stomping and hooting as he promised, "There is one who is coming to save Louisiana." The messiah of which he was speaking, of course, was himself.

On the other hand, in a group of four or five legislators in the governor's office he was almost subdued and easily dissuaded from his arguments. One on one, in my experience, he seemed almost shy.

During the legislative session of 1984, Edwards proposed a tax package which exceeded a billion dollars in new and enhanced taxes. As a committee chairman, I was considered an administration floor leader and expected to vote for and help sell the package. It was agonizing. The economy was collapsing because of the disastrous drop in oil prices. The state was losing almost a billion dollars in annual revenue. Businesses were laying off personnel or closing their doors. Yet, representing a community such as Lafayette which had so much dependence on state government, it was hard to just vote no on all taxes. I knew that would mean crippling cuts to state workers, the University of Southwestern Louisiana, the University Medical Center (once known as Charity Hospital,) the Mental Health Center, Highway Department District Office, Vocational-Technical School and on and on.

Edwards had told us, in a meeting of committee chairmen, that he wanted us to personally let him know if there were any parts of the package we could not support. He also, of course, said that passage of the entire billion dollar plan was vital.

The votes were taken on one piece of the tax proposal at a time over a period of a couple of weeks. After I had held my nose and voted for about a half billion in taxes, I decided to go see the governor.

I was driving into Baton Rouge from Lafayette over the Mississippi River bridge when I called the mansion from my car phone. I figured I'd leave word and the governor would get back to me later. Instead, the state trooper handling the mansion switchboard took my message, asked me to hold on and came back in moments to tell me to come directly to the mansion. That was one thing admirable about Edwards and one thing that constantly endeared him to legislators. We always came first. We could always get him on the phone or get an appointment. Other governors I have known could have been a lot more successful by following that practice.

This was one of the few times while I was in the legislature that I was alone, one-on-one with Edwin. I expected to be overwhelmed by his persuasiveness.

He quietly asked what I needed and I told him there were at least two elements of the tax package I could not support.

"What are they," he wanted to know.

Part of the tax proposal was a 3% tax on real estate transactions. I told the governor, "The real estate market is collapsing in Lafayette as it is, I'm sure, in many other parts of the state. This will absolutely kill it."

He thought for a moment and said, "They're hearing that bill right now at the Capitol. When you leave here go to the committee room and tell Bill Roberts (the governor's executive counsel) to cut it in half."

I thought, "This is too easy," so I said, "I don't think that'll do it. The market just won't stand for *any* additional costs."

He said, "Well, tell Bill to try it that way and if it doesn't work, drop the whole damn thing. What else?"

"Man, I'm on a roll," I thought. I said, "Well governor, the bottlers' tax really bothers me." (This was an increase in taxes on soft drink bottlers.) "You know it would raise almost $10 million dollars statewide and there are only 9 or 10 major bottlers in the state. That's a million dollars each."

He said, "Ron, do you know how much money those people make? And, they can pass it on."

"I know they can pass it on," I said. "But even if the increase translates to 2 cents a bottle they'll raise the price at the vending machine by 5 cents and it's another hit on the consumers."

A gleam came in his eye and he asked, "You still own those radio stations don't you?"

"Sure," I said, wondering where that question came from.

"Oh, well, I understand. Coca-cola and Pepsi and all those big bottlers spend a lot of money on your stations, why didn't you just say so."

It was the age old syndrome of attributing one's own motivations to explain the actions of others. In Edwards' mind, as long as I was making money, it didn't matter whether my vote on the proposed tax was right or wrong.

Notable quotes from the legislative halls:

When asked who was supporting a bill to regulate bounty hunters, Representative Danny Martiny replied: "If I told you I'd have to kill you."

XI

"You go to the mike and say, 'I endorse Edwin Edwards for governor!' "

With our mutual distaste for each other's politics and philosophy of government, how did I become a committee chairman and floor leader in Edwin Edwards' administration?

Good question. I must admit I too was persuaded by Edwin's 1983 campaign rhetoric. I thought he really was ready to change. I had been made a floor leader in my freshman term under Dave Treen partly through the efforts of his executive counsel "Sonny" Mouton and partly because I was older and thus presumably more mature than any of the freshmen legislators. That gave me a taste for being in the center of the action. I believed in my leadership abilities and believed that Edwards truly wanted to use his vast powers and personal talents to right the ship of state. Due to the state's economic woes and his own personal traits, Dave Treen was simply not an effective governor.

Throughout my life, I had been fortunate in achieving leadership roles: as high school student government president, cadet Squadron Commander in the Air Force aviation cadet pilot training program, manager and owner of three radio stations, president of the Greater Lafayette Chamber of Commerce, Louisiana Broadcaster of the Year in 1979 and various other boards and chairmanships in business and community service. Now, at age 49, I preferred to be the driver not just a passenger. I was ready for a legislative chairmanship.

It was obvious that John Alario, veteran House member from Westwego, would be Edwards' hand-picked speaker of the House. John is an intelligent, articulate and highly effective legislator. He has a knack for making everyone feel he is their best friend. Although a long time ally of Edwards with a decidedly populist-liberal leaning, John could swing from either side of the plate when necessary. If a speaker of the House in Louisiana could be elected on their own merit, John would probably win hands down. Unfortunately, the speaker always has been, in effect, a designee of the governor.

In my first term I had served on the House Committee on Ways and Means which Alario chaired and found him to be fair as well as extremely helpful to a freshman legislator. Now, with Edwards' election, he asked that I support him as speaker and become part of the new team.

John Hainkel, from New Orleans, another long-time House member had been Governor Dave Treen's chosen speaker in 1980. Even with Treen's support, Hainkel had challengers, but with the support of the Acadiana group of legislators, won easily. I got along well enough with Hainkel. With the help of Lafayette's only Republican legislator, Mike Thompson, I got two choice committee assignments: Commerce and Ways and Means. Hainkel had also made me chairman (highly unusual for a freshman) of a special task force committee charged with investigating the problems with the construction of the new Southwest Louisiana Charity Hospital in Lafayette. I was also sentenced to Shady Wall's Committee on Retirement but, as a freshman, that was to be expected.

My major problem with Hainkel was that most of his prime committee chairmanships were awarded to Jefferson Parish and New Orleans area legislators.

Though Alario was the obvious choice as Edwards' speaker in 1986, Hainkel insisted on running. I wanted to give him the benefit of the doubt and met with him and other Acadiana legislators to discuss his challenge to Alario. During the course of the evening, I raised the question of chairmanships for Acadiana members. Hainkel could be a bit high-handed at times. He immediately said, a little sarcastically, "Okay, Gomez, you want to be vice-chairman of Commerce?"

I said, "Who'll be chairman?"

"Oh," he said, "I've already promised that to John Ensminger."

John Ensminger of Monroe was one of my favorite House colleagues and certainly deserving of a chairmanship but that wasn't the question.

We asked about other committees. As I expected, the choice spots had already been committed to members from other areas of the state. We left the meeting with Hainkel without making a commitment to his candidacy.

I met again with John Alario and he asked if I would be interested in taking the chairmanship of the Ways and Means Committee. This is one of the two highest profile, most controversial committees in the house, the other being Appropriations. Every tax and revenue raising measure in the legislature starts in the House Committee on Ways and Means. It's chairman is referred to as "The Taxman." Conversely, every spending measure is blessed first by the House Committee on Appropriations.

We discussed this for a while and I realized that Edwards would not be satisfied with the state's income stream as it stood in the wake of our state-wide depression and would be shooting for some major tax increases. I decided that would be a little steep and sticky for a second termer to negotiate.

John agreed but said he had felt obligated to offer it to me first although a former chairman of the committee had just been reelected and wanted the job. He was talking about Claude "Buddy" Leach of Leesville. Leach was known as a tough, sometimes rude person who had run Ways and Means with an iron hand. He had left the Louisiana Legislature when he was elected to the U. S. Congress from a northwest Louisiana district and then became embroiled in accusations of voter fraud in his election. The allegations were never proven but the stain was enough to get him beaten in his first attempt at reelection by the up and coming "Buddy" Roemer. Leach, showing amazing resiliency, than recaptured his old House seat.

Leach was a large, jowly man who looked a bit like the actor Charles Laughton and enjoyed great personal wealth. He was not known for his tact and some would call him arrogant. This was typical "Buddy" Leach: When we first met on the House floor the opening day of the 1984 Legislative Session, he looked up and down my five-foot-eight frame and said, "So you're the famous Ron Gomez I've heard so much about. I thought you'd be bigger. You're just a little fella."

Alario asked if I wanted to chair the Commerce Committee. But there was a caveat. Edwards had as a top priority the passage of what was called a "Multi-Parish Banking" bill. At that time in Louisiana a bank domiciled in one Parish was prohibited by law from buying a bank in another Parish. In addition, Louisiana state banks could not buy or be bought by an out of state bank. Most other states had long ago eliminated such restrictions. The bill had been introduced a couple of times in my first term. The banks in my area were generally opposed to it then so I had voted against the measure.

Alario said they needed someone with my credibility and business profile to handle the bill and the governor needed to be assured that I would actively support a "Multi-Parish Banking" bill in the new legislature. I said I'd get back to him.

I talked with several bankers in Lafayette and Baton Rouge about the issue and found that their stances had drastically changed. With the crashing economy, more and more banks were terribly extended on non-producing and defaulted loans. Most of the bankers I consulted felt a change in the law was the only way many banks could survive. If it came to a question of existence it would be much better to be able to sell or merge than to simply shut down. Still, some of the smaller, rural banks which, as a rule, had operated much more conservatively then their bigger city counterparts, resented the big banks' attitudes and vehemently opposed the change.

I told Alario, with the change of attitude among most of the Lafayette bankers I had talked with, I could support "Multi-Parish Banking." Then another problem arose.

The governor's ultra-gregarious brother, Marion, had heard of my pending appointment and told the governor, according to Alario, that I could not be trusted and should not get the chairmanship.

I told Alario I figured Marion was still smarting from a couple of incidents that had occurred between us over the last couple of months.

Shortly after Edwin defeated Treen he announced a unique fund raiser to retire his campaign debt. For $10,000, a couple could join the governor-elect and his entourage on chartered jets for a week-long fling in Paris, France. People were lining up to go. It didn't take long for the eager Edwards supporters and "wannabes" to nearly fill two large passenger jets.

About a month before the trip, I got a phone call from Marion. He said, "Ron, we haven't heard from you. You're going to Paris with us aren't you?"

I dodged, "Aw, Marion, I can't afford something like that, and besides I don't think I can get away at that time."

"Look, Ron," he said, "you've got over $6,000 leftover in your campaign account. You send that to me and you and Carol are on the trip."

I was astounded. He had actually looked up the campaign disclosure documents that all candidates file after an election and found out exactly how much I had in reserve, to the penny. I later found out that he and other staff members had done that on every candidate's report.

I declined. He insisted. I continued to decline. We didn't go.

Obviously it was a heck of a trip. Dozens of legislators and their spouses took advantage of the opportunity. Edwards and a group made a side trip to the French Riviera and Monte Carlo where Edwards bragged that he won $10,000. A huge banquet was held at Versailles, summer palace of the French Sun King, Louis the XIV. It was reported that one of Louisiana's fine legislators even attempted to make off with some of the silver dinner settings from the palace. He failed only because he lost his grip on the heavy load concealed in a napkin and spilled it all over the cobble-stoned drive on the way to the waiting buses.

Louisiana and Edwards made headlines nationwide. *People* magazine carried a spread on the trip that even exposed a vacation love affair involving a couple of the participants. Unfortunately they were both married - to other people who were not on the trip. That, needless to say, created a lot of grief for the ill-starred couple when they returned.

Another thing that had stuck in Marion's craw was that I had refused to join Edwards and other legislators on the flat bed truck used for a stage at his big wrap-up rally at Cajun Field in Lafayette the last week of the campaign.

Carol and I attended the rally at the urging of some good friends who were Edwards supporters. I fully intended to just sit in the stands and enjoy the spectacle. My election was over in the first primary when I received 82% of the vote over Bobby Babineaux, a member of the local union trades council. I had long felt that an elected official should not be so presumptuous as to endorse other candidates or try to tell people how to vote. I had studiously avoided publicly taking sides in this gubernatorial race in spite of the fact that I personally voted for Treen. My friend pulled his car into a valet parking area in the parking lot of the stadium. As I got out of the car, one of the Edwards team grabbed my arm and said, "The governor wants to see you in the press box."

Carol and our friends told me where they hoped to be in the stands and I reluctantly went up the elevator with the handler.

I couldn't believe my eyes when the elevator opened at the top. Legislators, parish, town and city officials from six or seven surrounding parishes were jammed into the press box. The noise level of conversations was on a par with a disco. My escort led me to Marion Edwards who was animatedly talking at the top of his voice with Senator Allen Bares of Lafayette.

When Marion saw me he ran over and shouted, "Good, you made it. Now, when we introduce you, you come to the mike and say 'I endorse Edwin Edwards for governor'."

I said, "What are you talking about?"

He said, "Ya'll are all going to be on the flat bed truck on the field in front of the stands. Edwin's gonna come running out of the chute where the teams come out. Then we'll introduce each of you elected officials. When you're introduced you come to the mike and say 'I endorse Edwin Edwards for governor.' "

"Marion, I can't do that. I never have and hope I never will endorse *anyone*," I said.

"What?," he shouted over the din, "I thought you wanted to be somebody. I thought you might want to be a chairman or something."

I just turned around and started walking for the door that led out of the press box to the stands. On the way I linked up with Representative "La La" Lalonde of Sunset. He looked at me and said, "You, too?"

I said, "Yep, I'm not doing that."

"I'm not either," he said.

Once we had made the long walk down to field level from the press box and the upper deck, I spotted Carol and our friends. On the field the introductions were underway. The press box crowd had come down the elevators and were driven to the flat bed stage in vans. Senator Armand Brinkhaus shouted, "I endorse my friend Edwin Edwards." No surprise there. Former Senator and now Senate candidate Edgar Mouton of Lafayette made his commitment. Of course he had served as Treen's executive counsel the previous four years. So much for loyalty. Incumbent Senator Bares, opposed by Mouton, jumped to the mike and, in a great display of political one-ups-man-ship, gave his pledge in English *and in French.*

I eased onto a seat directly behind Carol. She was intently watching and obviously scanning the field and didn't know I was behind her. I tapped her on the shoulder. She turned and immediately tears welled up in her eyes. "Thank God," she said, "you didn't do it."

Now, some months later with my appointment as a committee chairman in question, Alario suggested I meet personally with the governor-elect to counter Marion's opposition.

Edwards and I met alone in his office in the transition headquarters building on Perkins Road in Baton Rouge.

I told him I knew he must realize that I didn't share many of his populist and liberal views of government but that, with the assurances I had received from my friends in the banking business, I thought the "Multi-Banking" bill was right for the business and the state. I also conveyed to him my belief that he could be the most effective governor the state has ever had.

He said, "Look, I'll never ask you to do anything to compromise yourself. I just want you to keep an open mind and let me know, first, when you can't support me."

We agreed, shook hands and I became the first member of the House from Lafayette to chair a committee since the days of Richard Bertrand in the early 60's.

*   *   *

John Alario asked me to make the seconding speech for his nomination as speaker of the House. As a second term member, I was honored and I truly believed that John was the right choice at the time. Besides, he was Edwin's choice and, realistically, that was all that mattered. John Hainkel was still fighting the odds and refused to concede the election. He was promoting his election as speaker as a show of legislative independence.

I wanted the speech to carry a message other than just a nomination of a man, to reflect some of the observations I had made in my first term. So I wrote and delivered:

" 'Buster' Sheridan has been a member of the Louisiana House of Representatives for twenty years. Danny Lemoine for less than 24 hours. All the rest of us fall somewhere in between. But I believe if 'Buster' or Danny or almost any of us were to be challenged to point out the unique quality of this group, the one big difference in this group from practically any other organization you've ever had anything to do with...THE big difference is our differences!

"Before becoming a member of this House four years ago, I had traveled Louisiana quite extensively so I have been aware of the differences encompassed in our relatively small state, differences in economic needs, problems and bases. I was well aware of the broad range of speech patterns and dialects in our state, the diversity of interests and cultures and religions and races. But none of that past experience fully prepared me for seeing all of those diverse traits all together in one room... here at the Louisiana House of Representatives.

"I suppose that's when I realized, for better or worse, good or bad, we are, in truth and in fact, a mirror image of the people of this state.

"Here in this one chamber, 105 men and women bring together the hopes and needs and problems and beliefs and philosophies of people from 105 different and distinct areas of the state. *How can it possibly work? There are some who say that it doesn't, but, in fact, it does.*

"*In spite of these differences in the way we think and act and believe and speak. In spite of all the diversity, we work together, and that is the key word, together. We yell and scream and coerce and beg, but, ultimately, to make it work, we do it together.*

"*And when we elect a speaker, we are electing the representatives' representative. The person who will represent this body, speak for us, be our liaison with the administration and the other house and other branches of government. He becomes our mirror image just as we reflect our districts.*

"*I believe the election of John Alario as speaker of this House of Representatives will insure that all of us can best use our differences to work together even more effectively. That is the key to our future strength. Just as many different fabrics are woven together to make a stronger cloth, many metals blended to produce a stronger, more efficient alloy, thus we must use our differences, our varying interests and experiences to build a stronger legislative body.*

"*I believe John Alario intends to fully utilize these differences and strengths from throughout the state, without favoring one area over another, without concentrating power in one section of the state. I believe you will see this in the committee assignments, chairmanships, and, in the general day-to-day business of the House.*

"*As a member of the Ways and Means Committee, I have seen John Alario preside over extremely sensitive, potentially volatile situations with great skill, absolute fairness and always with a unique sense of humor that tends to keep things in a proper perspective when we start taking ourselves too seriously.*

"*John realized that not all committee members could relate, on a personal basis, with some of the capital outlay needs of their colleagues, so he initiated interim committee meetings held throughout the state so we could see, first-hand, what the needs were. When Carl Gunter told us the hospital in his district was crumbling and decaying, we saw it for ourselves. When Jimmy Long spoke of the needs of Northwestern, we knew exactly what he meant, because we had been there. That, to me, is how you build a caring attitude and effectiveness into a system too often perceived as dehumanized and ineffective. And that's just one small example of the type of leader and the type person John Alario is.*

"Now, may I just say a few things about independence? It's a wonderful word, undoubtedly an admirable trait and a condition for which we all mightily strive. But, practically speaking, and, in particular within the context of what we're doing today, using independence as a rallying cry may be merely self-serving. After all, we are called public servants and we told the electorate we wanted to serve them. From whom are we trying to stay independent? If we were all to be totally independent, we'd each vote for ourselves. But, if we elect as our speaker a person who maintains an excellent relationship with a governor who is beginning an unprecedented third term with a whopping 62 percent voter mandate, are we relinquishing our independence or truly representing that electorate which sent us here to represent its wishes?

"Do you give away any kind of freedom when you elect a speaker who has paid his dues as a member of this House, a member of the Constitutional Convention of 1973, a chairman of one of our key committees, a person who has proven his abilities as well as his sincere feelings for all areas of the state? Is that giving up your independence, or is it acting in the best interests of your constituents to insure your effectiveness as a representative and the effectiveness of this House as we face the challenges of this new term?

"I have no problem defending my independence and voting for John Alario as speaker of this House. I believe we will be

reflecting the wishes of our constituents who spoke at the polls last fall and told us it is time to get moving in this state.

"I believe our election of John Alario today is a demonstration of responsibility, a dedication to cooperation for the good of the state, and a declaration of this House that we will truly fulfill our roles as representatives of our electorate."

John Hainkel conceded before a vote was taken and John Alario was unanimously elected as Speaker of the House. He would be faced with a reversal of the situation in 1988 when *he* would be arguing for legislative independence in a effort to be elected speaker over another representative chosen by a newly-elected governor.

Notable quotes from the legislative halls:

"I know that people in New Orleans take a keen interest in the political process. Some of them vote two or three times in the same election."

Representative Thomas Wright

Just sitting around in committee. Me and an out-of-focus Mike Thompson, Lafayette with Speaker-to-be Jimmie Dimos, Monroe in background.

Elias "Bo" Ackal (deceased), New Iberia, former chairman of the Acadiana Caucus with John Alario, Westwego; Speaker of the House 1984-'88, 1992-'96.

"Best wishes from Governor Edwin Edwards."
I'll bet he wrote that to all the legislators

(Times of Acadiana)

Governor Buddy Roemer with his mother "Miz Adeline" during the first
year of his administration, 1988

(Photo by Bob McManus)

Governor Dave Treen, on hand to cut the ribbon for the grand opening of our state-of-the-art new radio studios for KPEL and KTDY in 1983.

(Times of Acadiana)

My early House "mentor", Mike Thompson, Lafayette.

Looks like hard times for the chairman of Ways and Means hemmed in by (L.to R.) John Alario, Westwego; S.J. Theriot, Marrero; Clyde Kimball, New Roads and Allen Bradley, Deridder. Fiscal reform hearings 1988.

(Hank Wilson, Baton Rouge Morning Advocate)

Political cartoon depicting members of the Ways and Means Committee during 1989 fiscal reform debate. Top (L.to R.): Chairman Gomez; conservative Republican Charles Lancaster, Metairie; Sean Reilly, Baton Rouge; John Alario, Westwego; Kip Holden, Baton Rouge; Bottom row: Don Bacque, Lafayette; Republican Art Sour, Shreveport; Irma Dixon, New Orleans; Wilford Carter, Lake Charles and an unidentified member with an honest answer.

John Hainkel, House Speaker 1980-'84; Senate President 2000-.

Jimmie Dimos, House Speaker, 1988-1992.

(Photo by author)

My buddy, the "grenade thrower" Robert Adley, Bossier City.

(Times of Acadiana)

Charles Dewitt, Lecompte, elected Speaker, 2000-, after Governor Foster
withdrew his support for previous Speaker Hunt Downer, Houma.

XII

"Lightning done hit the bell cow!!"

In spite of the smoldering fights of 1988 and 1989 involving Buddy Roemer's new initiatives and fiscal reform, 1986 still stands out as the most frustrating, tedious and soul-wrenching year I spent in the legislature.

In the midst of floundering oil prices for the third consecutive year, 1986 started with dire predictions of a state budget which would be $800 million in the red without new revenues. Edwards, under indictment and facing a federal racketeering trial, announced that the only way to solve the revenue problem was to pass bills during a February special session legalizing casino gambling and a lottery in the state. That never came about. Edwards wouldn't even discuss the possibility of reducing the cost of government as an alternative. The legislature did that. And then the year ended with a special session in December which still accomplished nothing toward correcting the state's fiscal collapse.

In between, I was chairing the House Commerce Committee and handling a bushel full of legislation which would A) reform the civil justice laws of the state dealing with negligence or tort cases, B) rewrite the state's banking laws to allow interstate and regional purchases of bank holding companies, and, C) repeal the centuries old "Sunday Blue Laws." Meanwhile, Edwards federal racketeering trial began in April during the same week the legislative regular session started. It was some year.

Like so many of Edwin Edwards' proposals during the tight budget years, the casino and lottery ideas were poorly defined and obfuscated with rhetoric. At first the governor wanted more than a dozen gambling houses in the New Orleans area but proposed a three casino limit as a compromise. He said casinos would raise $250 million and create 100,000 jobs. He claimed the lottery would produce over $150 million in taxes for the state. He canvassed the legislators during January and February looking for votes for the gambling measures. He didn't find enough and finally, he admitted the votes were not there and abandoned the idea of calling a special session.

Before the opening of the regular session, the governor stumped the state, speaking to civic clubs and other groups, trying to sell his idea. He maintained that this was the only answer to the revenue shortages in the state budget. He even threatened to resign his office if the legislature did not approve his plan. He would not cut the budget. When the regular session finally met, he had several gambling legalization bills introduced. In order to get the casino bill through a House committee, he agreed to give half the revenue to the city of New Orleans. That raised serious questions about his motivation for passing such a bill. Had he not said that the state needed all of the money? The House voted 53 to 33 to table the bill without even allowing it to reach the floor for debate. Edwards deplored the vote, "New Orleans may have lost its best chance for jobs and economic survival," he said. "The state may have lost its best chance to balance the budget without raising substantial taxes or creating hardship by more budget cuts." Representative (later Senator) Diana Bajoie of New Orleans moaned, "Our people are unemployed, starving to death. We want to help ourselves pull us up by the bootstrings (sic)." Though the lottery had a bit more support than the casino idea, it too was doomed for that session.

As required by law, the governor had presented the legislature with a balanced general appropriations bill. Unfortunately, the budget he presented was dependent on oil prices averaging $19.50 a barrel for the fiscal year. They were then stuck at $13 a barrel and less. His budget also assumed revenue to be produced by gambling casinos and a statewide lottery as well as a state property tax. Even if such had passed the legislature, it was highly unlikely that they could be implemented fast enough to impact the state's 1986 - 1987 fiscal year. The governor's budget was an insulting and ludicrous pipe dream.

Edwards taunted the legislature by daring them to try to cut spending. His legislative leaders, Senate President Sammy Nunez and House Speaker John Alario announced that they would cut the session days by a third saving several hundred thousand dollars. It would amount to a drop in the bucket. We would be asked to complete the session 25 days early. Many of us felt the administrations' real plan was to end the session without an approved budget thus building the pressure for passage of the gambling proposals in a special session.

As the contentious session dragged on it became evident that the legislators were in no mood to raise substantial taxes to fill the budget gap. It was equally apparent that the governor, now mired in court with his federal trial, would not help solve the problem short of passage of the gambling bills. He even, half-facetiously I presume, suggested that legislators should forego getting paid for six or seven days to save the state more money and stay in session long enough to reach an agreement on the budget. Mike Thompson and I called his bluff. Mike said, "I wouldn't object to that. After all, the governor hasn't been able to collect his pay because of the unemployment problems he blamed Treen for." (Edwards had magnanimously said he would not take his gubernatorial pay until the state's unemployment figures were reduced. He hadn't counted on the oil price crisis to linger so long.) I told a reporter, "I'd be glad to do it. But remember, when I proposed two years ago that we all take a 10 percent pay cut, I was almost laughed out of here."

Rather than roll over and wait for the governor to act, some of the legislators, notably Bo Ackal, Robert Adley and others starting working on a new, legislature-initiated budget. Unheard of heresy!

In the last week in June, the legislature broke an age old tradition by approving an operating budget which it had crafted without the direction of the governor. When the final vote was taken in the House, Representative Carl Gunter shouted, "Lightning done struck the bell cow!"

The final budget called for over $600 million in cuts. Edwards had little to say about the outcome. He obviously deplored the reduction in spending and hinted strongly that a special session would be needed later in the year to raise taxes. Generally speaking, legislators sounded pleased with the turn of events. Representative Kathleen Blanco of Lafayette (elected Lieutenant Governor in 1995 and 1999) said, "The Legislature has matured, this was the first year it acted like I always thought a legislature should act. It's been the most interesting and fruitful session I have experienced. It's also the toughest." My only comment in the press was, "It was a very historic session, government was run without a governor."

While the budget battles were waged I was busy with the rest of my legislative package. Louisiana was one of the last states in the union with universal "Blue Laws." Only essential goods, such as groceries or gasoline could be sold on Sunday. I had voted against the repeal of the law on several occasions based on the arguments I heard during committee hearings at the Capitol over the years.

As Chairman of the Commerce Committee, I decided to have the committee really study the issue. I knew that our surrounding states had repealed most of their similar laws and Louisiana retailers along our borders felt they were operating at a huge disadvantage. I scheduled a series of committee hearings in various areas of the state so that we would get input from people who may not ordinarily come to the Capitol. It didn't take long for many committee members, including me, to start changing our minds on the issue. The religious arguments were still there but seemed less and less strident.

By the start of the 1986 regular session, I knew it was time for Louisiana to join the parade. In a bitter struggle that sharply divided both the House and Senate, we finally passed the repeal of Louisiana's "Blue Laws" effective December 1, 1986. To soften the blow for some opponents, we included a provision that local governments could place into law their own closing laws before that date, if approved by their citizens. When I drive past large shopping centers and malls now on Sundays and see their parking lots overflowing with shoppers' vehicles, it's hard to believe that could not be seen in Louisiana just over ten years ago.

While we were busy moving into the 21st Century in retailing, I was busily moving my interstate banking bill. This too would bring Louisiana laws in line with practically every other state. We had already passed the multi-parish banking bill allowing mergers and buy outs of banks across parish lines. The interstate bill would allow Louisiana banks to merge or buy banks in other states and other states to invest in Louisiana banks.

The only real opposition to the bill came from an unexpected source. It wasn't really opposition but a move to change the provisions of the bill. Congressman "Buddy" Roemer objected to the geographic terms of the bill. This was the first time I had dealt with the future governor at any great length. He served on the congressional banking committee and had some experience in the formation of some Louisiana banks so I respected his opinion, to a point.

We had drafted the bill with the full input and agreement of the Louisiana Banking Association as well as the Louisiana Banking Commissioner. The region to be approved in the bill included the Southeast United States Banking Region and the state of Texas. Roemer, for whatever reason, wanted to add several other states to the mix. He called me almost daily from Washington, D. C. While I was on the floor of the House, Roemer would implore me with arguments for his position. He was, after all, a former national debate champion, and could be quite persuasive. I passed his arguments on to some of the banking experts in our midst and they were opposed to his suggested changes.

Buddy's close friend and my sometime adversary, Robert Adley, was on the Commerce Committee and attempted to get the Roemer-supported amendments placed on the bill during the committee hearings. I prevailed and they were defeated. We got the bill to the floor of the House and Adley again went the distance for Roemer but we were able to defeat his amendments by extremely slim margins.

We went to the Senate Commerce Committee for hearings. When I finished my presentation on the bill before the committee, I stood up from the witness table, turned and almost ran into none other than Congressman Buddy Roemer. He had flown down unannounced from D. C. to testify before the committee in favor of his amendments. I asked my committee secretary to go to my office and pull the entire file on the subject and bring it to me.

By the time Roemer had finished an impassioned plea, I had in my hands what I wanted. I went back to the table to close my arguments on the bill. I urged the committee to pass the bill as it had come from the House and told them I wanted to read a letter to them concerning this subject. I suppose Buddy had forgotten the letter he had written to me almost a year earlier. In that letter he said there was no more important issue to come before the legislature than the passage of a regional banking bill and that nothing should be done to delay such a bill. I read the letter to the committee closing with, "Signed, Congressman Charles "Buddy" Roemer."

The committee passed the bill as it had come through the House and it was ultimately signed into law. As I walked out of the Senate committee room, Buddy approached, we shook hands and he said, "You're a worthy adversary." Little did we know how closely we would be allied in the coming years when he became governor.

Win some, lose some. My package of bills on tort reform, civil justice reform, lawsuit abuse reform, whatever you might call it, was doomed from the beginning. 1) It was too large and cumbersome, 11 bills on intricate legal matters. 2) The House Committee on Civil Law was stacked with legislators who were plaintiff trial attorneys in real life. 3) The Louisiana Trial Lawyers Association mobilized their wealthy membership into a major lobbying force, even paying "consumer advocate" Ralph Nader $10,000 to appear at a committee hearing and to hold a press conference opposing the bills. 4) Probably most importantly, there was then no grassroots support for the effort. Most people had no idea what we were trying to do. Only individuals who had been sued or business owners who were fighting the liberal tort laws for survival could relate. As one reporter wrote, *"Rep. Ron Gomez' liability package fell apart when a committee full of trial lawyers attacked and made it look like insurance companies were to blame, even though Gomez points out that even self-insured companies are paying huge court awards."*

Lawsuit abuse reform became a passion with me over the years. In 1992, an organization called "Citizens Against Lawsuit Abuse" was formed. I became executive director for the group a couple of years later and we worked to educate and inform the general public on the abuse the civil justice system has undergone through decades of liberal legislators, governors, judges and a small but politically powerful group of plaintiff trial attorneys. The 1996 elections brought major changes in the legislature as well as a business owner who was elected governor. That combination, along with our organization and many other business and industry groups combined for passage of several reform measures which have seriously curtailed some, if not all, of the abuse. It only took ten years.

*　　　*　　　*

In February of that strife-torn year 1986, I was invited to speak before the Louisiana Broadcasters Association. Of course, my radio stations were members of the association, I had served on the board and had been selected to receive its Broadcaster of the Year award in 1979. I figured I'd be among friends and decided to unload some frustrations and pent-up irritation.

Little did I know the print media would pay that much attention to a speech before some broadcasters. I also should have realized that you can't take on the governor, the head of LABI (Louisiana Association of Business and Industry) and the former chairman of the Appropriations Committee in one speech and not expect to be challenged.

My comments were built around the theme, "What this state doesn't need." I said, "Louisiana doesn't need a governor threatening to quit if he doesn't get his way (Edwards had said if we didn't pass his gambling proposals he would resign,) a business leader insinuating the state's education system sucks or an influential legislator portraying Louisiana's people as just plain dumb." I was referring to Governor Edwards' comments, Ed Steimel's recent remarks about the education system being sucked down into the mire, and Representative Kevin Reilly of Baton Rouge, former Chairman of the House Appropriations Committee. Reilly had recently been removed from that position by Speaker of the House John Alario after he publicly criticized the governor. Reilly, the very wealthy executive officer for Lamar Outdoor Advertising Company, had appeared in *People* magazine the previous month wearing farming coveralls which were so short they exposed his bare ankles over a pair of brogans. He was standing next to a pickup truck with the traditional shot gun slung across the rear window. He was quoted as saying all it took to make Louisianians happy was a pickup and a shotgun. That was one of the more generous quotes.

I must admit, I was frustrated and angry over the whole political atmosphere in the state and went a little over the top on this one. I said, "We don't need the governor saying, 'I'm going to resign if my one idea falls through.' I think we need the governor to govern, he's a brilliant man. We need him to use that brilliance to try to solve the problem in ways other than coming up with one solution and saying, 'If you don't go with that, I will resign.' "

Referring to Steimel, I said, "We don't need the leader of business and industry in this state telling us, in so many words, that education sucks. Steimel is saying, 'We can't get business and industry in this state anymore until we wipe out everything and start over.' That's as negative as anything that has gone on in this state."

I moved on to Reilly, "I don't think we need the former chairman of the Appropriations Committee, who served 14 years as chairman of that committee, who saw the budget go from a little over $1 billion to over $6 billion in that period of time, who saw it raised from $2 billion to $6 billion in the past five years alone, I don't think we need him to appear in *People* magazine with his bare ankles and shotgun talking about how dumb our people are in this state."

I couldn't leave well enough alone, "We don't need presidents of universities going around saying 'We're going to cut summer school out, unless you vote for gambling and lottery.' " (Several Louisiana university presidents had been persuaded by Edwards to make such pronouncements.) "These are scare tactics that have been used over and over in this state, especially in the education field."

I continued, "I don't think we need the Republican caucus, the conservative caucus and the Democrats in the House and Senate pointing fingers and screaming at each other."

"Now, let me tell you what we do need," I said. "We need to stop blaming and start working toward solutions. I feel as though there is a group of us in the middle of all this who are trying to calm down the rhetoric, trying to tell the governor, 'you can't get gambling passed, so please use your brilliance to do something else.' " I went on to suggest that leaders of business and industry and organized labor should understand that they may be fighting over a grave yard if the state continued on its fiscal downslide.

Steimel was and still is an icon in the business community. Reilly was very popular in his upscale Baton Rouge district. Both were well liked and respected by the owners and editors of the Baton Rouge *Morning Advocate* newspaper. An editorial was published the following week: *"What we really do not require."*

The editors, *"Regrettably disagree with Mr. Gomez. It is precisely the words and actions of the people he wants to be quiet that have brought about the Legislature's sudden concern with these problems. They are the people who were able to define the problems and bring them to the attention of the citizens of Louisiana. And it is these same people who, by continuing to voice their concerns, refuse to allow the issue to be swept quietly under the table."* The editorial continued for almost the length of a page concluding with, *"We'd like to replace Mr. Gomez' list with one of our own: What we really don't need is a State Legislator telling us that what we need is to hide our heads in the sand."*

I considered myself suitably chastised.

Funny how things go around and come around. When that smoldering 1986 regular session finally burned itself out, John Maginnis again compiled his "Best and Worst" of the legislature feature. I was listed as "Most Valuable Player" to business: *"Ron Gomez of Lafayette is not an attorney but he sponsored the liability reform package before the lawyer-packed House Civil Law Committee, a heretic before the inquisition. He mastered and cogently argued the issue in committee - to no avail, though the fault was in the lobbying, not in the sponsorship. Gomez also guided through the interstate banking bill which will change the face of banking, again, in Louisiana."*

Notable quotes from the legislative halls:

"Close the machines Mr. Clerk. Trial lawyers 26, insurance companies 66. The bill for insurance disclosure fails."

Speaker Pro Tempore Emile "Peppi" Bruneau

XIII

"The cotton plants didn't talk back."

Charles E. "Buddy" Roemer III, governor of Louisiana from 1988 to 1992, was, by turns, one of the most intelligent, stubborn, humorous, dour, logical, unpredictable, charming, cold, challenging, distant, interesting and exasperating people I have ever known or worked with.

I thoroughly enjoyed the long hours we spent, with other members of his administration and legislators, working on legislative projects, planning bill-handling strategy, fighting the battle of "fiscal reform" or just talking. With his brilliant, quick-study mind and Harvard training, he was delightful to work with in unsnarling difficult scenarios and procedures. Usually.

At other times he could be maddening, closing his mind to the most logical arguments if they disagreed with his stance and abruptly shutting off debate when he wasn't winning the argument. One person, on visiting with Buddy for the first time, observed that he was "socially dysfunctional." His mood swings were monumental and could have been attributed to his serious case of diabetes which required him to inject insulin at least twice a day. I personally could never judge to what extent the disease contributed to his unpredictability. Still, I truly liked Buddy and desperately wanted for him and his administration, called "the Roemer Revolution" to succeed.

The most logical explanation I ever heard for Buddy's personality traits came from Adeline Roemer, his mother.

When Buddy and his wife Patti separated in late 1989, Miz Adeline, as she was affectionately called by one and all, took over the first lady or hostess-coordinator duties at the governor's mansion. She was the epitome of a southern plantation noblewoman. Fittingly. The Roemer's had owned a 2,000 acre plantation, "Scopena," near Shreveport for years. Buddy's father, Charles Sr. (Budgie) was indicted and convicted along with reputed Mafia boss Carlos Marcello in the early '80's on charges stemming from his time as Commissioner of Administration under Edwin Edwards in the '70's. The convictions ultimately were overturned because of a quirk in the law but only after the senior Roemer and Marcello had served several years in a federal prison. The family holdings had been severely decimated because of the legal problems and the elder Roemers were now living in Baton Rouge.

On this particular day in 1990, the governor's chief of staff P. J. Mills and I were meeting with the governor in his office at the mansion. I was then serving on Roemer's cabinet as Secretary of the Department of Natural Resources. P. J., a former legislator, candidate for state office, insurance company executive and the first administrator of the Louisiana Offshore Oil Port (LOOP), had been brought in midway in the term as the governor's chief of staff to bring some maturity and experience to the office.

There was an especially thorny decision to be made that day. We were under a tight deadline and needed the governor's direction. For whatever reason, Buddy did not want to talk about the subject at hand and kept drifting off into other areas. P. J. and I, becoming more and more exasperated, were almost begging him to get to the matter and make a decision. Finally, he said he had other things to do and invited us to leave. We told him we had to have a decision before we left the office. He threw his feet up on the desk and said, "Well, you're not going to get it so you might as well leave."

We stormed out of the office. As the door to the office slammed shut behind us, I said to P. J., "That's the most stubborn son of a ..." and spotted Miz Adeline sitting at a small secretary's desk in the hall just outside the office ... "gun I've ever dealt with. Oh, excuse me Miz Adeline, I didn't know you were there."

She gave me her sweetest southern matron's smile and said, "Oh, that's all right Ron, I understand how you feel. What you've got to understand is, when Buddy was winning all those debate and declamation contests in high school he'd go out in our cotton fields and practice.... just talking and talking to the fields. And, you see, the cotton plants never talked back."

I frankly still believe that Buddy Roemer could have been one of Louisiana's greatest governors. The state's horrible financial condition when he took office, his dependence on an inexperienced and sometimes rashly immature staff in his first year or so, an overly-ambitious legislative agenda and his own unpredictable dealings with individual legislators all contributed to the failures he suffered. Ultimately, all of these factors led to his running third, as the incumbent, in the 1991 gubernatorial election.

Others, real historians, will undoubtedly better relate the details of his four years in office. From my viewpoint, his problems started the night of the first primary in 1987 when Edwin Edwards shocked the state by announcing that he would concede the election, after running second. There would be no second primary.

It was my opinion early in the 1987 election, and I still believe, that then-Congressman Roemer had entered the governor's race primarily to get a statewide forum for his hot fiscal-conservative rhetoric and thus get wider name recognition to put him in position to challenge U. S. Senator J. Bennett Johnston in the 1990 senatorial election.

With other high profile politicians in the running against Edwards, an incumbent who had never lost an election, Roemer was not given much of a chance. But, Buddy, even with his pronounced north Louisiana twang, was and is a dynamite orator who could light up an audience with his first two sentences. When he got wound up it was truly evangelical and, he made sense. His wiry, five foot seven, one-hundred thirty-five pound frame would seem to uncoil and grow as he outlined his vision as a fighter against crime, corruption and waste in government, poor education, taxes and industrial pollution.

As other candidates peaked and waned, ran short of money or merely shot themselves in the foot with ill-advised statements or strategy, Buddy made his move with about six weeks left in the campaign. In a series of one-on-one type, almost "talking head" TV commercials, he ignited the voters with his homey red-neck dialect and down to earth promises to "scrub the budget" and "brick up the top three floors of the Education building." Surprise, surprise, little Buddy Roemer led the pack in the first primary with 33% of the vote.

But then Edwards, second with 27%, conceded. The election was over and Roemer never got a chance to truly flesh out his vision for the state. His strategy in the first primary was to win big in north Louisiana, run respectably in the other areas of the state and ignore the time and money demands of campaigning in New Orleans. That combination, he believed, would get him into a runoff election. It did. But now, he would never have a chance to get over 50% of the vote and never campaign and get properly recognized in the state's largest city. He was cheated out of a mandate. When the going got rough a couple of years deep into his term, 67% of the voters could say, "I never voted for him."

Suddenly he was the governor-elect. People all over the state, but especially in New Orleans, including legislators, were asking "who is this guy?" One of my aunts, who lives in New Orleans, called me the day after the shocker. In her Brooklynese-sounding New Orleans dialect she said, "Ronnie, who's this north Louisiana preacher we got for governor? Anybody know him? You know him?"

Additionally, he simply was not prepared to be governor-elect. Naturally, little thought had been given to appointing key administration officials, dealing with the legislature and, worst of all, dealing with the catastrophic reality of a virtually bankrupt state. The only focus was beating Edwin Edwards, "slaying the dragon" in the runoff. Now there was no runoff.

The phenomenon of Roemer's election and defeat of Edwin Edwards was being hailed as the "Roemer Revolution." Buddy's election staff was composed primarily of his congressional legislative aides. They were young, smart, aggressive and, sometimes, very cocky. Some in the media quickly labeled them "Roemeristas." They were more than comfortable and competent in the relatively slow pace of Congress and extremely energetic in election activities. However, they were not attuned to the nuances of dealing with the Louisiana Legislature and running a state government. In fact, many of the staffers, all in their 20's or early 30's, showed a marked disdain for a lot of the legislators and, unfortunately, had little first-hand knowledge of the movers, shakers and players in Louisiana politics.

Chief of staff was Len Sanderson, a former journalist from Shreveport. Sanderson, with his blond hair spilling to below shoulder length, stepped on so many toes and got into so many faces that he didn't make it into the second year. The inner core of the revolution included Steve Cochran, a very bright social and environmental activist who Roemer had discovered waiting tables at a Washington, D. C. restaurant. Cochran eventually took Sanderson's place as chief of staff and later resigned to take a position as executive director of the organization formed to save Lake Ponchartrain from shell dredging and other forms of ecological plunder.

Bob Munson was the tall, gangly and highly energized son of a long-time, high-profile former Louisiana legislator. Munson proved during the fiscal reform referendum campaign in 1989 to be one of the most efficient political fund raisers in the state. He moved on to form a political consulting business operating in Texas and Louisiana. Scott Woodward, short and stocky with curly hair and an infectious smile, was the youngest of the bunch but the one with the coolest head and most logical mind. His poise under fire was learned as an outstanding performer during his teens in junior tennis circles. He is still involved at the Capitol as a highly respected and successful lobbyist. Lawrence Guidry, the only black member of the entourage, was Roemer's closest personal aide, gate keeper, confidant, gofer and shadow. Guidry, once on general staff in the military, had more recently been an appliance salesman in Shreveport.

I was frankly shocked at some of the early recommendations from this team for appointments to sensitive positions during the pre-inauguration transition period. It was obvious that the "Roemeristas" meant well, were highly motivated and totally dedicated to Roemer. They just didn't recognize or know of the alliances and backgrounds of many of the people who immediately showed up looking for jobs and swearing they were Roemer supporters.

One of Buddy's earliest and wisest appointments was Brian Kendrick as Commissioner of Administration. The Commissioner of Administration is probably the second most important position in Louisiana state government. He, or she, is the budget master, the exchequer, the contracts' manager, the state's business manager. Kendrick was chief financial officer for a large chain of department stores headquartered in Baton Rouge and was loaned by the owners of the chain to the governor.

Roemer had not yet taken office so Kendrick was an interim appointment and was having some trouble convincing some of the state's lower level bureaucrats to cooperate with him.

Buddy appealed to Edwin Edwards. He agreed to immediately hire Kendrick as his Commissioner of Administration. He now had total access and authority. He began combing the books. He soon found the frightening facts that not enough of us fully realized. The state was broke. Some of us in the legislature had finally drawn the line on new taxes and revenues and held Edwards' feet to the fire in the previous legislative session and forced budget reductions and cutbacks. The state's fiscal year would end on June 30, 1988. The new governor was to take office in March.

One big problem. Legislatively, the budget had been cut but Edwards ignored the cuts and continued to finance the departments as if nothing had happened. Therefore the reduced budget would only pay for state government through March of 1988. In other words, Edwards would leave office right about the time the money ran out and with three months still left in the fiscal year. In real terms, this meant there would be *no* money to meet April 1st payrolls. There would be *no* money for any cash expenses in the entire state government.

Kendrick's early appointment by Edwards as Commissioner of Administration gave him a head start in identifying the monumental financial problems in the state. It also meant that Kendrick and Roemer, not Edwards, would take the official blame for whatever cuts and layoffs were found to be necessary.

Kendrick, with his real-life experience in the high finance of the business world, immediately started to take innovative, emergency measures. He put off paying everything he could until the new fiscal year. As soon as the legislature came into session we started taking emergency corrective action. As Chairman of the House Committee on Ways and Means, I introduced a bill that allowed the state to sell Revenue Anticipation Notes (RAN). This was a practice fairly common to struggling businesses trying to avoid bankruptcy but not a normal practice in government. The governor, Kendrick, the supporting members of the legislature and I were all roundly criticized by the Edwards carryovers in the civil service ranks of government and the still-loyal-to-Edwards legislators who owed nothing to the new governor. They hardly knew Roemer and he had nothing to do with their elections. He also had no state money with which to deal.

When Kendrick and Roemer then discovered, in reality, the state was not only broke but owed nearly a billion dollars, we approached the legislature with another innovation dreamed up by Kendrick, The Louisiana Recovery District.

Simply stated: The state's bond and credit ratings were so bad that it could not borrow money to pay off the debt in the usual manner. In the Louisiana Recovery District plan, the entire state would be declared a taxing district similar to water or sewer districts in local governments. That taxing district would then be granted one cent of the state's sales tax base. With that guaranteed, recurring income stream and no other expenses, the taxing district could than borrow approximately $800 million to be serviced directly by the dedicated proceeds of the tax over a ten year period. The money would be used to pay off the debt and reduce the debt service on other bonds. Theoretically, this would raise the state's bond rating and reduce the interest rate for other bonding, such as capitol outlay.

If you and your spouse did this you'd call it a debt consolidation loan.

Again, the critics were howling. Included was my friend Dan Juneau at the Louisiana Association of Business and Industry. As I told Dan, "There were no options, it was doomsday, you had to be there." There simply seemed to be no other way to bail out this horrendous financial morass that the friend of the poor people, Edwin Edwards, had left. As fate would have it, oil prices eventually stabilized, the economy drastically improved and the Recovery District bonds were paid off early.

This economic and legislative turmoil was all happening in Roemer's very first days in office and with an unprepared administrative and legislative staff.

Buddy himself, unfortunately, shared his staff's disdain for many of the legislators. In a conversation just days before the inauguration, I suggested to Buddy that he needed to do more schmoozing and stroking of the legislators. I told him many had already complained to me that their phone calls to him or staff members were being ignored. In my usual immodest way, I was lecturing the guy who had just pulled off a miracle election, "You know Buddy, when you're in public office you have two constituencies, the ones who elect you and then the ones you have to work with."

And in his usual sardonic manner, he said, "Gomez, how do you work with some of those idiots."

Obviously, this was going to be a bumpy ride.

Buddy and I still stay in touch a couple of times a year and I still consider him a friend though I'm not sure if our definitions of friendship would be the same.

Notable quotes from the legislative halls:

Representative Steve Windhorst: "Mr. Lancaster, is there an urgent need for this Senate bill?"

Representative Charles Lancaster: "Compared to what?"

XIV

"I love grenade throwers!"

The morning after Edwin Edwards shocked the state by
conceding the 1987 gubernatorial election to Buddy Roemer my
phone rang before 7:00 A.M. I had been asleep about four
hours.

Except for brief intervals, I was on the phone all day and
into the night. Edwards had made his concession announcement
on statewide TV well after midnight. That didn't stop the
political hot line from getting an early start. The first few calls
were from friends and relatives around the state, such as my New
Orleans aunt. Most just wanted to marvel at the turn of events.
Some wanted to know what I knew about Roemer, whether
someone had threatened Edwards with a federal indictment to
get him to pull out and various other wild scenarios. Most were
from colleagues and allies in the legislature who were winding
up a reelection campaign or facing a second primary. I had
enjoyed the luxury of a free ride in the election, running
unopposed.

I walked around the house with the cordless phone
alternating from one ear to the other. I drank coffee and
munched on a biscuit for breakfast while on the phone. Carol
fixed me a sandwich at noon which I ate sitting on the patio of
our home while talking on the phone.

Around eight in the morning, Allen Bradley, a
Representative from DeRidder who had just easily won his
second term in office, called.

Allen is an attorney and was easily one of the brightest and most promising of the 1984 freshmen. He knew Buddy Roemer well and had worked closely with him in the past. He started speculating on who Buddy might tap as the new Speaker of the House.

"Well, Allen," I said, "I know one that has to be scratched from the running, John Alario." One of the memorable images of the previous night's startling announcement by Edwards was the sad face of the current Speaker of the House, John Alario, standing beside and slightly behind Edwards. He and Senate President Sammy Nunez of Chalmette had unconditionally supported and worked for Edwards' reelection. They both desperately wanted to continue in their legislative leadership positions.

Allen felt as though Buddy would have to make a quick decision to head off Alario before he worked his considerable charm and started calling in chits for his reelection as speaker.

I disagreed. After all, there were almost five months left before the new governor and legislature would take office in late March of 1988. I said, "I'd really like to recommend to Roemer that he take his time, let the shock of this situation wear down and, maybe, for a change, let the House exercise some independence and choose its own speaker."

Allen said, "You know that's not going to happen. Never has. If you give Alario a couple of weeks he'll have commitments all over the state. Why don't you run?"

"To tell you the truth I've never thought about it. I'd consider it but I still think this is all moving too fast. You're right. The House has never elected a speaker on its own, but it also has never elected speaker opposed by the governor. So Alario is out."

"Look," Allen said, "I'll get us an appointment with Buddy tomorrow. Let's talk with him, see what he's thinking. In the meantime I'll make some calls to some of the members of the

Rural Caucus. You call around Acadiana and let's see what's going on."

I agreed and hung up. The phone rang. Another colleague from New Orleans wanted to talk about who we could support as speaker and would I be interested. It continued throughout the morning and afternoon.

Between incoming calls I called some of the Acadiana delegation. At one point I talked with Jimmy Dimos of Monroe. Jimmy and I had served on the Commerce Committee together for eight years. He was a fiscal and social conservative but, as a practicing trial lawyer, he had fought all of our previous efforts at tort reform. Still, we were friends. Jimmy said he had talked with Bradley and wanted me to know he would support me if I chose to run for speaker. Then Jimmy said, "But, if you become speaker, I don't want to be a committee chairman. In fact, I'd just as well not even have any committee assignments. I need to pay more attention to my practice."

In mid-afternoon Allen called back. We had an appointment with Governor-elect Roemer at his Baton Rouge election headquarters for three o'clock the next day. He'd meet me there. Allen had been a busy young man. I started getting calls from all over the state saying they had talked with Allen and thought it would be a good idea for me to make the run.

Finally, about 9:30 P. M. the calls subsided. I flopped on the living room sofa and Carol and I started talking about the day's events. I must admit the idea going for the speakership was beginning to sound appealing, especially after all of the encouraging calls. But, I still felt that Roemer should not make a hasty decision, even if it was to endorse me. Besides, in spite of all the calls, I would still have a long way to go to get to a majority — 53 solid votes. And, of course, there was another important factor. The state was in the depth of the oil price induced recession. We had unwisely bought another radio station, this one in Sulphur, Louisiana, just west of Lake Charles at about the time the crash started. We had already lost a considerable sum of money in that venture and the prospects were not good for the near future. As a matter of fact, we were actively trying to sell the station at a reduced price in order to stop the bleeding. At the same time our Lafayette radio stations, though still profitable, had suffered a severe loss of revenue. On the upside, I had good management in place at the two Lafayette stations and hopefully would sell the Sulphur property soon.

At close to ten o'clock that night the phone rang again. It was New Iberia Representative Ted Haik. Ted and I had known each other from way before my first election to the House. We were on friendly terms though, as a trial lawyer, he disagreed strongly with my attempts at tort reform legislation. He, too, had been closely aligned with the Edwards administration and, like most attorneys serving in the legislature, his law firm had benefited from state contracts. Ted wanted me know that he would whole-heartedly support me for Speaker. He mentioned several times that he wanted to be a member of the "Roemer team." We talked a few minutes and when I hung up I told Carol, "Now that call surprises me. I don't think Ted would commit to supporting me unless he knows Alario can't win."

Monday afternoon Allen and I met at Roemer's Baton Rouge election headquarters which was now the temporary transition office for the new administration. It was a vacant store in a strip shopping center and, typical of most election headquarters, was in total disarray. Signs, brochures and reams of paper were strewn about on temporary tables and desks surrounded by folding chairs. Posters and maps were hanging from the walls and there was at least one phone per every ten square feet. Several Baton Rouge legislators were hanging around the offices including Louis "Woody" Jenkins, staunch conservative whose ideology strongly bordered on libertarianism. John Hainkel had been there and was expected back soon. We were told that Buddy's appointment schedule was running late and we waited until about 4:30 before we were called in.

Buddy had set up shop in a tiny office at the back of the store that may have been the janitor's office at one time. At least it afforded him some privacy. We knew time was tightly rationed and got down to the business at hand immediately. Buddy told us he had to leave Wednesday to go back to Washington, D. C. for the final days of the congressional session and to begin wrapping up his business there. He said John Alario had already visited with him and had pledged total loyalty if Roemer would support his candidacy for speaker. Buddy asked our opinion.

Allen and I both agreed that Alario had the experience and ability. We also told him that just a nod from the governor-elect would wrap up the election for Alario very easily. But, we said we were uncomfortable with his participation in Edwards' campaign and especially with the specter of his sad and somber face looking over Edwin's shoulder the night of the concession. Bradley was not in the legislature during the Treen administration, so I told him and Roemer of the constant presence and influence of Edwards on the legislative process, many times with the help of Alario and others, throughout that four years. That, of course, culminated in Treen's defeat and Edwards anointing Alario as speaker.

At first Buddy had seemed to be truly leaning toward Alario's candidacy. As I worked with Roemer over the next couple of years, I learned that was a favorite ploy: appear to be leaning toward a decision in order to illicit an argument or acquiescence. When Bradley and I finished our analysis, Roemer broke into his boyish grin and said, "You can believe, Alario will not be speaker of the House while I'm governor. I just wanted to see how you all felt."

He threw some other names at us: Robert Adley. We both agreed Robert would be a great floor leader and team player for the "Roemer Revolution." Adley and I had become good friends and allies over the eight years we had served together in spite of our early donnybrook over increased racing dates for Louisiana Downs. During our first term together, an astute legislative observer had described Adley to me as "street smart" and a "street fighter." He was dead on.

I told Buddy, "Adley's one of the best in the House. He's totally unafraid to stand up for his beliefs and, because of that, he's rubbed some of the members the wrong way. He's sort of a grenade thrower."

Roemer put on that impish grin again and said, with relish, "I love grenade throwers!"

I had forgotten I was talking to one of the real mavericks in Congress. This was the same Congressman Roemer that had repeatedly introduced his own federal budget to Congress. The same one House Speaker "Tip" O'Neill referred to as, "Often wrong, never in doubt."

Bradley also expressed his admiration for Adley's abilities but reminded Buddy of the geographical problem. Traditionally, a governor would choose a Speaker and Senate President from areas of the state other than his own home base. Adley, of course, was from Bossier, just a stone's throw from Buddy's home.

Other names were mentioned: Hunt Downer from Houma, a solid member of the House since 1976. (Hunt eventually became Speaker in 1996 with the Mike Foster administration and, in my estimation did a terrific job before being unceremoniously dumped by Governor Foster after the fall 1999 elections.) Woody Jenkins and Raymond Laborde of Marksville were discussed.

Eventually the conversation got around to the potential of my candidacy for speaker. I told Roemer my feeling that he should not rush, that he should go back to his business in Washington and let the House work its way through this. I told him I just didn't believe Alario could lock up the votes considering his closeness to Edwards and without the blessing of the governor-elect.

Bradley told Roemer he thought I would be an excellent choice. He said, "Ron has a lot of respect from a lot of different factions in the House. I know the members of the Rural Caucus (in which Bradley had a leadership role) trust him. There are 23 members of his own Acadiana Caucus and he has a good relationship with most of the Black Caucus."

We talked about some specific issues with which a new speaker would be dealing. Roemer expounded on some of the initiatives he would be introducing in his first session. By 6 P. M. or so I was beginning to feel as though I should start preparing for a run for the speakership.

Roemer asked me if I was staying overnight in Baton Rouge. I had not planned to. He said, "Look, stick around town a few hours and call me here at about nine. I may have some news for you."

As we were leaving the office we met Senators Sydney Nelson of Shreveport and Allen Bares of Lafayette going in for a meeting with Roemer.

An attorney, Nelson had been a Senator since 1980 and had been actively campaigning for Senate president ever since the previous legislative session. We had gotten word that he had traveled the state meeting with Senators in their home districts in an attempt to unseat Sammy Nunez, a member of the legislature since 1964 and a Senator since 1968.

Nunez had become Senate President in 1982 when the previous President, Michael O'Keefe of New Orleans, was indicted and ultimately convicted. Nelson, very professorial looking with his wire-rimmed glasses, was extremely meticulous in his approach to legislation. Although I thought his voting record was too liberal and trial lawyer oriented, I liked the way he had conducted his campaign for Senate president. He was going after the presidency no matter who was elected governor.

Bares, of course, had served starting in 1972 in the Lafayette House seat I now held and became a Senator in 1980. He was a solid conservative vote, scored very high in the LABI (Louisiana Association of Business and Industry) voting analyses and had recently been named in journalist John Maginnis' session wrap-up *"The best and worst of the 1987 Legislature"* as the most valuable Senator to business interests.

I later found out that Nelson had asked Bares to run as president pro-tem of the Senate in conjunction with his run for president. That way the president would be from north Louisiana and the pro-tem from the south. Of course Roemer, like Nelson, was from the Shreveport area. Their visit with Roemer was intended, of course, to get his endorsement and support.

Bradley and I talked for a few minutes with some of the staff before leaving the headquarters and heading for a nearby restaurant. We had a leisurely meal and killed time until nine when I called Buddy. I was told to call back in fifteen minutes. I did. I was told to call back at 9:45. This time Roemer came on the line. He said, "Look, this things falling into place real fast. Where will you be tomorrow morning?" I told him I'd be at my radio station office in Lafayette. He repeated the number I gave him to an aide and said, "I'll call you before noon." He then added, cryptically, "Get ready to go to work."

Driving back to Lafayette I ran through all the good side, bad side scenarios of running for speaker. I decided if Roemer offered me the opportunity I would ask him not to announce it immediately and give me a chance to contact all of the members of the House personally to get an individual reading. I would start on a statewide tour Wednesday morning to visit every member personally. If I determined I could get the necessary votes, I would publicly announce my intention and Roemer could immediately follow with his announcement of support. I hoped this plan would at least show some semblance of legislative independence and individual initiative.

I hardly slept that night. I was getting pumped.

Tuesday morning I met with my secretary and started clearing the calendar in anticipation of being out of the office for about a week or more. The morning passed. No call from Roemer. I had a sandwich brought in and ate in the office. Finally at about 2:00 P. M. I got a call from Baton Rouge.

One of the governor-elect's staff, Bob Munson, was on the line.

Munson, hyperactive as usual, got right to the point. "Ron, Buddy has made a decision on Senate President and Speaker of the House and we need you on board."

I was puzzled by the tone and structure of the comment. "What does that mean, Bob?"

"He's going with Allen Bares as president of the Senate. Since you and Bares are both from Lafayette he's decided to go with Jimmy Dimos as speaker of the House. Are you on the team?"

I was shocked, to say the least. Remembering Dimos' conversation with me two days prior that he didn't want a committee assignment much less any leadership role I said, "Has anyone talked with Jimmy about this? He told me he didn't want any more responsibilities in the House."

Bob said, "Ron, when the governor asks, who can refuse? And isn't that great for Lafayette to have Bares as president of the Senate? So, are you on the team?"

I could easily have said, "I'll have to think it over and get back to you." Instead I said, "Bob, this is going to be a very hard sell, on both sides, but I'll do what I can to help." More than anything, I wanted this administration to be successful and I felt it would be harmful and self-serving for me to hold out for the possibility of becoming speaker.

When I said it would be a hard sell, it was not to demean either Bares or Dimos. They were both deserving members of the legislature. But Dimos had never taken part in any of the leadership areas of the House and Bares had not, to this time, been considered a leader in the Senate except, perhaps, for LABI-supported business interests.

Munson said, "Great. Now, Buddy wants to know if you want to be speaker pro-tem."

I said, "Bob, I'd be bored silly in that job. No, thanks. I'll do what I can to get Jimmy elected then we'll talk about a committee chairmanship."

What had happened since 10 o'clock the previous night? I was totally baffled. Had I misread Buddy's signals? (During the next four years I found that was not hard to do.) What had happened to Sydney Nelson and his months long campaign? How did Bares leap-frog him?

Over the years, I pieced together the sequence of events that occurred. This may not be totally accurate but, following the rules of investigative reporting, I have at least two corroborating sources.

When Nelson and Bares left Buddy's office Monday night, they felt assured he would support the two as they wished, respectively as Senate president and president pro-tem.

Tuesday morning Buddy had two long conversations. One was with newly-elected Senator John Hainkel. John, of course, was a former speaker of the House, a Republican, a member of a prominent New Orleans law firm specializing in corporate and defense work and a very forceful proponent of his own opinions. (He was elected president of the Senate in January of 2000 making him the first Republican in that position and the first legislator to have been elected as both speaker of the House and president of the Senate. Prior to the new Constitution of 1973, the Lieutenant Governor served as president of the Senate. Taddy Aycock served as speaker of the House and, as Lieutenant Governor, was president of the Senate. But, only Hainkel was *elected* by both the House and Senate to their highest positions.) John, according to my sources, did not want Sydney Nelson to become Senate president. His reasons were very logically based on Sydney's liberal and trial lawyer leanings. Nelson was a solid and effective opponent of every effort to reform the extremely liberal workers' compensation and unemployment compensation laws of the state.

The other conversation was with Ed Steimel, then-president and one of the founders of the powerful Louisiana Association of Business and Industry (LABI.) Hainkel and Steimel were long-time political allies. Steimel echoed Hainkel's problems with having Nelson as president of the Senate. Steimel loved the idea of Bares becoming president. Bares had carried a lot of LABI's water over the years and particularly in the previous legislative session.

Buddy, according to my sources, told Steimel he was convinced I would be the best candidate for speaker of the House. Moving Bares up to the first position in the Senate created a major problem as both Bares and I were from Lafayette.

Steimel's response was that the LABI's interests were well represented in the House but they still always had major problems with their legislation in the Senate. He said he had to have Bares in the Senate and they could find someone else in the House.

Steimel also thought the world of Jimmy Dimos, personally and politically. In spite of Dimos' unswerving defense of the trial lawyers in the tort reform battles, he was a good "business" vote on practically every other issue. Dimos was also a long-time personal friend of Buddy Roemer.

So it was decided. Allen Bares would be tapped as the governor-elect's choice as president of the Senate and Jimmy Dimos would get the anointment as speaker of the House. They both agreed to pursue the offices though Dimos still had reservations.

As predicted, it was a tough sell. When Roemer made the announcement it was met with various degrees of surprise, speculation and even bewilderment. It was akin to George Bush choosing the virtually unknown Dan Quayle as his running mate later that year in New Orleans.

Alario and Nunez were even more determined to maintain their positions of power. They both sensed that Roemer's choices would not be universally accepted by the two houses. Alario immediately had the backing of organized labor, the black caucus, many members from the New Orleans and Jefferson Parish delegations and a healthy number of other House members whom he had helped and to whom he had ingratiated himself over the years. I, too, had mixed feelings. I considered John a friend and a very capable speaker. He had been very fair to me in our negotiations in 1984 culminating in my becoming Chairman of the Commerce Committee. It was just that damn Edwards connection.

Dimos had no natural constituency base in the House. He had never been a committee chairman and was not strongly aligned with any of the numerous House caucuses.

Nunez also had the strong backing of organized labor, the black caucus and New Orleans area Senators.

The cajoling, dealing and nose counting continued over the months leading up to inauguration day in March. The governor-elect, his staff and LABI pulled out all the stops. Those of us who had pledged to help called and recalled members.

The showdown finally took place on inauguration day, Monday, March 14, 1988. It started out as a classic shoot out and ended in an anti-climax that left every member of the legislature emotionally drained.

Both Alario and Nunez insisted on holding out until the last minute. They said they were determined to bring the elections to a vote.

In the House, the Dimos supporters felt we had a comfortable margin with at least 60 hard votes. Fifty-three, of course, was the number needed. Things weren't as clear-cut in the Senate. Twenty votes were needed to elect the new President. The governor's staff told us Bares had either 19, 20 or 21.

I had been asked to give the nominating speech for Jimmy Dimos. I walked around with my mixed emotions for a week before the day came and agonized over what I should say. I did not want to offend John Alario or his supporters. I still considered most of them friends. But I felt that John's insistence on carrying on the fight in the face of the facts was creating an unnecessary split in the House. On Monday morning I sat down and hand wrote the speech I would use to nominate Representative Dimos and, at the same time, try to pull the House back together.

There was a lot of tension in the air as I started:

"On June 16, 1858, a great and honorable man first uttered the now famous phrase, 'A house divided against itself cannot stand.' The man was Abraham Lincoln.

"Today, we, elected representatives of the people of the state of Louisiana, must see to it that this House not be divided.

"The people of this state are begging us to display leadership toward making positive changes. We simply don't have the time to waste on internal conflicts.

"If we do, in fact, continue to be distracted by personality conflicts we may well find ourselves presiding over the total

collapse of a state rather than helping to guide new courses to recovery.

"That is why I believe, and I think the majority of us in the House believe, that it is vital to elect a speaker dedicated to forming a partnership with the executive branch to work toward positive change.

"Notice I said 'partnership', not servitude. Divisiveness in the name of independence will only succeed in obstructing progress. And, with this monstrous agenda facing us in the coming months, we cannot, we must not allow self-serving motives to get in the way.

"Another honorable man, speaking on statewide TV just last week said, 'The most important thing, regardless of who wins the speaker's race, is to try to bring everybody back together. We've got some difficult things to do in this state, we've got some serious problems and it's going to take all of us pulling together. A division in this House of Representatives is not going to be good for anybody.' "

I looked across the sea of faces and made eye contact with John Alario before I continued, *"I could not agree more. The quote is from the Honorable John Alario speaking on LPB (Louisiana Public Broadcasting) last week."* John didn't blink an eye.

"Believing that the majority of us want to start this new term in harmony with the voters who voted for change, and to show our intent on forming a positive partnership with the new governor of this state, I therefore place in nomination for speaker of the Louisiana House of Representatives the Honorable Jimmy N. Dimos.

"For those who would ask if Representative Dimos is up to the challenge of this position, I would only remind you that this is a man who arrived alone in New York City at age 12 after a lonely flight from his home in Belgrade, Yugoslavia. He could

not speak English. He would not see his mother for another six months when she would finally be allowed to come to America.

"In New York, this 12 year old found that his continuing flights to Monroe, Louisiana, where his father waited, could not be completed for two more days.

"From this shaky start in this new world, Jimmy Dimos proceeded to learn English, put himself through high school, college and law school and serve three previous distinguished terms in this House of Representatives.

"Yes, he is a man of courage - a man of integrity, and a man who I am proud to nominate as speaker. May we stand united. He and we who are committed to working toward those changes so desperately needed in this state will need your understanding, your guidance, your tolerance and ... your prayers."

I knew we were nearing the end of the drama when the acting speaker did not call for the seconding speech but instead recognized John Alario for the floor.

John spoke with great emotion. After a few brief opening remarks he said, "I do not now have the votes. Please, understand I am not quitting. That's not part of my character. I gave my word that if I did not have the votes, I would not bring it to a vote on the floor."

Then John decided to take a few jabs at some of the conservative legislators he felt had stymied many of his friend Edwin Edwards' programs. I felt he was also staking his claim to continued leadership of the Roemer opposition. "While we struggled to see that the doors of the schools were not closed to the children and the doors of our hospitals remained open, there were those who would turn a deaf ear. Those who shouted the loudest and threw the most stones now have an opportunity to show us that they were right and we were wrong," he said.

Alario said, "We were right when we warned that this state was heading for financial disaster. We didn't get their (the conservative opposition's) help. They said all we needed to do was cut the budget." Alario conceded the speaker's election to Dimos and received a standing ovation.

I was then convinced that I had been right in supporting Roemer's choice. Alario had pledged his loyalty to the new governor when discussing the choice for speaker, but it wasn't based on philosophy or beliefs. He would be loyal and helpful only if he got what he wanted.

In accepting his election as speaker of the House, Jimmy Dimos thanked Alario for avoiding a potentially divisive vote, "I want to thank John Alario for what he did. Louisiana desperately needs us to work together, to look forward, to bring ourselves up. We have that opportunity if we work together."

Following a practice which I abhorred (begun by Alario when he replaced Hainkel as speaker in 1984,) Dimos then gave Alario his choice of committee assignments and let him name committee assignments for several of his staunch supporters. Alario was also awarded a suite of offices with staff and funding to maintain it. He also was granted an apartment in the Pentagon barracks. I just could not understand the naiveté. All of these elements would be used to bring down the Roemer initiatives.

Representative Hunt Downer was chosen speaker pro-tem by acclimation. Over in the Senate, a similar but even more rancorous scene was played out as Sammy Nunez, also taking a few shots at the incoming administration and the Senators who had chosen to support Bares, withdrew his name from consideration for president. Allen Bares was to begin a very rocky reign as president of the Senate. Nunez and his allies would wait two years before pouncing and unseating him.

Notable quotes from the legislative halls:

Addressed to a colorfully and nattily dressed Representative Kip Holden: "Mr. Holden, I just got a very important phone call from Motel 6. They want you to return their shower curtain that you're wearing as soon as possible."

Representative Warren Triche

XV

"Louisiana's Fiscal Alternatives"

As long as I can remember being aware of political debate in Louisiana, I have heard the recurring theme that the state's tax structure must be reevaluated, must be changed, is out of date, is unbalanced.

As far back as 1944 the Louisiana legislature created the Louisiana Revenue Code Commission and asked it to "recommend ways to simplify the meaning, verbiage and administration of the tax laws of the state, to improve the tax laws in ways which would encourage businesses to locate in Louisiana, to eliminate discriminatory taxes," in other words, to straighten out the mess that was the Louisiana tax code. As has happened so many times with reform measures, no major changes were made in the state's tax structure as the result of the Commission's findings or recommendations.

Another chance to reorder the tax system was missed when the State Constitution was rewritten and ratified in 1974. The new document did not adhere to the accepted parameters of most government Constitutions by setting broad tax policies and practices which could be flexible with changing economic and fiscal fluctuations. This constitution set specific fees for motor vehicle license tags, fixed income tax rates by percentage and dollar indexes and further nourished Louisiana's sacred cow, the homestead exemption. A $3,000 homestead exemption was written into the Constitution. It was quickly raised by constitutional amendment to $5,000 and again, at the urging of conservative Republican Governor Dave Treen, to $7,500. With land and residential improvements assessed at 10 percent of their market value this means that a private home owner with a home worth $75,000 or less pays no property tax. It also means that businesses pay over 90 percent of the local property taxes in the state. Since the state levies no state property tax, the limitations mandated by the state affect only parish governments and school district property taxes. Thus the state controls a large element of local government and school board revenue potential. No state in the nation has a homestead exemption even a third the size of Louisiana's.

The personal automobile license tag fee was set in the constitution at $3 per year. Personal income tax rates were set at 2, 4 and 6 percent and tied to *1974* income levels. Therefore no adjustments could be made as income levels naturally increased over the years.

There were many other provisions incompatible with sound tax structuring but none of this seemed to matter as the oil and gas revenues continued to flourish and then started gushing with the change in the severance tax laws in a special session in 1973.

In a brilliant move, first term Governor Edwin Edwards got the legislature to change the basis of taxation of oil from volume to value. Whereas the previous rates had been 18 to 26 cents per barrel, the new rate was 12.5 percent of value. State revenues from oil alone jumped from $112 million in 1973 to $186 million in 1974 in spite of the fact that actual production had peaked in 1972 and was beginning to fall. That was just the beginning. The world oil market dramatically changed and prices began to soar, eventually reaching over $38 a barrel. In 1982 the state collected $809 million in oil severance taxes alone, *a 722% increase in 10 years*. Additional revenues from natural gas severance taxes, royalties, rentals and bonuses swelled the take to over $1.6 billion. The ominous fact was that oil and gas revenues in 1982 accounted for over 49 percent of the state's total revenue. Then the bottom dropped out.

The Middle East coalition of countries comprising OPEC opened the spigots and oil prices fell quickly to the $12 and $13 per barrel level and domestic production fell with the prices. Those who had warned of a terribly unbalanced tax system in the state were suddenly being heard again. When Edwards started his third term in office in 1984 the state's economy was shattered. Revenues were down almost a billion dollars annually. Being the liberal, populist politician that he was, he knew of only one solution. Raise taxes. He proposed over a billion dollars in increased taxes. The economists and conservatives wanted to know what effect such a drastic move would have on the state's economy. The stark realization was that nobody knew.

In 1983 the Council for A Better Louisiana (CABL), headed by its Executive Director Ed Stagg, had created a special committee to study the state's financial situation. As the 1984 Legislative session got under way and Edwards' massive tax package was revealed, Stagg met with Senate President Sammy Nunez and House Speaker John Alario. Together they put together a coalition of selected members of the House and Senate, the Department of Revenue and Taxation, the Public Affairs Research Council, Gulf South Research Institute, Louisiana State University and Tulane University.

I was one of the House members chosen to serve on this task force. We were charged with pulling together a long-range study of state finances and immediately realized that we needed a professionally organized, comprehensive, economic study of the state's tax structure. Dr. James Richardson of LSU was chosen to conduct this massive undertaking. There could not have been a better choice. Jim Richardson is a soft spoken, gentlemanly professor with a computer-like mind, the patience of Job and a pragmatism uncommon among his profession. Not only did Jim organize an outstanding working group from several Louisiana universities as well as private think tanks, he took on the task with a passion which continues to burn to this day.

Through the many years that I have known him, I have been constantly amazed at his level of fervor for this cause in spite of the innumerable set backs and frustrations. He has spent countless hours testifying before, explaining to and stroking legislative committees. He has been insulted by mental midgets who accused him of shilling for every special interest group imaginable. His expert and tediously formulated logic has been scorned and rebuffed on countless occasions. Yet, I have never seen him show anger. Frustration maybe, weariness with the task occasionally, but always calmly and patiently explaining and re-framing his message, hoping to break through the barriers of ignorance or selfishness or self-protectionism.

The CABL study was completed in eighteen months and was presented at a two day conference in Baton Rouge in January, 1987. Its findings and recommendations were published in a book edited by Dr. Richardson called *"Louisiana's Fiscal Alternatives."* It ultimately led to a movement in Louisiana known as "Fiscal Reform."

Jim Bob Moffett became CEO of Freeport McMoRan in the early '80's and almost immediately moved the headquarters for his massive international oil, gas, sulphur, phosphate, copper and gold mining operations to New Orleans. He had graduated from the University of Texas in 1961 and he and his partners, operating primarily in Texas and Louisiana had parlayed some brilliant geology, nerveless investing and a bit of luck into a massive conglomerate. Moffett hoped he would be a pied piper for other Fortune 500 companies to join him in the city he loved. As the economists were arriving at *"Louisiana's Fiscal Alternatives,"* Jim Bob was forming a juggernaut aimed at massive fiscal reform for Louisiana.

Tall, good looking, with a gift for leadership and an enthusiasm for near-hopeless causes, Jim Bob used Freeport McMoRan's impressive clout and massive financial reserves to assemble business and industry leaders in his drive to pull Louisiana into the 20th century.

He rounded up a dozen or more expert economists, lobbyists and consultants and put them on handsome retainers. He and they devised a plan that involved changing the entire tax structure in the state to make it more stable, fairer and more predictable. Sales taxes would be reduced, they were too volatile. Income tax rates would be adjusted to fit more realistically the realities of Louisiana's economy. Property taxation would be revisited and, yes, even the Homestead Exemption would no longer be sacred. Most importantly, business taxes would be restructured so that Louisiana would be competitive with other states. The tax structure at the time was decidedly unfriendly to businesses, large and small. It was, of necessity, a complicated plan and Jim Bob hit the road to try to sell it to the voters of the state in simplified form. He called his organization the Louisiana Council for Fiscal Reform (LCFR).

For his public presentations, he had large cartoons blown up to four by six foot posters. One depicted the past with a group of fat and happy politicians on board the "Louisiana Hayride." The hay wagon was being pulled by a sleek and well-muscled steed. Oil money and exorbitant business taxes were keeping it rolling and everybody was merrily going along for the ride. The next poster showed the hay wagon broken down and lying in a ditch. This was Louisiana in the 1980's. The steed now looked more like a starving mule lying in the road with ribs protruding and tongue hanging out. The riders had fallen off and were scrambling in the muck.

Jim Bob hit the civic clubs and the chambers of commerce around the state. I had seen the presentation several times when I overheard a woman commenting on it as she left one of the meetings. Someone had asked if she thought the plan had a chance. She said, "Well, he's as good-looking as a movie star, as rich as a sheik, and has the balls of a bull-fighter, he just might do it."

When Buddy Roemer won the 1987 election by default it was widely assumed that fiscal reform would be one of his highest priorities and generally agreed that some sort of reform plan was destined to be passed.

As the stark reality of the fiscal plight of the state was uncovered in Baton Rouge, all the fiscal reform plans were put on hold. As previously related, the problem of simply making a payroll far overshadowed any complex restructuring of the tax laws. Jim Bob and his group were pushing hard for introduction of a package of bills in the 1988 Regular Session. They were understandably disappointed when a besieged Governor Roemer announced that he could not support fiscal reform in that session. He explained that there were just too many other previously smoldering fires to extinguish before planning for the future.

As chairman of the House Committee on Ways and Means, I was relieved that Buddy had decided to wait before attacking fiscal reform. Our committee was already under a lot of stress to pass the emergency measures, such as the Louisiana Recovery District Commissioner of Administration Brian Kendrick had dreamed up.

When I agreed to chair the committee, I fully understood what a battleground it could become. With the state floundering near bankruptcy, a new administration, a large number of new legislators and, unfortunately, a large number of Edwards-related older legislators in the House and Senate, the tax writing committee of the state would be the vortex of the whirlpool.

Before accepting the chairmanship, I asked for and got some assurances from Roemer and Speaker Jimmy Dimos. First, I wanted the size of the committee to be held to 15 members. House committees ranged in size all the way up to 21 members. I felt strongly that more than 15 would be a difficult number and could be an unruly crowd. Second, I wanted to have a majority of reform minded and, preferably, veteran representatives on hand. Once the session got under way, I got neither. Dimos said he couldn't find enough seasoned members who would serve on this volatile committee, and couldn't leave off some who requested committee membership. I ended up with 17 members, nine were freshmen. In addition, the leader of the opposition, recently deposed Speaker John Alario requested and, of course, was granted appointment to the committee. Within a week I was being asked to take on two new members.

Sherman Copelin was elected in 1986 representing District 99 in New Orleans. Forty three at the time, he already had a dossier a foot thick. Among his innumerable business ventures, he, at one time, had the franchise for concession sales at the Louisiana Superdome in New Orleans. Rumors and scandals swirled around that operation for seven years. He had been, among many things, a teacher, a New Orleans tax assessor, vice chairman of the National Business League, and a prominent member of the National Black Caucus of State Legislators. He was and is the personification of the modern entrepreneur and opportunist. Exceptionally smart and articulate, he could also be overbearingly arrogant and insulting. He was already an extremely wealthy man but seemed to still be struggling for acceptance and respectability among his legislative peers.

Always immaculately dressed in tailored suits perfectly draping his slim physique, Copelin would zoom into his parking space at the State Capitol driving his late model, top-of-the-line Mercedes. It was always hard for me to understand how he found the time to serve in the legislature with all the profitable ventures he had working.

He was publicly very honest, if not blunt about his ability to make money and his motivations. He had served on the Ways and Means committee in the previous administration. Once, during hearings involving the Louisiana Public Finance Authority (LPFA) and a proposed bond issue, Vic Bussie, head of the state AFL-CIO and then chairman of the LPFA, was urging passage of the measure allowing the issuance of the bonds. It was a very large transaction and would thus create sizable fees and commissions to attorneys and bonding institutions. Copelin proposed an amendment to the bill that would require a "set aside" of 10% on fees and commissions for black owned law firms and brokerage houses. (At that time "set asides" were a popular way for a specific percentage of government contracts to be granted to minorities.)

Some of the committee members and much of the audience in the committee room snickered or even laughed aloud when Sherman read his amendment. "Set asides" had never been proposed in this type of transaction. He was dead serious. Even Bussie, a close ally of the black caucus, was taken aback at the suggestion. He said, "Now, Mr. Copelin, you know I am supportive of much of your minority legislation and no one has been more sympathetic to your causes but, in truth, there are just no brokerage houses or law firms that are black owned that are big enough to handle even 10% of this issue."

Sherman didn't even blink, "You give me thirty days and I'll have one of each," he said. And he meant it. He didn't get the amendment passed but everybody knew exactly where he stood.

Since that time Copelin went on to become House speaker pro tem during the last Edwards administration and the chairman of the Legislative Black Caucus and moderated his words and methods enough to gain more respect throughout the legislature and among lobbyists and observers. But he was obviously not taking care of business back home. He was defeated in November of 1999 by a political newcomer who charged, among other things, that Copelin not only did not live in the district but, in fact, lived in a luxurious home well outside of the urban area he represented. One of the highlights of the campaign was a billboard featuring a picture of Copelin's residence with an offer of a large cash reward for anyone finding "this house in District 99."

But in 1988, with fiscal reform the number one priority, I did not want Sherman Copelin serving on Ways and Means.

First, Dimos approached me. "We need to put Sherman on Ways and Means," he said. "He wants on real bad and he can help us get some of the votes we'll need to move Buddy's programs." There were already four members of the Black Caucus on the committee.

"Don't do this to me, Jimmy, I've already got too many members, too many freshmen and John Alario. This stuff is gonna get real sensitive and I don't need someone like Copelin stirring things up and disrupting my committee. You know he can do that," I said.

Next, it was Governor Roemer. We were in his fourth floor office with a meeting of committee chairmen and floor leaders. Buddy, without looking up from his desk said, "Gomez, I need to put Sherman Copelin on your committee."

I was waiting for that. "Fine," I said, "be sure to make him chairman, because you just lost this one."

"Aw Gomez, you don't mean that. Copelin says he'll help us as much as he can if he gets on, but he'll kill us otherwise."

"Have at it Governor, I've got better things to do."

Roemer looked at me for several burning seconds and said, "OK, we'll talk about it later."

We did. When everyone except Dimos had left, I told Roemer we had to settle the Copelin matter. He asked me to think about it. I said I already had and I just was not going to put up with the disruptiveness of having him on the committee. Buddy then partially relented and said he'd talk with Sherman.

During the next two meetings of the Ways and Means Committee, Copelin decided to show me how important and persuasive he could be. He merely strengthened my argument that he would be a disruptive member of the committee. During witness testimony he would come up behind the members-only portion of the platform and hold louder-than-a-whisper conversations with Alario or one of the black Representatives. He was baiting me to admonish him and I finally did. He answered, in a loud voice that he, as a member of the House, certainly had a right to confer with his colleagues. I told him, "Mr. Copelin, your rights end here when you are disrupting this committee."

Later, on several votes, he would walk around talking with members of the Black Caucus and indicating that he was advising them how to vote.

Roemer tried one more time. Again, I told him to find a new chairman if Copelin was to be assigned to the committee. He gave up and said, "All right, YOU tell him that you don't want him on."

I said, "If that means you and Dimos will drop it, I'll gladly tell him."

That afternoon, I was handling a relatively unimportant bill on the floor of the House. Whenever I was at the microphone, I could count on Copelin to exercise his right to ask questions. Needless to say, he was never supportive of the bills I was handling. He got up and performed his contentious routine on me and we finished the process on the bill. I left the well and walked directly to his desk. I said, "Sherman, Buddy asked me to tell you in my own words why I don't want you on the Ways and Means Committee. I find you to be arrogant, discourteous, insulting and disruptive to proper committee decorum. So, as long as I am chairman, you will not be a member."

He looked at me coolly, started a slight smile and said, "OK Gomez, at least now we understand each other."

The *Morning Advocate* photographer who patrolled the chamber sidelines looking for photo opportunities got a shot of that exchange. Of course, he was out of earshot and the caption described the scene as two Representatives discussing the merits of a bill.

Sherman and I completed our mutual time in the House in relative peace and respect. I moved on and he remained to become a veteran statesman until his surprising defeat in 1999.

Dimos used my little victory in dropping the Copelin issue as an opportunity to add two more members to the committee so we were now ready to take on the budget crisis and fiscal reform with nineteen members, nine of whom were first year legislators. We needed ten votes to get anything passed.

In late May, Buddy was experiencing even more pressure from the fiscal reform people to "do something." He called a small group of us together and said, "I cannot deal with everything going on right now and work on fiscal reform too. So this is what we're going to do. I'll set aside two or three hours each Sunday afternoon and we'll all meet at the mansion to work on it. We can work from say, five to eight, have sandwiches along the way and put this thing together."

We looked at each other, some rolled their eyes, some dropped their jaw. I couldn't help myself. "Buddy," I said, "this is a full-time job for you but it's not for the rest of us. I'm pretty possessive about my weekends."

He was not to be dissuaded. "Come on Gomez, we've gotta put this thing together. You can bring Carol sometimes. Yeh, you guys can bring your wives and kids every so often and we can have a picnic on the mansion lawn."

Wow! I couldn't wait to give Carol that great news. A picnic with the governor on the grounds of the mansion! Be still my heart!

Buddy's persuasiveness and enthusiasm prevailed. We decided to give it a try.

The cast of characters changed somewhat from Sunday to Sunday but, generally speaking, the group consisted of Dr. Jim

Richardson; David Conroy, Chairman of the Council for A Better Louisiana; occasionally Speaker Jimmy Dimos; Dr. Tim Ryan, economist with the University of New Orleans; Bill Oakland, economics professor at Tulane; Mike Baer, Secretary of the Senate; LSU economist Dr. Loren Scott; Senate President Allen Bares and Senators John Hainkel and Randy Ewing; Representative Robert Adley and various members of the House and Senate fiscal staffs: Robert Keaton, John Rombach, Donnie Vandal, John Carpenter and Bill Black and me. I'm sure I'm leaving some important contributors out. Usually there was a working group of five to seven people plus the governor and some of his staff. Depending on the subject matter, various experts might be called in for specific briefings. Some of Jim Bob Moffett's fiscal reform cadre were also regular visitors.

This continued throughout the summer. That Sunday afternoon drive from Lafayette to Baton Rouge was terribly depressing. Many times I would leave a sun-drenched summer afternoon at our home with family and friends just beginning to set up the grill and hit the road at four o'clock to tilt the windmills at the mansion. I believe there were seventeen Sundays in all. I felt as though I had gone through a crash course in governmental economics. It was frightening to contemplate the enormity of the task before us if we truly wanted to properly reform the state's tax structure.

One thing we all recognized and agreed on, this could not be done piecemeal. It had to be a total package. Correcting the sales tax inequities alone would simply create more disparity in other areas. Adjusting the income tax rates would affect the entire revenue status of the state. It had to be a rounded, cohesive, restructuring. Additionally, we also realized that, to have any chance with the legislature and the state's voters, it had to be revenue neutral. This package could neither raise nor reduce total revenue for the state. Rather, it would give the state a balanced tax base which would be less volatile, less affected by unpredictable forces and would grow with and encourage economic growth.   One other vitally important point was obvious and daunting: a large part of the package would involve one or more Constitutional amendments. That would mean *two-thirds* approval by the legislature *and* a state wide referendum.

*   *   *

Naturally, the meetings on fiscal reform were not air tight and some of the discussions were leaked to legislators and the media.   By August, speculation was rampant and mostly negative. Everything was on the table. We discussed radical changes we all realized were impossible but needed to be explored to forward the debate and broaden the discussions. We fashioned innovative tax code scenarios just to test their viability. After constant molding and massaging, we decided we had to run with what we had concocted even if it wasn't perfect.

Roemer announced a special session for October 2nd. He let it be known that all of the revisions to the state tax code would be contained in *one* bill and *one* Constitutional amendment. Legislators were advised that they would get copies of the bill and amendment by the first week in September and I called the Ways and Means Committee into a series of daily meetings beginning two weeks prior to the session.

Before the ink was on the paper, the speculation reached a fever pitch. The media was reporting that the package included lowering the homestead exemption to $25,000; raising the $3 automobile license fee to $10 for every $10,000 value of a vehicle; imposing a state property tax to equalize funding for poorer parishes. That was all true, but little was said about reducing state sales taxes from 4 to 2.5 cents; reducing business taxes; adjusting the income tax schedules to more equitable levels and various other positives.

Senator Armand Brinkhaus of Sunset, long standing ally of Edwin Edwards was quoted as saying, "It's a roll of the dice. It's a yes or no vote. The big question is whether he can get it through the House and Senate with a two-thirds vote. There's a chance that if some say they like four out of five things but they don't like that one thing so much that they'll vote against the whole thing."

Representative Kathleen Blanco of Lafayette felt that Roemer had brought the all-or-nothing concept from Congress, "It's the omnibus bill concept. If you're for the more important parts of a bill you have to be for the whole thing. It's designed so people can't vote for the more palatable parts and against the more controversial parts."

As drafted, the original bill filled 1,204 pages. In a speech to the Alexandria Rotary club in the last week of August, I said, "We're trying to recreate a tax system that will be broad-based, equitable, fair, reliable and predictable. Doing that is like taking a blob of jello and trying to shape it into a perfect sphere."

The bill that I sponsored and which was presented to the Ways and Means Committee would accomplish, among other things, the following:

- Consensus revenue forecasting. The current system consisted of the governor's office making their forecast and the legislature making its own guesses.

- A mineral revenue stabilization trust fund by which any more than $750 million per year in oil and gas revenues would be set aside. This, hopefully, would lessen our dependence on that unpredictable source of revenue.

- Reduction of the state sales tax from 4 cents to 2.5 cents.

- A uniform telecommunications utility tax.

- Reduction of the state corporate income tax from 8% to 6%.

- Restructuring of the personal income tax starting with a top rate of 2.5% which would scale up to a top rate of 4% in 1992. There would be lower limits for lower income brackets.

- A natural gas severance tax based on value rather than volume.

- Raising the basic personal auto license plate charge from $3 per year to a basic rate of $10 with an additional $10 for each $10,000 in value of the vehicle over $10,000.

- Allowing local governments and school boards, by two thirds vote, to eliminate state-mandated sales tax exemptions, thus shifting control of local taxes to the local governments.

- Property taxes on business inventories would be repealed.

- Cigarette taxes would be increased as would the state wine tax. Both would be more equal to the surrounding states.

- (THE BIG BUGABOO)   Lowering of the homestead exemption from $75,000 to $25,000 with (the opponents never added this) **a roll-back of millages for revenue neutrality**. Then local governments could call for millages <u>with</u> voter approval and also have voters decide whether homestead exemption would apply. Additionally, families with income of less than $20 thousand and those with heads of household over 70 years old would retain the $75,000 exemption.

- A state wide property tax of 2 mills would be levied to finance a fair market assessment of all taxable property equally throughout the state. This would give the State Tax Commission the authority to set standards and **equalization of assessments** statewide. It would have ended the control of Parish assessors to arbitrarily and sometimes capriciously set property valuation for assessment purposes. This is what really uncorked the state's assessors. It didn't help when Roemer was quoted as saying, "I tried to find a way to have no property tax at all, do away with the tax assessors and everything in the system. I worked for two months to do that. It couldn't be done."

It was a massive and very comprehensive plan.

A thorough analysis of all provisions of the package showed that it was *almost* revenue neutral. The state would take in only about $11 to $18 million more revenue in the first year. The big winners in the program would be people making less than $25 thousand a year. The key provisions would insure state revenue growth tied to economic growth; a much fairer tax system for lower income families and much more predictable and stable revenue forecasts.

On the eve of the special session, after seven full days of committee hearings, I told Mike Hasten, state editor for the Lafayette *Advertiser*, "In its present form, I think it (the fiscal reform bill) will be very difficult to pass." I pointed out the four problem areas that had arisen during the hearings: lowering homestead exemption, removing the federal income tax deduction, dropping the inventory tax and allowing local government more freedom in calling tax elections. I said the homestead exemption change is not the main part of the plan but, "it has turned into the lightning rod that is catching most of the heat. The plan, as far as the state's budget is concerned, certainly can be done without even mentioning homestead exemption. It's just another option given to local governments so that local people can make local decisions. Reduction of homestead exemption also serves as a means to eliminate local sales taxes because, as people start realizing that they can write off property taxes on federal tax returns but they can't write off sales taxes, this whole controversy over homestead exemption will seem ridiculous."

I told the reporter I was amazed at the opposition to allowing more local responsibility. I had always been told that the most responsive government is the government closest to home. "Obviously," I was quoted as saying, "the legislators are thinking that local officials have more guts than we have because they think that if we give them the authority they're going to go hog wild and raise all kinds of taxes.

"I don't believe that to be a fact," I continued. "They're closer to home. They're going to get a heck of a lot more heat than we will and they're going to have to prove their case. Two thirds vote (needed to impose a local tax) is tough to come by for anybody."

The special session began October 2, 1988. It was set to run 24 days. I introduced the massive fiscal reform bill.

Governor Roemer opened the session with an impassioned, yet carefully reasoned speech. He told the joint session of the Legislature, gathered in the House chamber, "Our proposal is thorough, complete. It will let us build a new Louisiana and will mean jobs for our people. No plan is perfect. No plan will get your total support on every single issue, nor should it. But I'm asking that you put Louisiana first. Look at the long run and the big picture.

Roemer asked the legislators to remember two things as they considered the tax plan:

"One, we must address the whole problem, not just a part. If you change a single part you impact the rest of the package. Let's be careful and complete. Two, we must act and act now. The status quo is a proven loser, schools that don't work, roads on which you cannot drive and jobs that never come. If you like that kind of Louisiana, vote against our proposal or any constructive alternatives to it and the status quo will bury you and your constituents."

I opened Ways and Means Committee hearings the next morning and things immediately began to fall apart. We had completed two weeks of hearings before the Special Session began but I had ruled that they would be for information and discussion only, no votes had been taken. We started working our way through the bill one section at a time.

The first casualty came on Wednesday, October 5th. Louisiana was the only state which allowed individual taxpayers to deduct their federal income taxes from their state returns. The fiscal reform bill would eliminate that. Of course, there were some other areas of the bill which would offset the resulting increase in taxes, but the opponents of the bill cleverly focused on only this one provision. They made it appear as if it stood alone and was not a part of a bigger picture. We got thoroughly thrashed in a heated debate which ended with the committee voting 15 to 3 to continue allowing the deductibility. Former Speaker of the House John Alario, who our Speaker Jimmy Dimos placed on the committee over my objection, led the opposition.

While that part of the plan was being shot down, a proposed compromise on local government's sales tax alternatives was being rejected by a group of about 40 representatives of various business groups. "Our crowd just didn't like it at all," said Ed Steimel, president of the Louisiana Association of Business and Industry. Again, even our so-called supporters focused on one part, not the whole.

The one small victory we could claim that day was the defeat of an amendment, supported by local governments to continue the way sales taxes were being collected. The bill mandated that each parish would have only one tax collector. Many parishes had individual collection offices for each city and town, the parish and the school board. The local government representatives wanted no changes.

So after just three days we could detect the patterns: business would oppose us on individual parts of the bill, the local municipalities on others, assessors on anything to do with property taxes and on and on. Of course business wanted the elimination or rewriting of corporate tax laws and elimination of the inventory taxes, the locals wanted the increased authority on local taxes. It was the same old story. The special interests were gathering around their oxen to prevent the individual goring.

The chief ox herder for homestead exemption status quo was Jefferson Parish Assessor Lawrence E. Chehardy. His father, Lawrence A. "Big Lawrence" Chehardy had almost single-handedly enshrined in the 1974 state Constitution the exemption on homes valued up to $30,000. It had since grown to a $75,000 exemption. "Little Lawrence" had succeeded his father in a fine display of Louisiana politics. He qualified for his father's position at the very last minute before qualifying for the office closed. His father, who had been unopposed, then announced he would retire. "Little Lawrence" got a free ride into the office. Chehardy represented a parish with one-ninth of the total population of the state and 19 legislators.

"He is the ringleader of the assessors who have been the prime lobbyists against our effort to reform the tax code," said Rep. James Donelon of Metairie in Jefferson Parish. Donelon was one of only two of the parish's House members to stand up against Chehardy.

On October 13th, Chehardy engineered a 55 to 50 vote in the House on an amendment to the fiscal reform bill which effectively left the homestead exemption untouched, status quo.

In an earlier Ways and Means Committee hearing, Chehardy and I had our first confrontation. He had studiously avoided discussing the bill with me, preferring to do his lobbying through John Alario.

On this day, LABI president Ed Steimel had even agreed with Chehardy's position on a proposed amendment. The leader of the assessors flashed a rare smile and pumped his fist in the air like an NFL running back crossing the goal. When Steimel had finished, Chehardy came to the witness table. A couple of days before, a New Orleans newspaper had run pictures of Chehardy before and after the fitting of his new toupee. As he sat down, I suggested to Chehardy that Ed Steimel, who was quite bald, might want to consult with him on his choice of suppliers.

"Does it really look that good?" Chehardy asked.

"Well, you never talked to me before so I don't know what you looked like except in the newspaper," I replied.

Chehardy scowled up at me, "I met you before, you just have a short memory, that's all."

A newspaper report on the exchange noted that Chehardy's approach "would often be defined by his confrontational, humorless, unyielding style."

Another scolded me for my discourteous treatment of the leader of the state's assessors

A couple of days later, appearing again before the committee, Chehardy went into great details on his philosophy of taxation and why he was opposing the reform movement. He said, " We want to see that the office of assessor is preserved."

Nothing in the fiscal reform bill threatened the existence of the offices of assessors. It would, however, lead to more authority of the State Tax Commission to oversee statewide property assessment practices and assure fair and equitable property tax procedures throughout the state.

I told Chehardy, "It absolutely amazes me. You are elected as a tax assessor. An assessor. Not a policy maker. That's the role of the legislative branch of your parish government. You're supposed to assess the rolls. Would you also like authority over the budgets of local government bodies?"

"Yes," Chehardy said. "Some of the things I've seen, fancy cars being driven. I'd like to have that authority." It may have been one of the most honest statements he'd ever made.

I could only shake my head in awe, "Demagoguery at its best, Mr. Chehardy. You're the best."

The next few days would border on the bizarre. The fiscal reform package required the passage of two different instruments.   HB (House Bill) 1 was a Constitutional

Amendment which granted the *authority* to make the changes. HB 2 contained the actual changes in the tax structure. Both required a two-thirds vote (sometimes called a super-majority) of both houses. Two thirds meant seventy House votes and twenty-six in the Senate. In addition, the Constitutional Amendment would also require ratification by a majority vote of the citizens.

On October 13th I went to the well of the House and pleaded for passage of HB 1. The measure had already been amended to such a degree to make it almost unacceptable to the pro-reform, administration group. The homestead exemption was preserved at $75,000 for current millages but local governments were allowed to lower it in future property tax elections. I and others felt this would lead to a crazy-quilt pattern of property taxation among the parishes and would be used by local governments to compete unfairly with their neighboring parishes. Nonetheless, we decided to move for passage to the Senate, hope for possible changes there and dive into the quagmire awaiting HB 2.

When HB 1 passed by a vote of 72 - 32 it was hailed as a real breakthrough by some media reports and some opponents of the bill. Rep. Raymond "La La" Lalonde, one of those opposing the measure, said he had not expected it to pass on the first try and thought it would take two votes before Roemer could convince enough of the opposition.

Rep. Kathleen Blanco of Lafayette (later Lieutenant Governor) wisely stated, "We all know that these are not final votes on this package. But, I think that what we have is a bill that a lot of legislators think will have a chance of passing at the polls. There's a lot of concern that the voters might reject."

The group of legislators, economists and staff members who had been working on the tax reform for months, met each night after the day's procedures either in the governor's fourth floor office at the capitol or at the mansion. The night the Constitutional Amendment bill was passed I said to the group,

"They're setting us up. They know this means nothing. They can go home and say, 'I voted for fiscal reform.' They're getting ready for the slaughter of the real bill, (HB 2.)"

The next day, we brought HB 2 before the House. The debate raged for hours. I only remember how tired I was when I finally sat down at my desk after the opening presentation of the bill and the endless questions from the opponents. I believe I was at the podium close to three hours. In the Senate, a questioner must come to the well and go face to face with the person speaking on the bill using the same microphone. In contrast, each House member has a microphone at their desk. They push a button on the desk and it lights a display at the speaker's desk notifying him of their wish to ask a question. Then, they just stand at their desk and fire questions. I believe the Senate procedure, while somewhat awkward, is a little more dissuasive of needless arguments.

Not only did the bill not get the 70 votes needed for passage, it only got a less-than-majority 47 votes. There were 55 against. According to the rules of the House, a bill that receives less than a majority cannot be brought up for a second vote unless a member who voted on the *prevailing side* (in this case against) makes the motion to reconsider.

Governor Roemer, meeting with reporters in the hall outside of the House chamber after the vote said, somewhat condescendingly, "They are nervous. Some of them don't understand fully. They just didn't understand everything quite yet."

Nice spin, guv. At least two months of media reports on the proposed plan; two weeks of well publicized committee hearings prior to the special session; two more weeks of intense debate and "they don't understand everything quite yet?"

Roemer, to his credit as an optimist, spent four hours that night, a Friday, talking with individual legislators, asking them to give the tax reform a second chance. I was there for most of the discussions. There was a lot of whining, and subtle and not so subtle horse trading.

My comment to the media was, "This bill is still alive technically, I don't know how viable it is. I'm very disappointed with the vote. I thought there was a lot of short-sightedness in the House. I don't think they ever once took a look at the entire tax structure that we were submitting. They looked at bits and pieces of it and you can tear those apart easily if you're going to be single-minded and tunnel-visioned."

Some of the opponents even had the nerve to suggest that the Constitutional Amendment (HB1, passed the day before) should be presented to the voters before another attempt at passage of the specific provisions in the fiscal reform bill (HB 2.) My reaction was immediate. "We're not going to present to the people a shell that would say we're going to eliminate the current rates on income tax but we're not going to tell you what we're changing them to. The Constitutional Amendment allowed change but this (HB 2) specifically identified that change." It was obvious that those who wanted to kill fiscal reform and the Roemer revolution wanted to be on record as supporting fiscal reform but would also be content to see the voters reject it for lack of details.

We decided to delay any further debate to give the House some breathing room from the serious stress they had been under for the past two weeks. We also hoped it would give time for constituents who understood the fiscal reform concept to contact their representatives. Meanwhile the Senate started working on HB 1, the Constitutional Amendment. The Senate Revenue and Fiscal Affairs Committee voted on dozens of changes to the proposal. Among them was the restoring of the administration's homestead exemption provision cutting the exemption to $25,000 on new and renewed millages for education, police and fire protection and drainage or erosion protection. Senior citizens and veterans would retain the current exemption.

Senator Jack Doland of Lake Charles, a former college football coach and former president of McNeese State University, surprised everyone by proposing an amendment to reduce the number of New Orleans assessors from the unwieldy, but politically profitable, number of seven to one. The assessors were obviously caught by surprise by the move and it passed.

On hearing of the Senate's actions, Representative John Alario pronounced them "unacceptable to the House."

Representative Allen Bradley, once a staunch Roemer supporter but now a vocal opponent and a leader of the influential Rural Caucus, said, "If those changes stand, it will destroy any compromise in the works. The wheel is off the wagon!" Bradley, Alario and other opponents claimed they were working on alternatives to the Roemer plan. I never saw any of them.

The governor said, "I'll look at anybody's plan that will improve Louisiana. I have been very careful. I have tried to exhibit some patience. I am looking forward to meeting with them (the opponents)." They didn't come.

HB 2 was brought up for a second vote on Tuesday. The governor's meetings with legislators, intense lobbying by some business groups and constituency action had made a major impact. The bill got 68 votes, two short of passage. Now what?

We were in a quandary. With the solid defeat of HB 2 on the previous Friday and another failure Tuesday we were technically out of innings. The only way HB 2 could get another hearing would be with a two-thirds vote to suspend the rules. Not likely.

We simply introduced a new bill. To satisfy House rules against submitting an identical bill, this one was 99% the same as HB 2 so technically, it was a new bill bearing number HB 21. I introduced the bill and moved for immediate referral to the Ways and Means Committee while simultaneously calling a meeting of the committee for the same afternoon. We held a five-minute committee meeting and the "new" bill was unanimously approved and sent to the floor of the House. Now the clock became a real factor. Because the Constitution requires that a bill be read before the House on three separate days, we could not bring it up for a vote until Friday October 21st. The special session could run no later than 6:00 P. M. Tuesday, October 25th. Even if we got the 70 votes on Friday, we still had to get the act through a Senate committee and the full Senate. Additionally, if the Senate adopted any amendments, the whole thing would have to return to the House for concurrence and, failing that, would then have to go to a conference committee and subsequently back to both chambers for concurrence.

The new bill made another attempt at resolving the homestead exemption stalemate. The proposal to lower the exemption to $25,000 was changed to $50,000 and would still apply only to all new and renewed millages approved by the voters and still grandfathering in seniors, the poor and war veterans.

Suddenly, we were not only fighting with our known opposition but picking up new criticism from our friends. Mark Drennen, then president of the private, non-partisan Public Affairs Research Council (he later was chosen as Governor Mike Foster's Commissioner of Administration) said, "If we don't do the income tax (eliminating the deduction for federal taxes) and we don't do anything significant with homestead exemption, I'm not sure what's left of fiscal reform."

Former House Speaker and now Senator John Hainkel was quoted as saying, "I've generally been recognized as being a friend of, and supportive of, Governor Roemer, but never in the 21 years that I've served have we created a 'Lazarus' bill. When a bill is dead, it's dead."

It should have been and, ultimately, it was.

We stroked, harassed and cajoled, to mention only the nice actions, enough to get HB 21 passed and sent to the Senate. After substantive amendments, the bill got only 22 votes on the first try on Monday but finally got the 26 vote super-majority, sending it back to the House Tuesday afternoon for concurrence in some Senate amendments. The House balked again and a motion was made to submit the bill to a conference committee. Two House members and I were assigned to the conference committee and met with the three Senators. It felt like a final appeal before execution. Nerves were frayed, everyone was physically and emotionally drained. We agreed to leave the bill alone and resubmit it as passed by the Senate. I felt like the prize fighter Roberto Durand who had thrown up his hands in defeat and shouted, "No mas, no mas." (No more.)

It was after 5:00 P. M., the final hour of the Special Session, when we submitted the signed conference committee report. I made one more plea to the House, "This is the last stage. You defeat this at this point now and the House will have failed. I ask you to concur for fiscal reform and restructuring of this antiquated tax system in this state."

Every member of the House voted. The final vote was 60 for and 45 against. It failed. It was over.

Buddy Roemer, looking even more tired and drawn than the rest of us, held a final press conference. Would he give fiscal reform another try? "I don't know that we can give it another shot. If we approach fiscal reform again, I've got to approach it differently. But, I can't wait around for that. We've got to proceed with the world as it is. I am not a quitter. I will keep fighting for a better Louisiana. I have put in 12 to 15 hours every single day. I will not surrender to those who would trade the chance for a better Louisiana for politics as usual, something for nothing, or the easy way out." He also ominously pointed out that he must now shift his focus from tax restructuring to budget cutting.

Notable quotes from the Legislative halls:

Representative Juba Diez, urging passage of the bill to repeal the law mandating helmets for motorcycle riders:

"If you like Governor Foster, vote for this bill because he wants it.

If you don't like Governor Foster, vote for the bill so he can go down the road on his motorcycle and split his head open."

XVI

"David Duke? He's just another freshman."

Between the failed fiscal reform special session in October, 1988 and the regular session of 1989 we were all licking our wounds, trying to regroup and trying to find areas of compromise. Naturally, those who were opposed to the fiscal reform effort felt that the October defeat should have ended the entire discussion.

The opposition generally fell into three categories: 1) those who would oppose anything Roemer and the reformers proposed, the idea being to cripple him so bad that there would be no hope for a second term; 2) those who wanted to be able to vote individually on the elements of fiscal reform, to pick those parts that made people feel good and reject the areas that caused some discomfort; and 3) those who had legitimate, if not totally logical, disagreement with the provisions, such as the assessors regarding equalization of assessments.

In the midst of the turmoil, there were two elections called to replace members who had run successful campaigns for other offices in November. Representative Kathleen Babineaux Blanco of District 45 in Lafayette had been elected to the Public Service Commission and Charles "Chuck" Cusimano from District 81 in Metairie was elected as a District Judge.

Jerry Luke Leblanc, whose father had preceded Blanco in the House seat and who had served many years as his father's legislative aide, was elected in District 45.

Notice of his election was almost overwhelmed by the donnybrook that ensued in District 81. The voters in the district were 99.6% white. The area was a classic "white-flight" bedroom community of majority black New Orleans. John Treen, older brother of the former governor, was matched in a runoff with David Duke, a former grand wizard of the Ku Klux Klan. Both were Republicans. Duke had run for state Senator in the same general area twice before. Now, he was running as a Republican and he had learned to speak in codes. In spite of his relative young age, 38, he had been doing this a long time. In his early twenties he dominated "Free Speech Alley" the open-air, informal student forum at Louisiana State University in Baton Rouge. He had traveled the country making speeches as the KKK grand wizard and had honed his message.

His new message was that he had left the Klan, shed the Nazi uniform he had proudly worn in many previous appearances and only wanted to serve the people. He eliminated his high-octane anti-Semitic rhetoric. He was particularly concerned with the plight of "European-Americans." He never blatantly spoke of race as a factor but referred to the "growing underclass." He used the tried and true demagoguery of class envy to sell his message: excessive taxpayers' money spent on welfare, school busing practices, affirmative action programs and set-aside programs. He also embraced a subject near and dear to every Jefferson Parish voter, protection of the homestead exemption. It was a hot topic since the reduction of the exemption had been the subject of heated debate in Governor Roemer's fiscal reform package. The District 81 race kicked off just after the October trouncing of the fiscal reform effort in the legislative special session. The first primary was set for January 21, 1989. Republicans John Treen and Delton Charles were odds on favorites to lead the field. David Vitter, a young Republican attorney, who very much wanted to enter the race, did not because he had not met the length of time of residency requirement, a detail that did not bother David Duke. Ironically, Vitter would become the state representative for District 81 in 1992 and go on to win a seat in the United States Congress over

David Duke and former Governor Dave Treen, among others, in 1999.

Fate intervened for David Duke. Five days before the primary, a Martin Luther King Day parade in New Orleans ended when a riot broke out involving a group of blacks beating and kicking pedestrians. It was all caught on TV videotape and broadcast over and over on the local stations.

When the smoke had cleared, David Duke led the election with 33 percent. Treen polled only 19 percent and Charles was third with 17 percent. A huge, glaring spotlight had just been switched on. The world was now watching Metairie, Louisiana.

John Treen was not a very dynamic campaigner and he was not very well liked by the political insiders in Jefferson Parish. The Chehardys, "Big Lawrence," now a judge, and "Little Lawrence," his successor to the throne in the assessor's office, were political enemies. The flamboyant Chinese-American Sheriff Harry Lee was quoted as saying the runoff election was "a choice between a bigot and an asshole." During the few head to head public forums Treen's advisors allowed, John wilted under the relative eloquence of Duke.

President George Bush and former President Ronald Reagan joined in the campaign against Duke. New Orleans Archbishop Philip Hannan felt that he could not formally enter the fray but did issue a statement to be read during Sunday masses throughout the diocese. The message, in part, read, *"The election will determine the convictions of the voters of the district about the basic dignity of persons, the recognition of human rights of every person and the equality of races..."*

The New York based Jewish Defense Organization weighed in. Little David was taking on a squad of Goliaths.

A relatively high 54% of the registered voters turned out for the showdown election. It was the only item on the ballot. The shock wave traveled around the world as Duke won by a 227 vote margin, not a landslide in a district of 20,000 plus voters but enough to send a former Nazi-embracing, Ku Klux Klan wizard to the Louisiana Legislature representing a portion of Jefferson Parish, the second most populace parish in Louisiana.

The Sunday following the election was much like the day after Edwards had ceded the governor's election a year or so earlier. The phone at my home started ringing early and was occupied the entire day. I talked with several House leaders in New Orleans including members of the Black Caucus. Everyone was in shock and in various stages of reaction, anger, revenge, denial, challenge and even acceptance. By late afternoon a consensus was forming. It was determined that John Treen and some of his supporters would challenge the election on the grounds that Duke did not meet the residency requirements. This had been rumored and discussed throughout the campaign and was probably true. But, since no one thought he would win, no formal action had been taken.

The House leaders and members of the Black Caucus agreed that the matter should be decided within the district, that no House member should get involved and we would follow the dictates of the courts.

Further complicating matters was the fact that Governor Roemer had called another special session to consider fiscal reform again beginning the Tuesday after the election, February 21, 1989. The two new House members would be sworn in as the session convened.

Sunday night, I got a call from Lafayette Representative Odon "Don" Bacque, Jr. Don was a first term member having defeated Mike Thompson in a bitter election in 1987. A former "Green Beret" with service in Viet Nam, and, like me a former president of the Chamber of Commerce, Bacque was an independent and lived by that philosophy. Highly principled, he could be very intense, and very stubborn. He asked what I was hearing on the Duke situation. I told him at great length of the day's discussions. Finally I said, "The good news is that Treen is challenging in court and it has been agreed that we would live by the outcome of that hearing. If the court rules against Treen, there will be no challenge in the House. We'll have him sworn in and when the media asks about him we'll simply answer, 'David Duke? He's just another freshman.'"

There was silence for a moment before Don said, "Ron, if no one else is challenging Duke, I'm going to."

I was surprised and said, "Why Don? He was elected in District 81. We have nothing to say about how they elect their representatives. If Treen has proof that he was elected illegally, it will come out in the hearing. If he doesn't, how can you challenge?"

"Because he doesn't live in the district."

"How do you know that?"

"I just know he doesn't and the House should investigate."

What Don was saying was correct. However, by now it had become irrelevant. Duke had indeed been living two blocks outside of the boundaries of District 81 when he decided to run in November of 1988. The residency requirement for state representative is one year. He quietly changed his registration at the Jefferson Parish registrar of voters office to a residence inside the district. Laws governing such things require a candidate's residency to be challenged within ten days of qualifying. But, in November of 1988, nobody was taking David Duke seriously and nobody protested.

I knew I could not talk Bacque out of his decision but I hoped to delay him long enough for others to try. I said, "Donnie, sleep on it. Think about the burden of proving that allegation from your position when others within the district have not. Even if you successfully challenge his seating it will lead to months of hearings and investigations. It will be a media carnival and the business of the state, the attempt at fiscal reform, will go down the drain. Let's talk about it tomorrow."

We hung up and I started making calls to others I thought might have some influence on Don including Buddy Roemer. I woke up the next morning with my radio on the station I had formerly owned, Newsradio KPEL. The newsman led with the story of the special session beginning the next day with the swearing in of Lafayette's Jerry Leblanc and Klan wizard David Duke. He then proceeded to report that Duke's seating would be challenged by Lafayette Representative, Don Bacque. He played a taped interview with Don explaining his reasons for offering the challenge. The news raced around the state and the phone lines were jammed again.

I asked Jimmy Dimos to do me one favor. Please swear in Leblanc and Duke seperately. I did not want Jerry Leblanc to be standing side by side with David Duke taking the oath and for that to be the picture on TV and in newspapers of his first moments in office.

The session was scheduled to convene at 10:00 A. M. with the oath-taking ceremonies the first order of business. The court hearing on John Treen's motion was to begin at 9:00 A. M. in New Orleans. We had arranged to have an open phone line from the court house to the speaker's office. A small group of us gathered there.

The first word was that a lower court had ruled against Treen and the lawyers were now walking the documents upstairs, literally, to a higher court. It was 9:45 A. M. By 10:10 the House members were getting restless and Dimos and Butch Speer, the clerk of the House left the speaker's office to start the opening procedures of the House, the roll call, the pledge and the opening prayer. They then proceeded to call Jerry Leblanc to the podium and administered the oath of office. It was now almost 10:30. Our phone correspondent in New Orleans came on the line and said, "We lost, Judge Clarence McManus threw Treen's motion out."

That was it. We moved into the House and the clerk announced that the next order of business would be the administering of the oath to David Duke. Don Bacque stood, was recognized by the speaker and announced, "I object."

The public balcony overlooking the House was filled. I had noticed as I came into the chamber that it was a different crowd than I had seen on previous opening days. There were no black faces. There were no school children in groups. It was mostly male and mostly 25 to 45 in age. They were intensely focused on the proceedings and they were ominously quiet. Until Don voiced his objection.

Then there was a low, rumbling, guttural sound that rolled over the House from the balcony. I got goosebumps.

Don went to the well and explained his feelings. He asked the House to investigate Duke's eligibility to serve. Quietly and without further discussion the House voted 69 to 33 against his motion. I had the utmost respect and admiration for Bacque and understood his determination to test the process. I knew how deeply he and his family felt about this. I also recognized how traumatic this could be to him politically. I still felt it was better to honor the court's decision and move on without further elevating Duke to the role of martyr and victim.

Duke took the oath and proceeded to walk through the chamber, shaking hands along the way with his new colleagues. I had not seen David in person since the mid 1970's and couldn't believe the change. He had come into our radio station while visiting Lafayette in his role as KKK grand dragon. My news director at the time was just beginning the job and was very young and relatively inexperienced. He excitedly came into my office and said, "David Duke, you know the Ku Klux Klan guy? He's in the news studio. He wants to be interviewed about his visit to Lafayette. What should I do?"

I told him I'd do the interview. If something was going to be said that would threaten our FCC operating license, I wanted the personal responsibility.

I went back and met Duke. He was still in his mid 20's and very non-descript. Tall and slimly built, he had a very prominent nose, flat cheek bones, a slightly receding chin and straight dark brown hair. The interview turned out to be quite innocuous and I hadn't thought about it again until Duke came by my desk and we shook hands. Who was this guy? Tall and well-built with a perfect nose, a model's cheek bones, prominent chin, blue eyes and freshly coifed blond hair, he looked like a movie star. He obviously didn't remember me from the radio encounter and I was content to leave it at that. As he approached Bacque's desk he extended his hand and Don merely looked up at him and did not respond. A *Morning Advocate* photographer got a shot of the moment as Don refused the handshake. It was widely distributed. Don received some pretty nasty phone calls, letters-to-the-editors and other malicious comments for that.

Duke was assigned a desk which was at the very back of the chamber. Standing in the well and looking toward the balcony it was the very last desk on the left and was the only one of the 105 not paired with another desk.

The TV cameras and radio reporters were assigned to that side of the chamber and Duke soon learned to use his position to great advantage. When he was recognized to ask questions from his desk, he would slowly rise, very deliberately pull the microphone from its receptacle on his desk and hesitate long enough for the cameras to swivel and focus before he started talking. He also got in the habit of wandering out into Memorial Hall during slow periods in the House. Many of the TV crews would set up in the hall in the afternoons to catch legislators as they were leaving for the day or to call them out for individual interviews. Duke would stroll by the camera set ups and ask if they wanted an interview. He got a lot of TV time from bored reporters.

I noticed when we reconvened later the day he was sworn in that the first three rows of the balcony had now been roped off to prohibit seating and there were several official-looking men standing on either end of the area. I later learned that the placement of Duke at the lone desk at the rear was not by happenstance. State police and other law enforcement entities had been working all weekend on security plans. Duke was a firebrand and a lightning rod. He drew adoration and hatred. Some of the hatred was spelled out in death threats and the state police were not about to let that happen. Sitting in the balcony, you could not see Duke's desk unless you were in one of the front three rows. Thus, those rows were blocked off. The desk was also only several steps from an exit and plain clothes state police were stationed nearby at all times ready to whisk him out of that exit.

It was hard to imagine the worldwide impact of that 227 vote margin victory by this egocentric young man. He soon appeared on ABC's "Nightline" with Ted Koppel and CNN's "Crossfire." He was masterful in staying cool and on message in spite of the penetrating questioning. This was just the beginning of his national media tour. The mail room of the House was overwhelmed with letters to him. Some contained money, some bore lipstick imprints of kisses. One was delivered from California that was addressed simply: "Duke, Louisiana."

Most of us in the House lived up to our determination to treat him like any other freshman. Ignoring him was the worse treatment he could get. He was the consummate egotist and stood out as such even in this high caliber arena of narcissism. One Monday he came into the chamber looking like a house fire survivor. His face was bright red and peeling. He was talking with some members near my desk and told them he had been on the beach that weekend with his daughters and had fallen asleep.

I noticed as I looked up from my desk that there was a perfectly straight line running along each side of his jaw from the ear to the chin along the jawbone. The upper side was burned, the lower was not. I also remembered that the entire Gulf Coast had been blanketed with rain clouds all weekend. I called my wife and asked her to describe the results of a chemical face peel. She described David Duke's face. Three weeks later he flew off to Chicago for a series of TV talk show interviews. His face was as smooth and pink as a baby's.

In spite of his quick mind and rhetorical glibness, Duke never really caught on to the House rules or to parliamentary procedure. He had a couple of good tutors in the Jefferson Parish delegation who tried to watch out for him. He really was a "one trick pony." I believe he was much more interested in the presentation than the substance. When appearing on national talk shows, he invariably answered any question with his prepared sound bite. Professional heat-seeking interviewers like Rowland Evans and Robert Novak were stunned that they could not break through his calm demeanor. In spite of their best techniques of badgering and baiting, he always stayed on the message he wanted to convey. Because he was so single minded, he never really became involved in the nuts and bolts of House rules and parliamentary procedure. It was just that shortcoming that led to the demise of most of his attempts at lawmaking.

He once presented a bill on the floor, one of the few which he had managed to get out of committee. He finished his opening presentation and strolled with great self-satisfaction back up the aisle to his seat. In his mind, he had spoken, made his presentation and that was that. Before he had even reached his desk and refocused on the proceedings, another first-term member had been recognized for the floor and immediately moved to table the bill. The House voted for the motions effectively killing the bill. That and similar procedures were used against him many times.

History has and is still recording the saga of David Duke. His tenure in the House was short and uninspired. Never has anyone parlayed an election by such a narrow margin to such a minor position to such international prominence. He has run for numerous other positions without success but has always had some effect, usually negative, on the outcome. He was running for U. S. Senate just ten months after taking the oath in the Louisiana House and forced incumbent J. Bennett Johnston into a tough, expensive race before losing 54% to 43.5%. He beat Buddy Roemer out of the runoff spot against Edwin Edwards in the 1991 election thus inspiring the second primary bumper sticker, "Vote for the Crook, It's Important!" Edwards responded by saying that he and Duke were both, "Wizards under the sheets." Large contributions flowed into the Edwards campaign from all parts of the nation, particularly the Jewish community. Edwin tried to appear humble.

Just weeks after Edwards beat him 61% to 39% he announced his intention to run for President of the United States. He had obviously gone to the well once too often. His campaign money didn't come in as it once had. He was forced to drop out after several forays around the country but still got unprecedented national TV coverage for a minor candidate.

He dropped out of the 1995 gubernatorial race after selling a mailing list to the eventual winner, Mike Foster for an exorbitant amount of money. That purchase came back to haunt Foster four years later resulting in a major ethics violation fine. He was back in 1999 running for the Congressional seat vacated by Rep. Bob Livingston. His surprisingly weak showing left him well out of the runoff which was won by State Representative David Vitter.

So in essence, David Duke won one election, getting just over 8,000 votes and by a whisker-thin margin. The only bill that I recall he got passed and signed into law was legislation which prohibited movie producers or book publishers to pay jurors for accounts of their court experience. He was very instrumental in having the voters defeat Governor Roemer's fiscal reform package. He campaigned ceaselessly state wide. He got reams of press. He labeled Jim Bob Moffett, one of the founders of the fiscal reform movement, "Jim God Profit." He's authored several books, is always available for a TV interview and has recently formed a new organization supposedly to protect the interests of the Caucasian race. He is still a relatively young man and I doubt seriously if the world has heard the last of David Duke.

Notable quotes from the legislative halls:

"At the beginning of the day I had a lot of questions, but right now, if I have any, I don't know what they are."

Representative Dirk Deville

XVII

"I've met God and he is an assessor"

I was invited to speak to various groups all over the state during the interim period between special sessions.   As the author-of-record for the failed fiscal reform legislation in the special session and chairman of the House Committee on Ways and Means, I was one of the most logical choices as spokesman for fiscal reform. Since Governor Roemer was not making many public appearances, I was also the most accessible. I wasn't aware of it at the time but I believe I had already subconsciously decided that I was not going to continue to serve in the legislature and I might as well give this undertaking my best shot. I felt very deeply that it was worth the effort.

One unforgettable meeting took place in Alexandria early in 1989.   The group I met with was the CenLa governmental coalition. I don't recall the official name but it was a gathering of elected officials from central Louisiana.   Municipal and parish officials from Rapides, Vernon, Natchitoches, Sabine, Grant, LaSalle, Avoyelles, Catahoula and others were present. A large turnout was expected and, driving to the meeting, I felt somewhat optimistic about the presentation since a big part of the fiscal reform concept was for the state to relinquish control on some aspects of local taxation.   The idea was that local taxation would best serve local needs rather than have the state tax, collect and then return money to the local level through appropriations and capital outlay programs. What a ridiculous assumption on my part that local politicians would want the opportunity to control their own tax programs. Huey Long had figured that out sixty years before when he started centralizing the power in the state. One of the mayors in attendance, whom I had met before, told me in the coffee session before the meeting, "You know, Buddy told me during the campaign that he intended to give more taxing authority back to us at the local level. Damn, if I'd a known he was serious, I'd a voted against him."

Once I had finished my twenty minute presentation on fiscal reform, the meeting became a little rancorous. They were intent on "killing the messenger." I got to hear all of the complaints against state government, all the pent-up resentment that our state's economic depression had aggravated, all the anger. After about a half hour of this, some of the delegates started feeling sorry for me and advised their comrades that I really was a good sport and had been more than understanding of their problems. That didn't work on one of them.

Charles Slay was the legendary assessor of Rapides Parish. I don't know how long he had served, but he was considered the Lawrence Chehardy of central Louisiana. Tough-minded, self-satisfied and iron-handed in protecting his territory of authority, Charlie had appeared before my committees on several occasions and was not the least bit in awe of a lowly state representative or the Baton Rouge process.

After most of the animosity had been spent, Slay rose and calmly but forcefully let me know what he and his fellow assessors thought about the property tax, homestead exemption and assessment equalization provisions of the fiscal reform package. He got a little louder and more vehement as he built to a climax. He assured me that none of those provisions would ever pass and that I and "that governor of yours" and the rest of us reformers could go straight to hell.

Later in the same week, I was speaking to a meeting of a group called Citizens of South Lafayette. I told them about the meeting in Alexandria and of Charlie Slay's travel plans for the governor and me. In hopes of lightening things up, I said, "I've met God, and he is an assessor." There was a reporter in the audience and the next week the Lafayette *"Times of Acadiana,"* in a box labeled "Quote of the week," printed the quote.

The next week I received a hand-written letter from Charles Slay, on official *Assessor, Rapides Parish* letterhead:

> *Dear Rep. Gomez,*
>
> *I vaguely remember this meeting, and with the crowd you have to work with can easily understand how you could be awed in my presence, however, when I told you to "go to hell" I was speaking from a lower authority - not a "higher authority." I only wanted to get you down here to give you as much hell as you have given the assessors.*
>
> *In the future I will be careful to more clearly identify myself.*
>
> *Charles Slay*
> *Assessor, Rapides Parish*
> *Extra-Ordinary, Plenti: Potentiary*

I never did figure out what that last title meant but I realized I had been thoroughly put in my place.

Notable quotes from the legislative halls:

"I haven't visited your landfill yet, but I will put it on my list of places for my summer vacation."

Representative Ernest Wooten

XVIII

"Don't tax you, don't tax me, tax the man behind the tree.

But there's nobody left behind the tree!"

Round two. Fiscal reform redux. February 21st, 1989. After the Duke oath-taking was over we got down to the business of the special session. Meetings had been held throughout the winter and we had expanded our group to include many more of the legislators.

The new bill which I introduced was a watered-down and much slimmer version of the October document. The homestead exemption proposals were abandoned. Mission impossible. In his session-opening address, Roemer told the legislators the plan was, "not everything I'd like to have but I think it's possible to pass. I think it will get strong public support and I know it will help the state. Louisiana needs it." Roemer said the new plan would reduce state sales taxes by $100 million, increase income taxes on the upper income level by $175 million, give businesses a $75 million tax break and a separate bill would create a highway, airport and port construction program through a 4-cent excise tax on gasoline.

Our numbers crunchers had assured us that the net impact would be an increase in revenue of $20 to $40 million which they felt was as near "revenue neutral" as you could get in a $7 billion budget. A reporter suggested to me that some people saw the plan as merely shifting taxes from businesses and putting them on the backs of the people. I said, "That's because we've operated so long under the rule of 'don't tax you, don't tax me, tax the man behind the tree.' Well there's no one left behind the tree. It's time to get realistic."

Naturally, the opposition took many forms. LABI, the Louisiana Association of Business and Industry was not happy that the lowering of homestead exemption had been dropped. They said they would push to have it put back in because the Roemer proposal "abandons this element of reform, undermining the attractiveness of the entire plan to business." They also took issue with the proposal to impose a one-mill statewide property tax. Our reasoning for this provision was to use the $11 million it would produce annually to strengthen the tax commission by giving it a standing to challenge inequitable and unfair property assessments in court. LABI felt a ¼-mill tax would do the job.

Others started coming out from behind the tree. A minor part of the new bill was imposition of tolls on a New Orleans bridge. The bridge had been built with the understanding that tolls would pay for its construction and maintenance. The tolls were removed in a magnanimous and blatantly political gesture by a previous governor. The area known as the West Bank of New Orleans, John Alario's home base, was not particularly pleased with our suggestion.

Several of the Republican members of the legislature were very uncomfortable with the income tax increases, especially since they affected only the upper income levels.

The governor was proposing a six-cents-a-pack increase in tobacco taxes and doubling of taxes on wine. The tobacco and wine lobbyists were very strong and very strongly opposed.

Before we even opened hearings in the Ways and Means Committee my staff had requests for drafting of 35 amendments.

After six days of committee hearings, we presented a much-amended but still viable bill to the House. Like October, the Constitutional Amendment bill was HB 1 and the enabling bill with detailed changes was HB 2. HB 1 passed the House on

Monday, February 27th and zoomed through the Senate Committee on Revenue and Fiscal Affairs Tuesday morning

As Yogi Berra said, it was "deja vu all over again." The House spent another wrenching, emotional afternoon fighting over the details of HB 2. By the end of the day it was loaded with gutting amendments. Satisfied that they had savaged the beast to their satisfaction, the opponents allowed me to end debate and move for final passage. We were still seven votes short, 63 for and 40 against. We couldn't even pass this emaciated pretense of a fiscal reform measure. Not much seemed to have changed in four months.

Roemer, after spending countless hours counseling and listening during the winter with many of those who voted against the bill, was furious. Immediately after the vote he was surrounded by reporters, microphones and cameras in the marble hallway leading from the House chamber to the speaker's suite of offices. Standing on the outer perimeter of the crowd, I was struck by the irony of the scene. The mob was standing in almost the exact spot that Huey Long, surrounded by a squad of body guards, encountered Dr. Carl Weiss in 1935 and was mortally wounded. I was looking at another wounded governor, not mortally in the physical sense but most probably in the political sense.

Roemer told the reporters he planned to address a joint session the next day to outline what budget steps would be taken if the fiscal reform plan was not sent to the voters. Roemer had warned that without a new tax plan the '89-'90 budget would face a $654 million revenue shortfall. The governors face was flushed and his eyes flashing as he said, "Look, money talks, lunches with lobbyists talk, lobbying talks. It's time for somebody in this state to talk, to call it like it is. The special interests now run the legislature and they're running it to the disadvantage of human beings." He then took aim specifically at the oil and gas and tobacco lobbyists who were successful in cutting out tax increases in their industries.

"I'm going to ask the House for two votes tomorrow. I'm going to ask for a majority vote for an amendment to make the bill right again by stripping all the amendments, and then ask for 70 of the 105 members to send the bill to the Senate. If they won't do it we'll shut down the session and start shutting down state institutions."

The next day, Roemer's appeal to the joint session was much more conciliatory than his anger-induced comments to the media. He was very straight forward in telling the legislators that the failure of the fiscal reform plan would leave him and them with no other palatable choices. There was a pall over the House chamber as the governor closed his address to polite, sincere but not overwhelming applause.

Somehow it worked. Between the one-on-one talks with individual legislators, constituency contacts, lobbyist's urgings and any thing else we could think of, the House passed HB 2 before the weekend by a whisker and sent it to the Senate. After hours of wrangling and votes on numerous amendments, the Senate was finally ready to vote on Monday. It came up two votes short. Two more days were left in the session. Back to the drawing board. Another long night of conferencing, pleading, trading, threatening, cajoling and praying.

Finally, on Tuesday, March 7th, the Senate approved HB 2 by a vote of 26 - 12. It was zipped over to the House and, with a minimum of debate, the exhausted members voted to send it to the governor by a vote of 76-25. One last hurdle was left. The Senate had sent back an amended version of the constitutional amendment, HB 1 and Roemer and others felt there was some last minute tweaking needed.   They had me ask the House to vote against concurrence in the Senate amendments thus sending the bill to a conference committee. As author of the bill, I was on the conference committee and after a relatively brief time I was able to honestly report to the House that the amended bill was "a better instrument than we sent out because of changes made in the income tax and natural gas severance tax provisions.

"I believe the two major changes are those that affect the income tax where it saves those people in the middle range from the proposed tax we had before and the proposed natural gas severance tax is agreeable to the industry." We had also determined that the overall impact of the bill was about $25 million to the plus side of revenue neutral.

I found myself getting emotional about the fact that we were about to finally send a fiscal reform package to the voters. Sure, it was a watered-down version of that ambitious 1200 page document we had presented the previous September. But, I told the House in closing remarks before the vote, "We have made a long journey trying to achieve something that will restructure the tax code of our state. While the tax reform will not solve all the problems, it sets the state on a good course.

"This is a small step, but it is a very meaningful step not only for our people, our businesses, the overall atmosphere of the state. We are finally taking some steps to correct our own problem rather than waiting for Saudi Arabia, the federal government or someone else."

The Senate voted 31-1 and the House 80-25 for the compromise plan.

We now had a date with the voting public on April 29th, 1989, a short seven weeks away.

Notable quotes from the legislative halls:

Representative Ed Murray: "Will you accept an amendment to make the bill better?"

Representative Mike Walsworth: "We don't want too good of a law."

XIX

"I just wanted to see if Buddy Roemer had sent us a Mexican"

Quite frankly, I never wanted to discuss fiscal reform again. I was mentally, physically and emotionally drained and ready for what my wife likes to call hibernation. The regular session was due to start in a couple of weeks and promised to be an exercise in futility as the state waited for the April 29th vote. My hoped for isolation was not to be.

Two days after the special session ended, Roemer asked me to come to a debriefing session at the mansion. All the principals were are on hand. There was a lot of congratulating and smiling. Then we got down to business. Educating the public on the merits of the fiscal reform package before the voting date would be a massive task requiring a lot of organization and money. Roemer's former chief of staff, Len Sanderson, had been heading a political action committee (PAC) with the unlikely name "Louisiana Is Worth It." The acronym LIWI was pronounced Lee-Wee. (I always felt the name was the losing entrant in a slogan contest.) Sanderson had recently moved on to another position in Washington, D. C. and Roemer and the political advisors decided that LIWI would be used as the campaign arm for fiscal reform. It made sense. It already had an office, address, was properly registered as a PAC and had a little money (very little) in the bank.

Then came the shocker. Buddy looked at me and said, "I want you to run the campaign. We'll give you all the people and support you need. Don't tell me you can't. You've got to."

I protested as best I could but, after going so far with the program, now seeing a light at the end of the tunnel (I didn't realize it was an oncoming train) and with everything riding on this vote, I said, "OK, let's do it."

We had sold our radio stations the previous year and with all the fiscal reform meetings and special sessions, I had virtually been a full-time legislator and really was semi-retired. I insisted, however, that I would not be paid for my work with LIWI and would cover my own expenses, including travel.

Roemer announced the decision in a press conference saying that I would chair an "information oriented" campaign. "It will be an informational task. Most voters don't yet know details of the plan," Roemer said. "We have a job to do in the next few weeks to let them know what the facts are, and then we will rest our case with the people. I predict that, if fully informed they will say, let's go!"

We quickly acquired a floor of offices in the famous, though somewhat seedy at the time, old Roumain Building in downtown Baton Rouge. (It would later be renovated and proudly stand as a building on the National Historic Register.) There were already some volunteers in place and Roemer cut loose two people from his fourth floor staff: Bill Conway and Bob Munson.

Bill Conway was one of those people who had done a little of almost everything and a lot of many things. Holding an academic doctorate, he had taught in various venues, then worked for the National Football League for a period of time before landing in Ruston, Louisisana teaching at Louisiana Tech University. In his early 50's, he was tall, slim and sinewy from his passion for running and athletics. Bill's long and prematurely creased face would be called by some "gaunt." On the other hand, many would call it a face with a lot of character and reminiscent of many memorable character actors in movies.

He was my chief aide, confidant and became a good friend over the course of our LIWI involvement and to this day.

Conway, an unabashed idealist, confided that by 1987 he knew he had to try to do something other than academics. He was inwardly fuming over the inconsistency, hypocrisy and corruption in state government and, like many of us, saw Buddy Roemer's campaign for governor as the last best bet for change. He signed on as a volunteer and worked the campaign in Lincoln Parish, home of Louisiana Tech and got to know Buddy casually. Roemer had a passion for baseball which Conway shared.

After the election, one of Roemer's inner circle, Danny Walker, called Conway and talked him into taking a leave of absence to go to work for the new governor. His assignment was to work on getting a major league baseball team for New Orleans. Even though Bill felt and strongly opined that the idea was hopelessly unrealistic, Roemer and Walker persuaded him to take the job and make the effort.

With his broad base of knowledge and experience plus his obvious maturity in contrast to the "Roemeristas", Bill was soon taking on other assignments and, like the good soldier, accepted the job of helping me with the unfortunately named LIWI. He ran the office, kept the books, scheduled volunteers and put out fires. And he did it all calmly and with equanimity.

Bob Munson, as I have previously related, was a money raising whiz. With his own connections and that of Roemer and his network, plus the efforts of Jim Bob Moffett, other members of the business community and highly placed lobbyists, LIWI raised a million dollars in less than four weeks.

The campaign was terribly condensed and terribly confused. By the time I had settled into the office and begun scheduling speaking engagements, editorial board visits and media interviews for myself, Roemer, other members of the administration and a couple of dozen legislators who had volunteered, we had less than six weeks before the election.

I soon discovered that my role, described at first by Roemer as the leader of the campaign, would become subordinated to some of the governor's other political advisors. A million dollar honey pot attracts a lot of bees.

George Kennedy was chosen by Roemer to produce and place the electronic media. This immediately created a riff with Representative Jim St. Raymond of New Orleans who owned an advertising and public relations firm. Jim had worked with us on passing the reform bills and claimed that he had been promised the job. Kennedy is the brother of Roemer's special legal counsel John N. Kennedy who later became Secretary of Revenue and Taxation in the Mike Foster cabinet and resigned to make a successful run for State Treasurer in 1999.

Elliot Stonecipher of Shreveport was hired by Roemer to handle polling for the campaign and Leon Tarver, brother of Senator Greg Tarver of Shreveport, was hired to coordinate the effort in the black community. (Leon now serves as president of Southern University in Baton Rouge.)

Not a day went by that Conway didn't report to me another attempt at a raid on the LIWI treasury: a demand for a contribution to assure the support of a black Baton Rouge minister; members of the governor's staff asking for expense money for travel, meals and whatever, including resoling of shoes (honestly.) People, literally off the street, claimed to have been sent by Roemer or one of his aides to be put on the payroll or reimbursed for some sort of undocumented service or expense. It angered the volunteers in the office to see these attempts to milk the campaign when there were so many that were spending their own time and money to try to get fiscal reform passed.

I didn't even attempt to influence the direction of the advertising campaign. It was obvious that Kennedy, Sandersen, Stonecipher and others had decided that this was Buddy Roemer's proposal and he would be the principal figure. They would use the same style that had been so successful in the closing weeks of the gubernatorial campaign, the persuasive Roemer, one-on-one with the viewer. There was one thing not taken into consideration: this was not the virtually unknown outsider railing against the waste and corruption in state government. This was the governor who had been severely damaged in his first 15 months in office.

The media experts recorded several TV spots in Memorial Hall of the Capitol with Buddy strolling through the massive, gloomy space and talking about his vision for the future. The spots came out of post-production so poorly lit that the whole batch had to be scratched and re-staged. Time was slipping away and money was being spent in many non-productive ways.

For me the six weeks went by in a blur of speeches, driving, interviews, driving, debates, driving.

The support was gratifying. We had a good coalition of business associations working hard for support of their members. Even Fred Skelton, director of the teachers' union, was on board and giving us the benefit of his organization. About forty legislators were actively working their districts and helping fill state-wide speaking engagements.

On the other side, state labor boss Victor Bussie unequivocally told a meeting of the AFL-CIO he would resign if the package passed. David Duke announced a crusade across the state to defeat the reform amendment. Strange bedfellows with Duke were most of the members of the Black Caucus. Robert Garrity, a fire-breathing trial lawyer from River Ridge also made speeches across the state. Naturally, Edwin Edwards, Lawrence Chehardy and John Alario were doing their mischief. "Woody" Jenkins got into the mix running anti-reform ads in the Baton Rouge area.

One of the real difficulties of selling our package was the complexity of it and the need to show how each part had to be carefully aligned to form the whole of fiscal reform. Though I was accustomed and trained to produce sales messages for radio and TV that had to say a lot in 30 seconds to a minute, I could only condense my presentation on fiscal reform to 22 minutes. We had a good product: elimination of some business taxes which were stymieing economic development; creating a fairer schedule for income taxes so that most would pay less and the rest would pay a higher but fairer amount. (Amazingly the upper income voters, who would pay more after fiscal reform, overwhelmingly supported the measure. Those in lower income brackets, who would have paid less in sales and income taxes and received more benefits, were told by their leaders that it would be a bad measure and overwhelmingly voted against it.) We could prove that the overall increase in taxes was only $26 million, less than one percent of the total budget of the state.

On the other hand, it took our opponents about two minutes to blithely make their claims that it was a massive tax increase. They would cite isolated provisions of the amendment that might have a negative effect standing alone as examples of the gross unfairness of the package. As has been said before, it takes months or years to build a fine building and only moments to blow it apart.

One evening in Monroe, Representative Robert Garrity, the plaintiff attorney from River Ridge, pollster Ed Renwick of New Orleans and I had been invited to address several hundred citizens in a large auditorium. I was first up and gave my 22 minute presentation. Garrity was next. He was a totally unrestrained opponent of Roemer, me, and all we stood for and he minced no words. He strolled up to the podium holding a large roll of paper. He looked over the audience for a few moments than slowly unrolled what turned out to be a full-color poster-size picture of dozens of snakes inter-coiled on each other. In his best trial attorney voice he said, "Do you know what this is? This is *'serpentas ophidian,'* that's Latin for snakes. And this," he walked over and pointed his index finger right in my face and yelled, "this is the chief snake oil salesman in the state." Isn't serving in public office gratifying and fulfilling?

Garrity then proceeded to very effectively, if not very accurately, destroy the viability of the fiscal reform package.

One of my more memorable trips to North Louisiana during the fiscal reform campaign was to the small town of Farmerville in Union Parish. The assessor of the parish, M. L. Graham, was a genuinely nice man. He had spent a great deal of time in Baton Rouge over the last year and most of it in the Ways and Means Committee hearings. On one hand, he was a part of the assessors' group which was vehemently opposed to the state's advances into property taxation or property tax equalization. On the other hand, he and I had struck up an easy friendship and he told me, I think sincerely, that he really hated to see me and my political career get sidetracked by this "darn fool fiscal reform stuff."

Nonetheless, once the election date for the referendum on fiscal reform was set and the campaign was underway, Graham was open-minded enough to invite me to speak to his civic club in Farmerville. He picked a date that seemed clear in my schedule book and I wrote it down.

During that month prior to the vote, the days and weeks started running together. I was driving morning 'til night between speaking engagements and media interviews. Occasionally, I was lucky enough to commandeer a private plane to take me to some of the more distant venues. I developed a bad habit of only checking my schedule calendar one day in advance. I almost became panicky when I checked my book one morning and saw "Farmerville, M. L. Graham, Noon" noted for the next day followed by "Hammond, 4:00 P. M., Warner." I must confess, with all my travels of Louisiana, I had never been to Farmerville and only knew it was in the Northeast part of the state. I also knew that Hammond, in Southeast Louisiana was a long way from anything "up yonder." I soon found that

Farmerville was between Monroe and the Arkansas border. Way up yonder.

After several phone calls I had ascertained that 1) M. L. was ready and anxious for me to speak at noon to his club, 2) the Hammond event could not be postponed and I could not find a substitute.

I finally found a supporter with contacts and he found a private plane and pilot to fly me from Baton Rouge to Farmerville and back to Baton Rouge by 3:00 P. M. for the 45 minute drive to Hammond.

It was a partly cloudy but very windy day as we swept over Monroe and started losing altitude for our landing in Farmerville. The pilot, like me, had never landed up here and only knew that the grass landing strip was just southeast of the town and very short. What we found upon arrival was that it was also surrounded by tall pine trees. It ran roughly north and south and we were experiencing a stiff northwesterly wind. Our twin engine plane would have to drop in over the pines at one end of the strip, crabbing against the wind, apply full flaps to bring us down quickly and immediately apply hard brakes on touch down.

We came in low and paralleled the runway on one flyby. I could see a small figure next to a car parked just off the center of the strip waving as we went by. M. L.! The pilot circled back, cut the engine, applied full flaps and dove over the pines. We hit the grass hard, started braking immediately and finally came to a stop about 30 yards from the other end of the runway.

As I jumped down from the plane, M. L. was already waiting next to the wing. "Man," he said, "that was all right. Ya'll made that strafing run, then just came on in nice and smooth."

The pilot muttered under his breath, "Right, don't miss the upcoming take off in a pasture near you."

Graham drove us into the picturesque little town of Farmerville and I delivered my 22 minute fiscal reform speech to about 25 civic club members in a room adjoining a small restaurant. The reception and reaction was about what I had come to expect with North Louisiana, rural audiences. They were very attentive but showed nothing, no agreement, no disagreement. There was no visible emotion. No nodding in approval, no frowning in disapproval. M. L. tried to loosen things up with a couple of questions after the speech. When I had finished and the meeting was adjourned, a small group was lingering and talking with M. L. and me. One gentleman, small, wiry and wearing the white and brown forehead tan of the farmer, was standing back, eyeing me warily. I decided to reach out and try to get him involved with the group. I put out my hand and said, "I hope you got something from my talk and can help us with a vote for fiscal reform on April 29th."

He gave me a heavily callused, yet limp hand and said, "Well, I don't know about that. I just came out 'cause old M. L. told me the governor was sending somebody by the name of Gomez up to talk to us. I just wanted to see if Buddy Roemer had sent us a Mexican." The group had a good laugh about that and M. L. drove me back to the air strip and I continued on the adventures of peddling "good government" to the vox populi.

*   *   *

The legislative session opened in Baton Rouge in late March and I split time between chairing the Ways and Means Committee and traveling the state. During this period I was strongly reminded how rural our state really was, how isolated some towns and communities were, and how that isolation was compounded in many cases by a lack of media coverage of state affairs.

I finished a speech to a civic club in Oakdale one afternoon and opened the floor for questions. The first question was from a very sincere, but obviously very skeptical, middle aged man, "Sir, I just listened very carefully to every thing you said and, you know what? James David Cain talked to us last week and everything he said was opposite of what you just said. Now who're we supposed to believe?" Cain had been the Representative from this district since 1972 taking office for the first time along with Governor Edwin Edwards. He had built a solid political career being friendly with Edwards and, naturally, opposed the fiscal reform amendment. He now serves in the Senate.

He was also a masterful politician. He had disciplined himself to make ten phone calls per day to constituents. He did it every day, absolutely without fail. His legislative aide would give him 3 x 5 cards with a voter's name, address, phone number, occupation and names of family members and other pertinent information as available on each one. James David would call ten of them a day, note on the card the subject and gist of each conversation and the aide would write a follow-up letter the next day. The subject of the conversation was not significant, the fact of the call was the important thing.

For instance, James David might open a conversation like, "Hey there Billy Bob, this here's James David, right, James David Cain. I'm calling you from the Capitol in Baton Rouge, how's your better half Clara Jane and the little ones? Uh huh, uh huh, well listen here Billy Bob, we got some fellow down here that put in a bill to put some kind of tax or fee on water wells. How many of them water wells you got on your place? Really? That many? Well we're just gonna have to do something to stop this bill."

He'd chat a little more and make some notes on the card. I heard such a conversation and started checking the directory of bills to try to find the water well tax. It wasn't there and never was and Billy Bob would never know it wasn't. He'd get a nice letter a couple of days later thanking him for his advice and letting him know that, because of that conversation, James David had had the bill killed. How can you beat that kind of "politicking."

In addition, many of the rural legislators would write legislative reports for their weekly newspapers and give their views on the news in the Capitol. Most of those newspapers did not have the manpower to send a reporter to Baton Rouge and many could not afford access to a news service such as Associated Press. The same was true for many of the small, rural radio stations. Many, if not most, would get their state government news by calling their legislator or having him come in to record a report on the weekend.

How could I possibly convince this gentleman in Oakdale that I was right and that the guy he had been electing for seventeen years and reading about and hearing on his local station was wrong?

By mid-April I was beginning to tire of trying to win this battle by being Mr. Nice guy. I was at a forum at the YWCA in Shreveport. I dropped my usual detailed outline of the fiscal reform package and told the group that the opponents of the proposal were not concerned with facts but with destroying the administration of Governor Buddy Roemer and ensuring that no reform governor would ever be elected again.

I told the group that much of the opposition was directly linked to Edwin Edwards and his attempt to return to power in 1991 (which he did.) "Critics aren't interested in facts," I said, "because they have opposed this proposition even when all their objections were eliminated.

"Let's see, who is in that good ol' boy network. Oh, here's a newcomer, David Duke, but then there's Lawrence Chehardy, Edwin Edwards, John Alario. Opponents are not for it because they don't want a governor who is reform-minded. Period. End of reason. Every time we made a change they wanted they found another target."

Former state Senator Virginia Shehee was a part of the forum and she told the gathering that there were four substantial business prospects looking at the Shreveport area. She said she knew that the April 29th vote would be a major consideration in their decision.

Seeing one newspaper after another endorse the plan, I was beginning to feel some cautious optimism. John Maginnis opined in the April issue of the weekly *Gris Gris, "There is one good reason to vote against the constitutional proposal. That is: you like things the way they are."* Maginnis went on to explain, *"About the same amount of money will be generated but the burden will shift some. The folks with higher incomes will pay more --- as is the case in the rest of the country, not in Louisiana now. Louisiana's poor and most of the middle class will get a break on sales taxes* **and** *income taxes. Some people don't think that's fair --- we do.*

"This election is about change, a change from volatility to stability in the state treasury. We can replace an unpredictable, regressive tax base with a fairer one that we can predict and rebuild on. The 1974 ratification of the current Constitution modernized our form of government. This amendment changes the substance with an historic shift of revenue source and policy. Also, the world has changed radically in the past 15 years, and not in our favor. Voting yes will recognize that change and enable us to catch up with a world that is leaving us behind."

Pollster Elliot Stonecipher was telling the governor we had better than 50% voting yes. I still did not feel that in the audiences I talked to and the people I met. I tried to listen without bias to the radio and TV spots the opposition was running and I could see how they sounded logical to the citizens.

It was bitterly disappointing if not totally unexpected. The turnout was fairly good for an issues election, about 46%. The fiscal reform amendment was soundly defeated by roughly 100,000 votes, 55% to 45%. Carol and I went to the mansion once the trend was evident and visited with Buddy and his wife Patti and other fiscal reform refugees. Buddy held a brief news conference on the front steps of the mansion and tried to be optimistic and put a bright spin on the bad news, "We cannot quit. We will keep building, just not as fast. We will not quit fighting for jobs, for schools, for the future. I wanted to win for Louisiana, but, I feel good about Louisiana. This state is a great state. We could have done a variety of things differently."

Representative David Duke was cheered by a couple of hundred people gathered at a labor union hall in Metairie when he said, "The people sent a message that they want a new approach to state spending policies. They want true fiscal reform. We've got to have welfare reform. We've got to replace welfare with workfare." Sometimes the right message just has the wrong messenger.

At least Vic Bussie didn't have to resign.

Driving back to Lafayette over the Atchafalaya Swamp at midnight that night I said, "You know what? The majority of the people of the state don't want to be saved. Why are we trying to do it?"

The president of the Public Affairs Research Council Mark Drennen said, "It means Lousiana will remain last in education, number one in unemployment. It means that the legislature will have to devote most of its time to the same thing that it's been dealing with for five years, and that is: where to cut the budget and how much do we raise taxes?" That statement would prove ironically prophetic eleven years later when Mark was serving as Commissioner of Administration for Governor Mike Foster. The state was again faced with the same dilemma - where to cut the budget and how much can taxes be raised.

The post mortems were swift and harsh. We were criticized for over-publicizing the referendum. "Too much TV," they said, "in California, where referendums are as common as our elections, you practically don't know there's an election going on unless you receive a direct mail piece."

Others criticized the LIWI campaign for using too much Buddy Roemer. They said Roemer made the vote a referendum on himself at a time when his job approval rating was low among the groups the tax proposal needed most, labor and blacks.

It was all of the above and more, or none of the above and dozens of other reasons. It was over.

Nothing had been accomplished in the legislative session still in progress. We all took a breather for a few days before Buddy decided to try to start salvaging whatever he could of the session and the future. Like the Sunday mansion fiscal reform sessions, he decided to meet with small groups of legislators every day at noon for a brown bag lunch in his office on the fourth floor at the Capitol. The core group of floor leaders and inside staffers were expected to be there every day. In addition, eight or ten different House members were invited each day.

One day we would have sandwiches, the next day pizza, then someone suggested we could make some points with former speaker pro tem Joe Delpit by getting some fried chicken from his restaurant. This went on for a couple of weeks until almost every member of the House had been included. I started dreaming of the day I could eat lunch using a table instead of my knees. Buddy would ask for input on how our fiscal problems could be solved, how we could find some unity between the legislature and the administration. There were some lively discussions. Some of the staunch opposition, namely John Alario and Bo Ackal were invited, would accept the invitation then would not show up.

Meanwhile Ackal and Alario were quoted in news articles as saying that Roemer was "holed up" at the mansion and wouldn't see anyone. They said he was obviously in a deep depression over the loss of the fiscal reform referendum and had virtually abdicated leadership.

I read a newspaper story with those allegations in it and blew my top. As the House was convening one afternoon, I went down to the press desk which faced the chamber and ran almost the width of the House on either side of the well podium. Several members of the print media were there. I said, "How in the world can you write something like this? Buddy Roemer's been in his office in the Capitol everyday and we've met with nearly 80 House members in the last two weeks. Just because Alario and Ackal say otherwise doesn't make it so!"

One of the reporters asked if I wanted to make a statement and be quoted on what I had just said. They said Alario and Ackal said Buddy would not meet with them. "They and every member of the House have been invited to meet. We've been doing this everyday at noon. Alario and Ackal just never show up. Look, why don't you go up to Roemer's secretary and ask to see a log of his appointments. It's all there. Everybody he meets with, everyday. He's not 'holed up' anywhere," I said.

One of the New Orleans reporters, normally quite accurate and efficient offered to quote me.

I said, "This is not an 'I said, they said' type thing. When I was a reporter we were taught that, if you had conflicting statements you should find the source of the truth. It's there, somewhere in between. Go prove it to yourself. Get the records."

The reporter said, "Ron, we don't have time to go chasing down things like that." So much for informing the public.

The excruciatingly long legislative session ground to a halt. We renewed $300 million of the sales taxes expiring on June 30th. The session became bitter and vitriolic. Old alliances split and new ones formed. Roemer was accused of submitting a bloated budget and allowing the Senate to add even more to it.

The July 4th weekend produced another dark comedy in the halls of the legislature.

The Senate added over $150 million in appropriations to the House passed bill. The House members had suddenly taken on a fiscally responsible mind set. After the defeat of fiscal reform, they needed to prove that they could manage the budget properly. They angrily rejected the Senate amendments and put the bill into a conference committee.

Theoretically a conference committee works this way: The speaker of the House and the Senate president each name three members. House rules are very specific and require the three members to be: the author of the bill, the chairman of the committee to which the bill had originally been referred (or another favorable member if the committee chairman and author were the same person,) and a member who opposed the bill. Typically, the Senate had no rules on this and the President usually named members who would vote the way he wanted them to. The committee is supposed to hold a public meeting to discuss the differences between the two houses and compromises offered and voted upon. If and when a consensus is reached, with four of the six members agreeing, the committee reports the compromise to the legislature at which time both chambers vote. Both houses must give the compromise a majority vote for it to pass (a super majority on tax bills and Constitutional amendments.)

In this case Speaker Dimos named Robert Adley, Chairman of the Appropriations Committee, Ed Scogin, who had opposed concurrence and me.

Representative Scogin, the salty old Slidell Republican had told the House, "I'm voting no on this bacon-wrapped budget. I'm one person who doesn't intend to be made a steer by the Senate. I refuse to be neutered and spayed. If you like pork, vote for this bill. I don't like pork."

Senate President Allen Bares was already under siege and rumored to be within a vote or two of being overthrown. He went along with the majority of the Senate which wanted to stuff the House on this question. He named B. B. "Sixty" Rayburn, the dean of the legislature having served since 1948. His picture was listed in the dictionary under "curmudgeon." Bares then named himself to the committee along with the Senator that many believed was the real leader of the Senate, Don Kelly from Natchitoches.

Somehow, it was decided that the committee would not meet as a body since such a meeting, expected to be rancorous and verbally violent, would have to be held in public and with media coverage. It was thought that we could resolve the differences by the members of each body meeting separately with the governor first, then holding a joint public meeting to ratify the agreement. It was June 30th, the beginning of the July 4th weekend. If we could solve our problems and get both houses to agree we could shut down the session and all go home. The three House members of the conference committee met with Roemer in the governor's office on the fourth floor of the Capitol for almost an hour and went over the provisions of the Senate version of the appropriations bill which we felt needed changing.

We then left the governor's office and waited in the office of the chief of staff, about 15 steps down the corridor to the East side of the fourth floor. The Senate members, who had been cooling their heels in an office on the West side of the governor's office were then summoned. They spent some time in discussion and the positions were reversed again.

This went on all day Friday. In the chambers, tempers were heating and members wanted to leave for the July 4th holiday. The media, in a fit because of the lack of a public meeting, were yelling, "Foul!"

The only way the session could end without an agreement between the chambers was the expiration of time.

The three of us on the House side decided to go over the bill item by item to try to find some compromises. After several hours we had a list. The Senate members moved in and out of the governor's office in less than 15 minutes rejecting our suggestions.

It was obvious the Senate conferees were not going to budge.

About 9:00 P. M. we got word from a legislative aide that the Senate's staff had been instructed to draft a conference report with no changes to the bill. The Senators intended to present it to the governor and us in a take-it-or-shove-it gesture. Robert Adley was fit to be tied. He asked some House staff to take the list of cuts we had proposed and to draft them into our own conference report. The job was finished about 11:00 P. M. We got the Senate's document, trashed it and sent them ours. Minutes went by. The legislative day, by law, must end at midnight. We wanted to get this over with, end the session and go home. The Senators would not respond. Adley called an aide and told her to set up a table in Memorial Hall and to notify the media we would be down shortly to sign a conference committee report.

When we stepped out of the elevator into Memorial Hall at about 11:45 it looked like a scene from "Tales From the Crypt" or "The Mummies of the Pyramids." There was a small table set up in a corner on the House end of the Hall and TV cameras had formed a tight semi-circle around it. Their bright lights were on and, because there were no lights in the rest of Memorial Hall, they cast weird, stark shadows throughout the cavernous space.

The three House conferees solemnly gathered around the signing table and made a few remarks about how right we were and how we hoped at least one Senator would come out of the barricaded Senate to sign the report to make the majority. Our words echoed eerily through the hall. We then each signed the document. John Maginnis reported that it looked like the surrender aboard the *USS Missouri*, except the Japanese didn't show up.

Suddenly, we heard the gravelly voice of Sixty Rayburn coming out of the shadows and through the maze of TV cameras, "What the hell's going on here? Why don't everybody just go home. The Senate needs more time to consider this thing." He turned to his old friend and colleague Ed Scogin, and said, "Ed, you and I can't sign this thing yet."

Scogin fixed him with a steely eye, offered him his pen and said, "I just did, Sixty."

The clock struck midnight and the legislative day ended. We adjourned for the night and left the capitol.

The major problem the delay caused, much more important than the legislators holiday time off, was that a portion of the sales tax expired at midnight that same night. Though the legislature had voted to renew it, the stalemate in the conference committee had delayed that renewal. It would cost the state considerable revenue to lose even one day of the tax. It also caused chaos with retailers. Saturday July 1st, all over the state, businesses and retailers whose registers had been programmed to eliminate the tax starting that day were in confusion and angrily calling tax collection offices, legislators, even the governor. They didn't know whether or not to charge the tax and whether they would be liable later if they made the wrong decision.

The matter was finally resolved. I reluctantly broke the tie. We were in Roemer's office Saturday morning when Senator Bares called to say he and the other two were meeting publicly, with media coverage, in a Senate committee room and had a counter-offer to make. Adley and Scogin were still steaming from the night before and were adamant. They would not compromise. I called down and talked with Bares and he outlined their offer to me. I was surprised. It really was a compromise. The Senators were willing to reduce the $150 million difference between the two houses to about $21 million. I suggested to Bob and Ed that we go down and magnanimously sign on, declare victory and get this session over with. They unequivocally refused. "Well," I said, "I'm for solidarity, and all that, but I'm also realistic enough to know we've won about as much as we're going to. Please excuse me, I admire your determination, but I'm going to sign it."

That settled the problem with the appropriations bill but the sales tax renewal problem wouldn't go away. Roemer decided to take the unprecedented step of letting the session end without full resolution and call a six-day special session to begin immediately upon sine die adjournment of the regular session. It took the Senate about one minute to adjourn one session and reconvene the other on Wednesday, July 5th, 1989.

There were an amazing number of bills introduced for such a condensed session. In addition to the renewal of the "temporary" sales tax on food, drugs and utilities, several members decided to approach fiscal reform on a piecemeal basis by introducing individual elements of the original proposal.

Almost twenty bills were signed into acts in that brief session. Many were innocuous but there were some of significance.

There was the change of natural gas taxation from percent of volume to percent of value. There was the elimination from constitutional protection of the $3 personal automobile license tag. There was even a bill reducing homestead exemption from $75 thousand to $25 thousand. Will miracles never cease? There were several instruments designed to give local governments more taxing authority.

And then there were the gambling bills. Casino, video poker, lottery, riverboat gambling, everything but mumblety-peg, all promising, naturally, to solve the financial problems of the state. The House Committee on Criminal Justice did its best to kill all the gambling bills it could, but somehow, a few bills sneaked out with unfavorable or "no action" reports. They were greeted on the floor of the House with bloody fights which further divided an already fractured body.

It became a contentious, vitriolic session. I told the House as I presented the natural gas tax bill, "We are asking you to do what every other natural gas producing state has done, put a tax on percent of value. Will it hurt the industry? I cannot believe that it will."

The House gave us 61 votes, nine short of passage. I had handled too many bills over the past two years that had to be voted on more than once. I gave up.

Representative Robert Adley, himself an oil and gas entrepreneur, lashed out at the industry's lobbyists and the legislators who had voted against the bill, "When you go home you will have to answer to people who will ask 'how could you vote for sales taxes on food, drugs and utilities and not vote for a tax on Texaco, Exxon and Conoco?' "

In his session-ending "best and worst" column, John Maginnis nailed it, "It was the worst of times, it was the worst of times."

Even his kind remarks about me did little to ease the frustration and depression I was feeling. Maginnis wrote, *"Ron Gomez proved that not all administration floor leaders have to be ineffective. He loyally and credibly advanced the administration's bills and held back counter revolutionary forces on the Ways and Means Committee."*

I realized then that I was burned out as a legislator. We had been in session 210 of the 485 days Buddy Roemer had been governor. In addition there were the pre-special session and interim committee meetings, the endless Sunday fiscal reform sessions at the governor's mansion and the innumerable other regular legislative-related meetings. Earlier in the year a reporter had quoted me as saying, "I tied myself to what I believed was a reform program. Buddy Roemer was the catalyst for that program." Now here we were with the "Roemer Revolution" in disarray and no redemption in sight.

Perhaps sensing my frustration, Roemer asked me a couple of weeks later if I would like to consider taking a position in his cabinet. What he had in mind was forming a new cabinet level office: Secretary of Communications. It really only amounted to a high paid, elevated press secretary. Thanks but no thanks.

A couple of weeks later, Roemer sent for me and suggested that I consider taking the office of Secretary of the Department of Economic Development (DED) should the current secretary Arnold Lincove resign, which he was rumored to be considering.

Now that was interesting. The more I thought about it the more excited I became considering the possibilities.

Roemer and Lincove were heading up a much-anticipated industry seeking trip to Japan in mid-August. Buddy said he would know when he returned what the future of the department would be.

Several weeks went by after they returned before I got to meet with Roemer again. He seemed distracted when I entered his office and I could never get the conversation to focus on the cabinet position. He finally asked me if he could talk to me about something totally different, in confidence. He told me his marriage was in serious trouble and proceeded to tell me his interpretation of why. Having experienced a divorce, I was totally empathetic but, it was no surprise. I told him it was obvious that he had taken up with a mistress two years before. The mistress was the governor's office and he spent every waking hour obsessed with it.

He was truly agonizing over the prospects of separation from Patti. There was not much I could say or do. As I left the office he added, as an afterthought, that Lincove would remain as Secretary of DED but that Dr. Ray Stephens, Secretary of the Department of Natural Resources (DNR) would be leaving at the end of the year to resume his private business and teaching. "Think about it," he said.

It became more intriguing the more I thought about it. Lafayette was the center of the oil and gas industry in the state and I had a lot of friends in the industry. Also, one of the key divisions of DNR was the Office of Coastal Restoration and I was vitally interested in the efforts to correct the terrible loss of wetlands along our coast. Carol and I talked about the possibilities and I told Buddy I would accept the offer.

I took over as Secretary of the Department of Natural Resources in January, 1990. It was a challenging and rewarding experience. I am most proud of the initiatives begun by Dave Soileau and Dr. Bill Good in the Office of Coastal Restoration and the accomplishments of the Oil Spill Task Force which I chaired and which was responsible for milestone legislation in 1991.

*   *   *

Since 1989 there have been no real concerted efforts toward comprehensive fiscal reform. However, all of the time and effort was not a complete waste. Many of the original elements of the program first espoused by Jim Bob Moffett's Louisiana Council on Fiscal Reform have been enacted into law:

The double taxation on Subchapter "S" corporations was eliminated in 1989 saving small businesses almost $40 million annually.

In 1990 the Revenue Estimating Conference was established in the Constitution, a true "balanced budget" amendment to the Constitution was passed, a Mineral Trust Fund was established in the Constitution, the constitutional protection of the $3 personal auto license tag was repealed, local inheritance taxes were prohibited, and the City of New Orleans was authorized to pass a millage for police and fire protection that *is not subject to the homestead exemption.*

A state tax credit for local inventory taxes was passed in 1991 saving businesses, large and small, about $100 million a year.

Sales tax collection agencies were reduced to only 64, one per parish, as opposed to the previous 164.

In 1998 the inheritance tax began a phase out.

But, in spite of the mountains of studies and rivers of blood, sweat and tears spent on discussing fiscal reform, the state continues to be overly dependent on sales taxes, totally bereft of federal tax-deductible property taxes and stymied by income tax rates which are buried in the constitution. We still follow the precepts of Huey Long and bleed business and industry for taxes such as the corporate franchise tax and wonder why we find it so difficult to attract industry other than that which must locate here because of our natural resources. We also still have a homestead exemption three times higher than any other state.

Now, at the dawn of the new millennium, the state is apparently again faced with a major revenue shortfall. The nation is enjoying the longest sustained economic boom in history. Sales taxes in the state have been soaring for the past several years. With Louisiana's traditional bellwether indicator, oil prices, at their highest level in over 15 years, with the tens of millions of dollars in blackmail-tinged tobacco money in the treasury and with virtually every kind of gambling known to mankind sanctioned and taxed by the state, there is a budget crisis of major proportions. Again, legislators and journalists hint at the need for "fiscal reform," for a total restructuring of the tax base.

Governor Mike Foster has been a champion of sales taxes during his tenure in office. He says they are a democratic tax since everybody pays them equally. He has staunchly defended the homestead exemption level in Louisiana and even suggested that it could be higher. But Foster now seems to be recognizing the depth of the problem. On March 20th, 2000 he opened a special session of the Louisiana Legislature which he had called to address the recurring revenue problems of the state. In his opening address to the joint session he admitted that massive tax raising measures were not the answer. He told the legislators, "Louisiana has a 1950's economy, a 1940's tax base and tax code and we're trying to compete in the 21st century."

Often with the state in similar financial disarray, Mr. Ed, Ed Scogins, the raspy-voiced ex-police juror from Slidell who reveled in his role of conservative conscience of the House, would purposefully stride to the well of the chamber. Standing behind the microphone, he would plant his right elbow on the podium, his hand against his jaw and cheek, take a deep breath and growl, "How long, Louisiana, how long?" He is yet to be answered.

Notable quotes from the legislative halls:

"We pass far too many bills in the legislature, which says to me , either a lot of stuff we pass doesn't do anything or it's not really being considered to the full degree that it should."

Representative Raymond Jetson

XX

C'est tout, finis, Mama

Dear Mama,

I just finished writing a bunch of words which may be of interest to some or found to be totally boring or meaningless to others. But I'm glad I did.

I wanted people to know some of the things I learned in my dozen years in public office: the elation, the frustrations, the satisfaction, the disappointments. I wanted them to become aware of the dual role in which we have cast people who seek and/or hold public office i. e. "politicians."

Tell someone you're considering running for public office and you will usually get encouragement and praise for your courage and selflessness. Tell a stranger you are an elected official and you'll most likely suddenly read mistrust, derision or worse in his eyes.

Almost ten years after leaving public office, I still have people urging me to run again. Most are sincere and I appreciate their consideration but many are the same ones who griped the most and supported the least.

We want, and rightfully expect, our public office holders to be honest, forthright, effective, independent and accessible. Yet, too many times, we paint them all with the same brush: untrustworthy, glib, immoral, overpaid, corrupt and uncaring. I guess it's just a natural human reaction to judge all persons of a class by the actions of the most flamboyant or obnoxious.

Mama, I know you had a very low esteem of politicians when you told me, "If you're not careful you'll end up just as crooked as all those other politicians." I thank you for saying that. I thought about it many times.

But, I truly believe that the vast majority of the office holders with whom I served and have known in my public life were honest men and women of integrity. They served with dignity and made a difference. Naturally, some were more effective than others. They decided to run for public office for many different reasons. Some were seeking the perceived power of a political position. Some honestly wanted to and felt they could make a difference. They had specific ideas and agendas they wanted to move forward (such as my "Cajundome" project.) Some ran because the position paid more or as much as they were making in private life, some for the generous retirement benefits available to some elected officials. (This, I found was a very popular reason among those who already were retired from a civil servant or teaching position.)

I also know many who entered the arena with a narrow, specific agenda of self-aggrandizement. A lot of them succeeded in that goal. They enhanced their personal futures and some made a lot of money for themselves and their associates using the power and advantages of their public positions. And then, there were some who started out sincerely but shifted gears once they found that most people thought they were dishonest, deceitful and untrustworthy just because they were "politicians." "What the hell," they said, "if I'm gonna be accused of it, I might as well do it."

The sad part is that it is very difficult in politics to tell the difference between "the good, the bad, and the ugly" without close and constant observation. Frankly, most voters don't have the time or the day-to-day interest or the unfiltered access to truly determine who's who among today's office holders and seekers.

Equally sad is the fact that the moral and principled majority of elected officials, especially those in part time offices such as the state legislature or city councils, tire quickly of the constant pressure to please a diverse constituency. Sometimes it feels as though each constituent wants something from you or the government and at the same time resents anyone else feeling the same way.

One phenomenon that I noticed early on was what I called the "black hole" syndrome. Every year, starting several months before the regular session, area legislators were asked to meet with various special interest groups or constituents. We would meet with the retired state workers, school bus drivers, teachers' associations, highway contractors, you name it, there is a "special interest group" for everyone.

During those meetings, most of the legislators seemed to be normal, friendly, mild-mannered, easy-going individuals (with maybe a bit more ego than the norm.) But once we moved into session and we sank into the black hole of the Capitol in Baton Rouge, we were surrounded by lobbyists anxious to please our every whim, laugh at our jokes and buy our meals. We were catered to by legislative aides, state troopers and state civil servants and saw our names and images and quotes on TV and in print.

The selfless public servants of several weeks before suddenly morphed into self-important statesmen. Some would, in private, legislators-only conversations, joke about how they had told a group of constituents one thing but fully intended to do the opposite, saying laughingly, "They'll never know the difference, none of'em keep up with the news from here anyway."

While known as dignified, sober ladies and gentlemen in their own districts, many would suddenly drop into the black hole and become party animals. Baton Rouge never lacked for entertainment, especially for legislators. I spent one memorable luncheon on the last day of a session at the wonderful restaurant, Chalet Brandt's, with three other legislators and a prominent business lobbyist. One of the legislators was from a north

Louisiana parish which was "dry." No liquor was sold. Even if it was brought in it wasn't consumed in public. This representative proceeded to order one gin martini after another until, within 45 minutes, he was well inebriated. "I don't suppose you're driving home tonight?" I asked him.

"Naw," he said, "I'm staying here and tying one on tonight 'cause, when I get home, I won't be able to have another drink 'til the next time my committee meets down here."

But, of course, none of these traits or habits are confined only to politicians. It's just that politicians are, more or less, ordinary people in extraordinarily high profile positions.

And, I learned some interesting things about lobbyists. Most of them are also hard-working, basically honest people. Their job is to disseminate information and cast issues in the best possible light for their clients. Sure, some get carried away and go over board with biased information. But, they are usually balanced by those on the other side. It's up to the individual legislator to sort out the information, not unlike any other decision making process in life.

In years gone by there were lobbyists who thought they could buy enough votes with favors and gifts. There were those who thought they could influence enough votes through intimidation or threats. Most of those have been negated through changed laws and changes in the intelligence and motivation of most legislators. I did say most. There are still some of all of the above to be found. The vast majority of lobbyists, however, know that they will be judged on the truthfulness and honesty of their information and know that the longevity and success of their careers are on the line daily. In truth, no legislator can research every bill that comes up. Lobbyists are invaluable sources for learning about legislation and arriving at informed decisions.

You know what Mama? I want to thank you for pushing that stroller down to the Capitol to see the funeral of Huey Long when I was 10 1/2 months old, I think maybe I got my interest in government by mere exposure to such a dramatic event.

And I thank you for letting me go to the Capitol when I was 9 and 10 years old while you were working at Rosenfield's. My curiosity of what those old men were doing sitting around and sometimes loudly arguing with each other in the legislative halls fed my desire to learn more about the process.

And I thank you for your own burning interest and curiosity about government and politics and people in general which fired mine. Rarely did I know anyone else with just a fifth-grade education who could reel off all the names of Louisiana's governors over a 60 year span — and in chronological order.

I must confess there were times I too became arrogant and sometimes too harshly critical of the system and of others with whom I was associated in politics. I let my patience run short with those with whom I could not reason. I did, however, learn to compromise even when I would have much preferred perfection.

And with all this said, I must also confess that I do not regret one minute of the experience of serving in public office. I hope some of my more negative observations in these pages do not dissuade others from seeking office.

When I was first elected, a young reporter recorded a thirty-minute TV interview with me. During the program, he asked what I hoped to accomplish as a state representative. Off the top of my head I said, "I would like to prove that an average citizen can serve with honesty, and dignity and without losing his family, his occupation, his pride or his integrity. I'd like to serve in a manner that would encourage others to seek public office." I repeated that phrase in similar terms many times after that. Often over the years, young men and women have told me they heard those comments or heard about them. They told me it was that statement that encouraged them to enter politics. Many of them have become successful in the field while maintaining that honesty and dignity.

Mama, I wish you had lived longer than three of my 12 years in politics. I think we could have had some long, interesting conversations about how government really works and what goes on behind the marble walls. I know you would have had some cogent and candid comments about some of my associates and activities. Maybe I could have convinced you that not all politicians are corrupt.

At least, I hope you could agree that at least one was not. I wanted you to see that you could be proud of a son who was a "politician." But, I think you know.

Love,

Ronnie

Acknowledgments

I have found that writing one's memoirs entails a lot more than shutting one's eyes and remembering. I had the advantage of being a "pack-rat." While I was in the legislature, I saved papers, documents and trivia that eventually filled a five-drawer filing cabinet. When I finally got around to cleaning it out, I was amazed at how much detailed information I had. I had subscribed to *Metro Press Clipping Service* in Baton Rouge during my ten years in the legislature. Many of the envelopes containing clippings had never been opened. Naturally, seventy to eighty percent of the items were not relevant and were thrown away, but the rest were invaluable.

Bob Hamm, a real-life professional writer and my media comrade in radio and television for almost forty years, was the first person I asked to read early chapters and drafts. He was not only helpful, he was candidly challenging and encouraging. Jim Patterson, a soccer-playing lobbyist with LABI who sports a wicked sense of humor first suggested that I open my speeches with the phrase, "My name is Ron, and I'm a recovering legislator." Su King, a stalwart source of knowledge and efficiency with the House Legislative Services in Baton Rouge, didn't know it but I still had a lot of her research in my files.

I first asked James Edmonds to look at a final draft and to consider editing the manuscript. He graciously made a few corrections and comments and encouraged me to finish it. As a former member of Governor Buddy Roemer's staff and an academician, Bill Conway was another of the half dozen or so people kind enough to read and comment and critique.

My brother Griffin, a lifelong journalist, read early efforts, proofed the final draft and was very encouraging throughout the process. His wife Camille, who at one time had worked as a proof reader, read and corrected the manuscript twice. Carl Bauer, a dear friend who had preceded me in the House and went on to serve in the Senate, read the entire final draft and made some suggestions and comments which I deeply appreciated. And, of course my wife Carol was asked to read and reread bits and pieces for the nine or ten months of conception.

I would be remiss without acknowledging the astute cardiologist Dr. Mike Mounir, the magnificent heart surgeon Dr. Ed Nagem and a truly compassionate staff in the cardiac surgery section of Lafayette General Hospital. When my life and the writing of this manuscript was interrupted by unexpected triple coronary bypass surgery in July of 1999, they made the potential trauma seem routine and the recovery a cake walk. I am blessed.

Index